LEGENDARY LOCALS

OF

# TOLEDO

OHIO

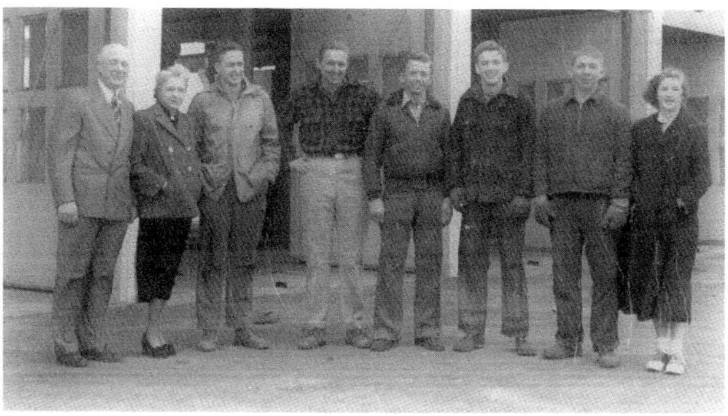

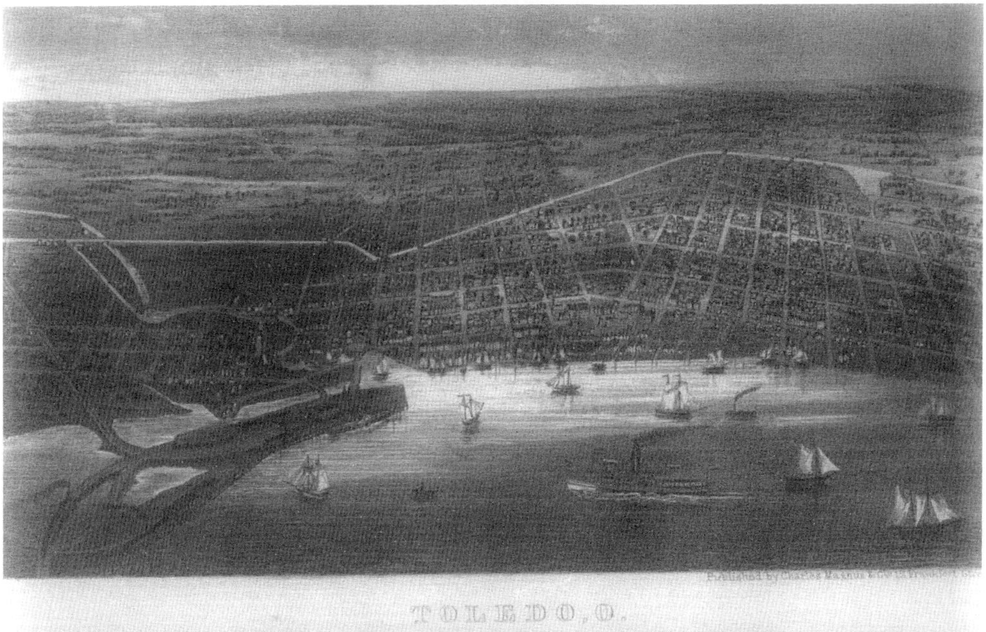


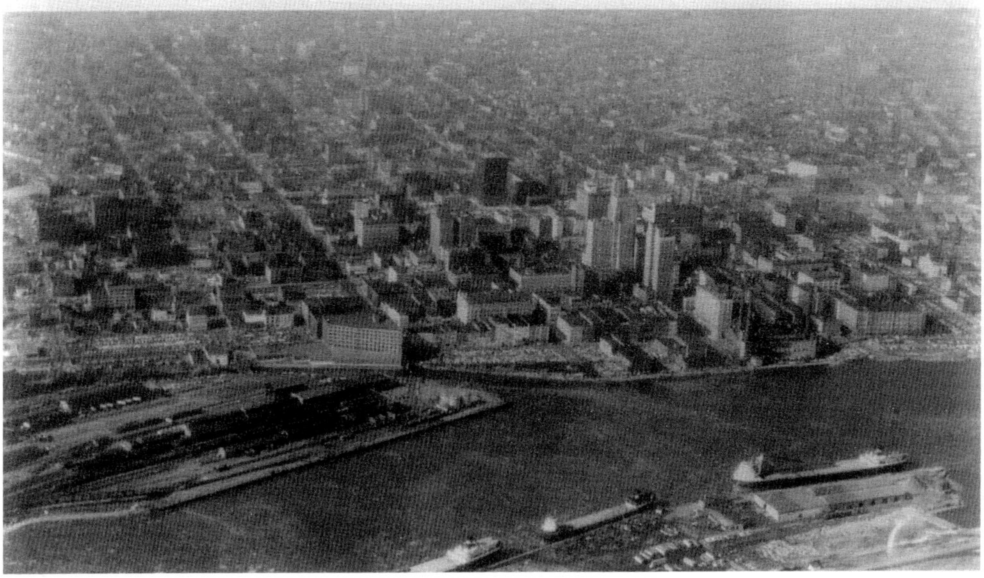

Toledo, 1850

Above is a rendering of Toledo, Ohio, from about 1850. Below is a photograph of the same location from around 1950. (Courtesy of the Ward M. Canaday Center for Special Collections, the University of Toledo.)

**Page 1:** Harold and Margaret Anderson

Pictured here are Harold and Margaret Anderson and their children, John, Tom, Bob, Don, Dick, and Carol. Harold Anderson founded what would become The Andersons in 1936, and in 1947 he brought his wife and family into the business. See page 70. (Courtesy of the Ward M. Canaday Center for Special Collections, the University of Toledo.)

LEGENDARY LOCALS

OF

# TOLEDO

## OHIO

BARBARA L. FLOYD

LEGENDARY LOCALS

ISBN 978-1-4671-0179-0

Legendary Locals is an imprint of Arcadia Publishing
Charleston, South Carolina

Printed in the United States of America

Library of Congress Control Number: 2014940555

For all general information, please contact Arcadia Publishing:
Telephone 843-853-2070
Fax 843-853-0044
E-mail sales@arcadiapublishing.com
For customer service and orders:
Toll-Free 1-888-313-2665

Visit us on the Internet at www.arcadiapublishing.com

**On the Front Cover:** Clockwise from top left:
Danny Thomas, actor (Courtesy of Ward M. Canaday Center for Special Collections, the University of Toledo; see page 104); Jamie Farr, actor (Courtesy of Ward M. Canaday Center for Special Collections, the University of Toledo; see page 108), Rep. Marcy Kaptur (Courtesy of Ward M. Canaday Center for Special Collections, the University of Toledo; see page 88), Edward Drummond Libbey and Florence Scott Libbey, founders of the Toledo Museum of Art (Courtesy of Ward M. Canaday Center for Special Collections, the University of Toledo; see page 47), Harold Boeschenstein, first president of Owens-Corning Fiberglas (Courtesy of Ward M. Canaday Center for Special Collections, the University of Toledo; see page 60), Ella P. Stewart, pharmacist (Courtesy of Ward M. Canaday Center for Special Collections, the University of Toledo; see page 30), and Edward Ford, industrialist (Courtesy of Ward M. Canaday Center for Special Collections, the University of Toledo; see page 44).

**On the Back Cover** From left to right:
Michael J. Owens (center, in long coat) with glassworkers at Libbey Glass around 1900 (Courtesy of Ward M. Canaday Center for Special Collections, the University of Toledo; see pages 48–49), Ward M. Canaday (seated in center of Jeep), celebrating the one millionth Jeep produced at Willys-Overland, 1952 (Courtesy of Ward M. Canaday Center for Special Collections, the University of Toledo; see page 54).

# CONTENTS

# ACKNOWLEDGMENTS

I would first like to thank my colleagues in the Ward M. Canaday Center for Special Collections for their assistance and helping to keep the Canaday Center running smoothly during the time I was at work on this project: Arjun Sabharwal, Tamara Jones, Sara Mouch, and Lauren White. It is wonderful to work with such talented hard-working people who are dedicated to collecting, preserving, and making available collections that help to document the history of our city. The collections of the Canaday Center are rich in their depth and breadth, and there is no better proof of this statement than the fact that most of the images in this book are from the center's collections.

I would also like to thank those at other archival repositories and organizations who provided images for the book: Donna Christen, local history and genealogy department, Toledo-Lucas County Public Library; Karen Mason and Janet Weaver, Iowa Woman's Archives; Phillip L. Kaplan and the *Toledo Blade*; Dan Saevig from his personal collection; and Mary Mennel, 577 Foundation.

Erin Vosgien, my editor at Arcadia Publishing, kept me on track, and I appreciate her support and help.

Lastly, I would like to thank my husband, Bill Little, for his support and assistance in everything.

Unless otherwise noted, all images appear courtesy of the Ward M. Canaday Center for Special Collections, the University of Toledo.

# INTRODUCTION

While a city is defined as a geographic region, it is really defined historically, socially, economically, culturally, and politically by the people who live within its boundaries. For some cities, there is a pervasive stereotype of the sort of person who lives there: Hollywood is full of celebrities, New York is a place for theatrical and artistic types, Berkeley is for the counter-culture, Chicago is the city of broad shoulders.

But what sort of person defines Toledo, Ohio? In the mind of many, it, too, has a stereotyped image. Toledo is a blue-color industrial city with strong union membership, votes primarily Democratic, and is gritty and hardworking and a little down-on-its-luck. Toledo is often the butt of jokes about life in the rustbelt and a stepchild to its troubled neighbor to the north, Detroit. Its nickname is the Glass City, named for the industry that once dominated its economy. Sometimes it is called Frog Town, a holdover from when the city was founded in 1837 in the middle of the Great Black Swamp.

But Toledo is much more, and Toledoans are much more diverse than the stereotypes that often describe them. Throughout its history, the city has produced revolutionaries who have worked to end slavery (Congressman James Ashley), fought for the rights of women (including Anna Mott, Olive Colton, and more recently, Gloria Steinem), and led the Progressive movement in politics (mayors Samuel "Golden Rule" Jones and Brand Whitlock). It has produced business leaders who developed technological innovation in many fields, particularly in the glass industry (including Michael Owens, who invented the automatic bottle machine.) It has produced one governor (Michael V. DiSalle), one Supreme Court chief justice (Morrison Waite), an ambassador to the Soviet Union (Foy Kohler), the longest-serving woman in the House of Representatives (Marcy Kaptur), and a Civil War hero (James Steedman). It has been the birthplace for one of the greatest jazz pianists of all time (Art Tatum), revered actors (including Joe E. Brown, Danny Thomas, and Jamie Farr), popular singers (Helen O'Connell, Teresa Brewer, and Jon Hendricks), and nationally known writers and artists (including Mildred Benson.)

In addition to the famous, other legendary locals are people you may never have heard of before. They include a boy born severely deformed whose personal determination and the care provided to him by the Toledo Rotary led to an international movement to assist children with disabilities that continues to this day. It includes a woman who wanted all children with developmental disabilities to have the chance to go to school. It includes a coach who made Toledo the center of the world's stage at the height of the Cold War when he brought an international wrestling tournament to the city that included athletes from behind the Iron Curtain. And it includes a basketball player who may have been the first African American to play on an integrated professional team.

Some of the people who were born here or made their careers here have influenced not only Toledo but the world. Some are not known outside of the city but are remembered for what they did to make Toledo a better place. Some made their mark in quiet ways that nonetheless improved our city. It is worth remembering who these amazing people have been. But of course, the people who are documented in this book as legendary locals were not successful on their own. Rather, they are the product of forces within Toledo that shaped them and of people who supported them and encouraged them: their teachers, religious leaders, coaches, family members, and friends. In many ways, these people are as legendary as those who achieved success, because without them, success would not have been possible.

While this book describes many of the people we might define as legendary, it is certainly not comprehensive, and to those I have overlooked, I apologize. There may be justified arguments over the inclusion of some of the people in this book, but each of them in some way are legends, either for what they managed to accomplish that brought them national prestige or for how they contributed to the city. We should all be proud to celebrate their connection to Toledo.

# CHAPTER ONE

# Pioneers

The dictionary defines *pioneer* as a noun, "a person or group that originates or helps open up a new line of thought or activity," and as a verb, "to open or prepare for others to follow." The people described in this chapter did exactly that, in many different ways and in many different fields. They include the obvious political leaders such as John Berdan, the first mayor of Toledo; and Jesup W. Scott, who proclaimed Toledo to be the future great city of the world and whose ideas continue to influence economic development in the city today. But also included here are pioneers who spoke out about issues that were at the time unpopular but whose actions shaped public opinion about these issues in significant ways. They include Toledo's congressman during the Civil War who saw that the only way to forever bar slavery from the country was to pass a constitutional amendment outlawing it and helped to draft what became the 13th Amendment. They include Scott Nearing, who only lived for one year in Toledo but who, through his radical views about economic inequality, brought unpleasant issues into the political debate. Also included here are women who paved the way as pioneers—Anna Mott and Olive Colton, who helped to found the Toledo Woman's Suffrage Association; and Ella P. Stewart, who was not only a woman, but an African American, yet still became successful in her field as a pharmacist. She was also an outspoken supporter of civil rights and world peace. And they also include those who led their chosen professional fields, like Dr. Nathan Brown in cardiology and Dr. Randolph C. Downes in local history.

While the people here are from all walks of life, they are all pioneers in their own way, and Toledo would be a different place without their contributions to the city's history.

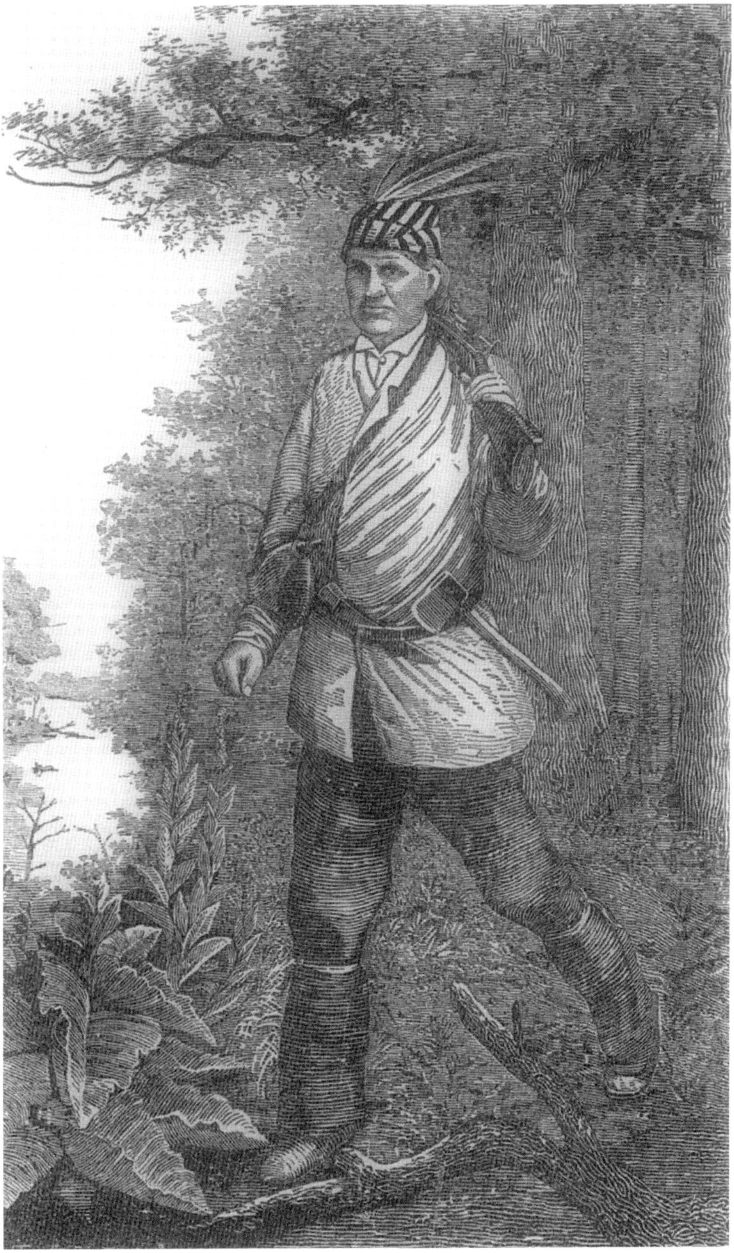

Peter Navarre

Peter Navarre was a pioneer in the traditional sense of the word. He was one of the first white settlers in northwest Ohio. Born in Detroit in 1785, he built a cabin on what is today the east side of Toledo with his brother Robert in 1807. He worked as a fur trader until the War of 1812 closed off the trade.

During that war, Navarre worked as a spy, and General Proctor, leader of the British forces, placed a bounty on his head. He successfully smuggled in Kentucky sharpshooters through British and Native American lines to reinforce Commodore Oliver Hazard Perry's forces on Lake Erie, helping Perry defeat the British at the Battle of Lake Erie. He also worked as a scout for Gen. William Henry Harrison at Fort Meigs. After the war, he returned to his cabin on the east side, where he died in 1874.

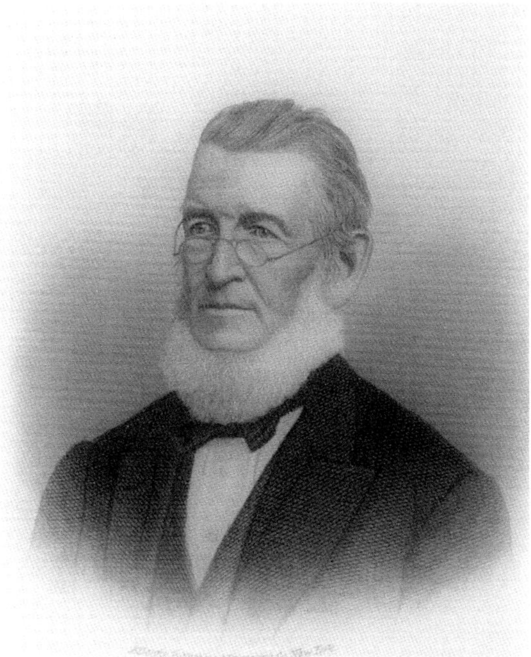

### Jesup W. Scott

There are few historical figures who have made such a lasting impression on Toledo as Jesup W. Scott. In 1832, he moved to Toledo and invested in the real estate bubble created by plans to build a terminus for the Miami and Erie Canal, buying 70 acres of land near what is today downtown. From 1844 to 1847, he was editor of the *Toledo Blade*. He also wrote articles for national periodicals of the day, including *Hunt's Merchant Magazine* and *DeBow's Review*, expressing his theories on the impact of geography on economic development.

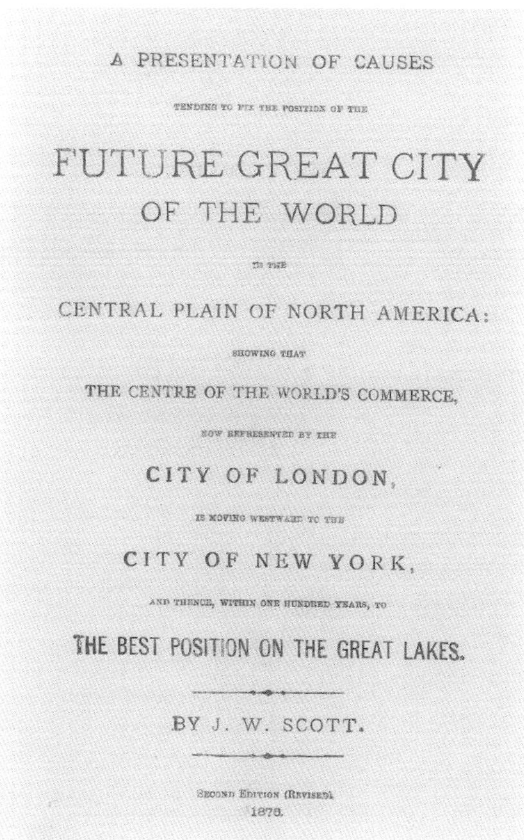

A PRESENTATION OF CAUSES

TENDING TO FIX THE POSITION OF THE

FUTURE GREAT CITY

OF THE WORLD

IN THE

CENTRAL PLAIN OF NORTH AMERICA:

SHOWING THAT

THE CENTRE OF THE WORLD'S COMMERCE,

NOW REPRESENTED BY THE

CITY OF LONDON,

IS MOVING WESTWARD TO THE

CITY OF NEW YORK,

AND THENCE, WITHIN ONE HUNDRED YEARS, TO

THE BEST POSITION ON THE GREAT LAKES.

BY J. W. SCOTT.

SECOND EDITION (REVISED)

1876.

### "Future Great City of the World"

In 1868, Scott expanded his ideas in a pamphlet titled "A Presentation of Causes Tending to Fix the Position of the Future Great City of the World in the Central Plains of North America." Here he theorized that since ancient times, the center of civilization had been moving westward, and as a result, the next likely future great city would be Toledo. To help Toledo fulfill its destiny, in 1872 Scott endowed the Toledo University of Arts and Trades, which would later become the University of Toledo.

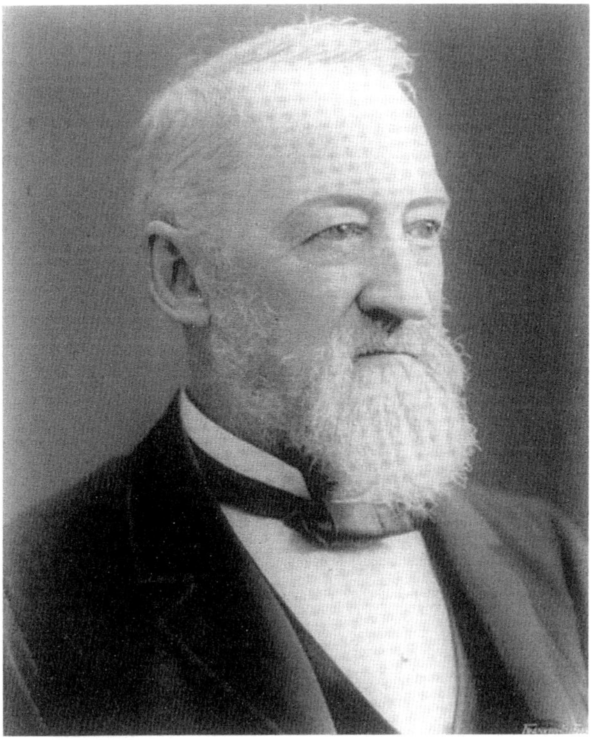

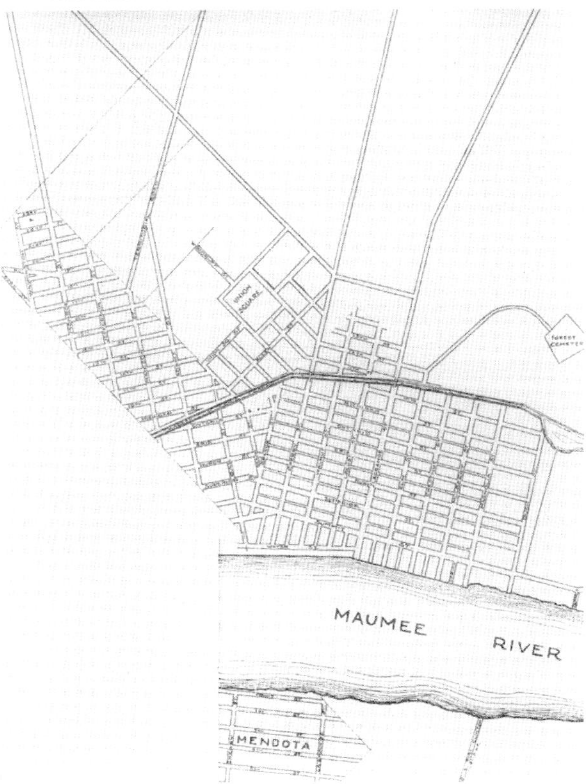


### John Berdan

The city of Toledo was incorporated in January 1837, and John Berdan was elected mayor by one vote that year.

Born in New York City in 1798, Berdan moved to northwest Ohio in 1835. He opened a shipping business with B.H. Peckham and built a warehouse on the Maumee River at Lagrange Street.

In the race for a one-year term as Toledo's first mayor, he ran against Andrew Palmer. His one-vote victory was succeeded by being elected to a second term. But he was unable to fulfill this term because he was appointed by the Ohio Legislature to the position of associate justice on the court of common pleas. He died in 1841. At left is a map of Toledo and at right the articles of incorporation for the new city of Toledo from 1837.

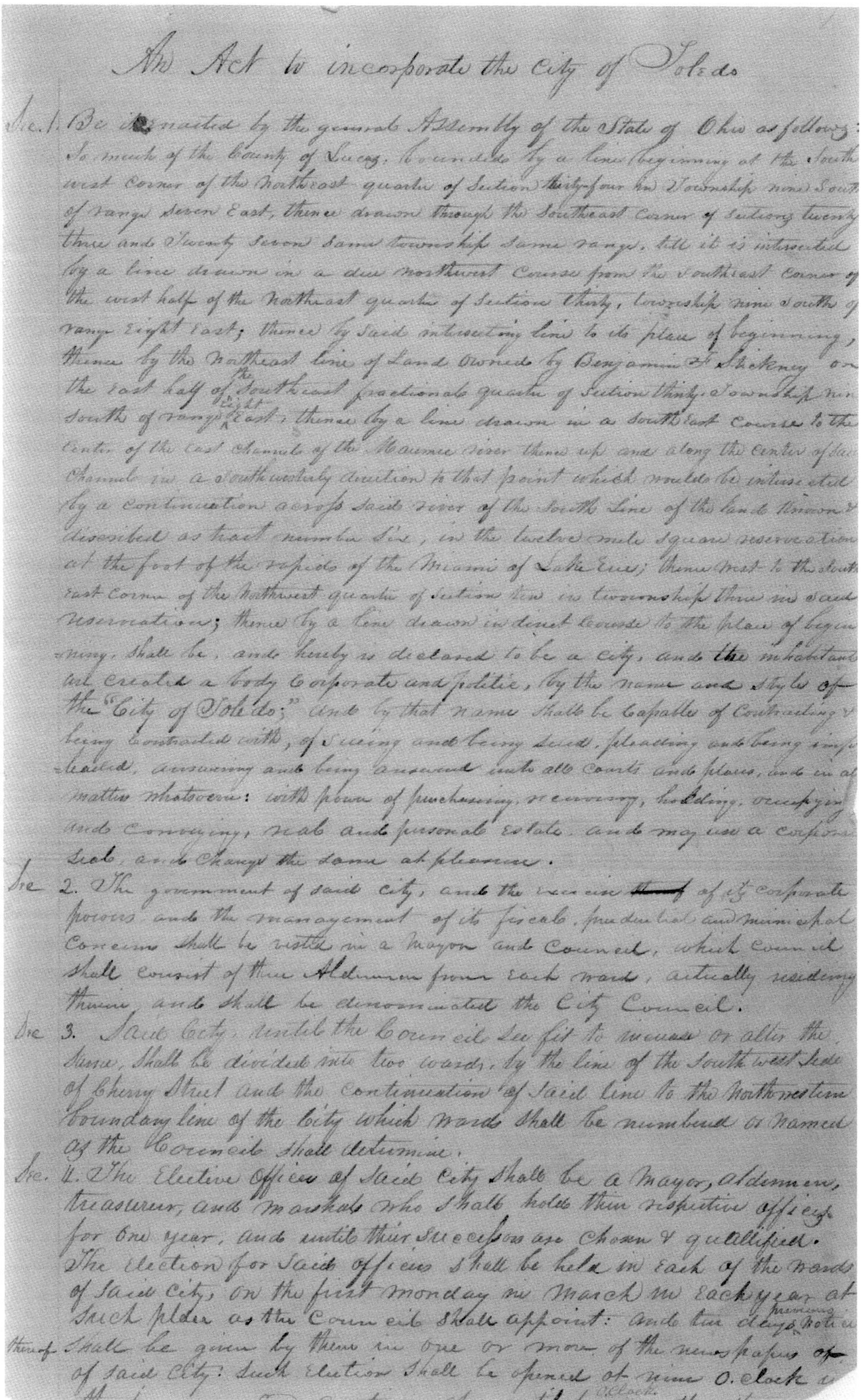

An Act to incorporate the City of Toledo

Sec. 1. Be it enacted by the general Assembly of the State of Ohio as follows:
So much of the County of Lucas, bounded by a line beginning at the South
west corner of the Northeast quarter of Section thirty-four in Township nine South
of range seven East, thence drawn through the Southeast corner of sections twenty
three and Twenty Seven same township same range, till it is intersected
by a line drawn in a due northwest course from the Southeast corner of
the west half of the Northeast quarter of Section thirty, township nine South of
range Eight East; thence by said intersecting line to its place of beginning,
thence by the Northeast line of Land Owned by Benjamin F. Stickney on
the East half of the Southeast fractional quarter of Section thirty Township nine
south of range eight East; thence by a line drawn in a southEast course to the
Center of the East Channel of the Maumee river thence up and along the center of said
Channel in a southwesterly direction to that point which would be intersected
by a continuation across said river of the South Line of the land known &
described as tract number Six, in the twelve mile square reservation
at the foot of the rapids of the Miami of Lake Erie; thence west to the South
east corner of the Northwest quarter of Section ten in township three in said
reservation; thence by a line drawn in direct course to the place of begin
-ning, shall be, and hereby is declared to be a city, and the inhabitants
are created a body Corporate and politic, by the name and style of
the "City of Toledo;" And by that name shall be Capable of Contracting &
being contracted with, of Sueing and being sued, pleading and being imp
-leaded, answering and being answered unto all Courts and places, and in all
matters whatsoever: with power of purchasing, receiving, holding, occupying
and Conveying, real and personal Estate, and may use a corporate
seal, and change the same at pleasure.

Sec. 2. The government of said City, and the exercise ~~thereof~~ of its corporate
powers and the management of its fiscal, prudential and municipal
Concerns shall be vested in a Mayor and Council, which Council
shall consist of three Aldermen from each ward, actually residing
therein, and shall be denominated the City Council.

Sec. 3. Said City, until the Council see fit to increase or alter the
Same, shall be divided into two wards, by the line of the South west side
of Cherry Street and the continuation of said line to the Northwestern
boundary line of the City which wards shall be numbered or named
as the Council shall determine.

Sec. 4. The Elective Offices of said City shall be a Mayor, aldermen,
treasurer, and marshal who shall hold their respective offices
for one year, and until their successors are chosen & qualified.
The Election for said offices shall be held in each of the wards
of said City, on the first monday in March in each year at
such place as the Council shall appoint: and ten days previous notice
thereof shall be given by them in one or more of the newspapers of
of said City: such Election shall be opened at nine O.clock in
the forenoon, and continue open until four O.Clock in the after[illegible]

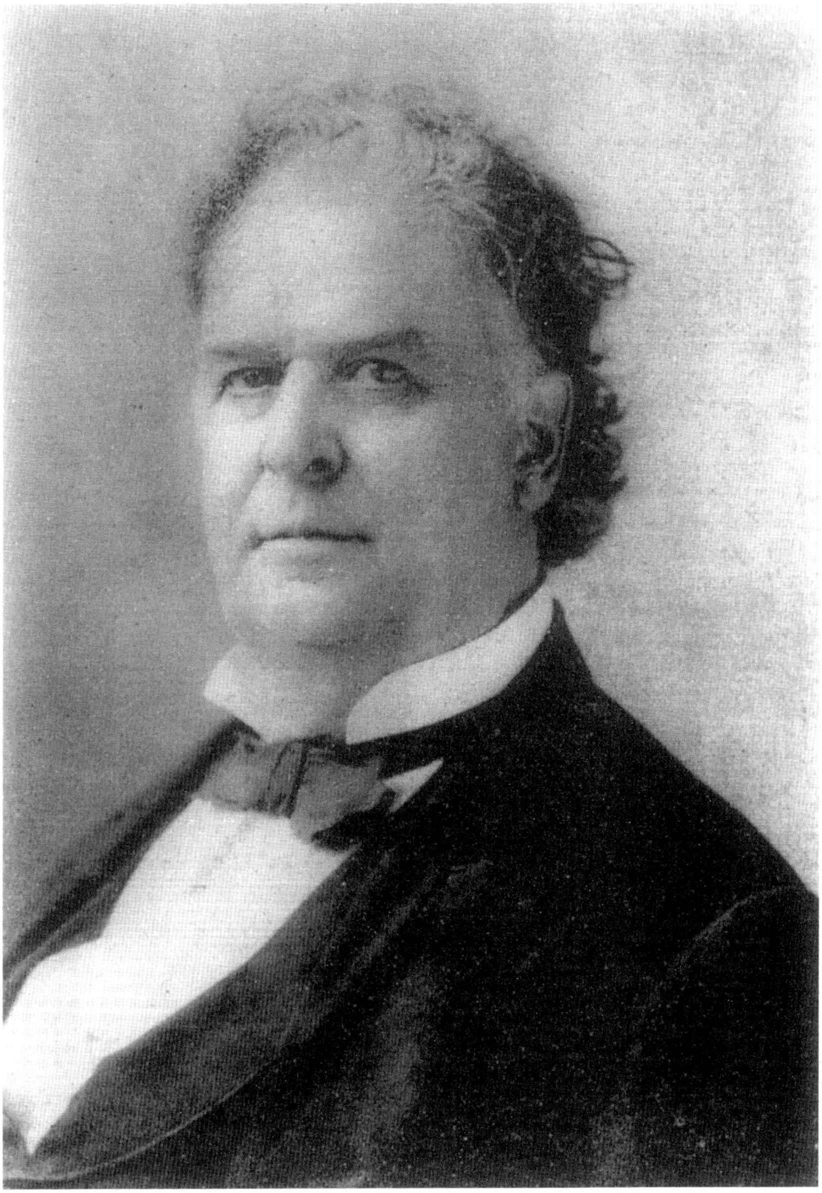

**James M. Ashley**

James Ashley was born in Pennsylvania in 1822. In 1840, he ran away from home and worked as a cabin boy on boats on the Ohio and Tennessee Rivers, where he witnessed the cruelties of slavery. "My earliest recollection of the criminality of slavery was the impressions which came to me direct from the shocking scenes of the whipping post," Ashley later recalled.

In 1851, he moved to Toledo, where he was active in the Democratic Party, frequently speaking out against slavery. Fearing that slavery would spread into western territories, he became a Republican and in 1856 served as a delegate to the national convention. His strong abolitionist views earned him the label "Radical Republican," and in 1858 those beliefs got him elected to Congress from Ohio's Fifth District. He was reelected in 1860 and helped to campaign on behalf of Abraham Lincoln. Ashley was elected two more times, in 1862 and 1864.

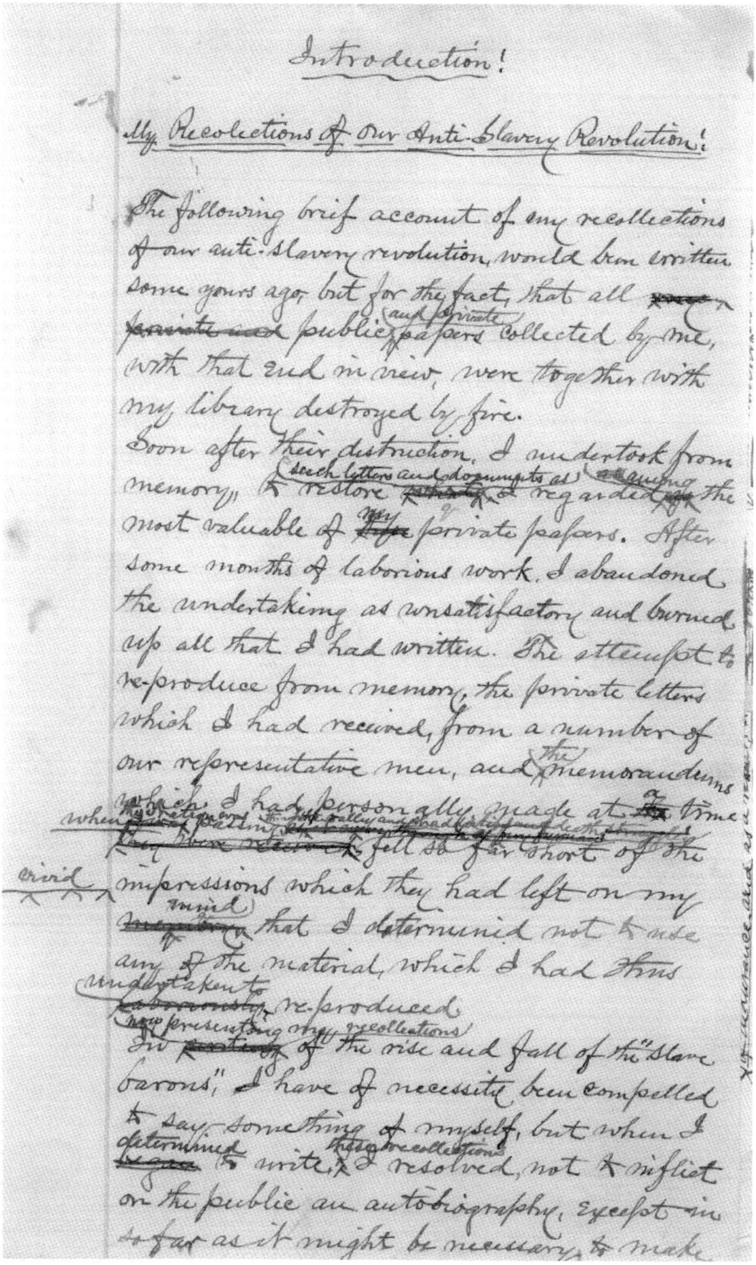

Introduction!

My Recolections of Our Anti-Slavery Revolution!

The following brief account of my recollections of our anti-slavery revolution, would been written some years ago, but for the fact, that all public and private papers collected by me, with that end in view, were together with my library destroyed by fire.

Soon after their distruction, I undertook from memory, to restore such letters and documents as I regarded the most valuable of my private papers. After some months of laborious work, I abandoned the undertaking as unsatisfactory and burned up all that I had written. The attempt to re-produce from memory, the private letters which I had received, from a number of our representative men, and the memorandums which I had personally made at a time when [illegible] fell so far short of the vivid impressions which they had left on my mind that I determined not to use any of the material, which I had thus undertaken to re-produced.

In presenting my recollections of the rise and fall of the "slave barons", I have of necessity been compelled to say something of myself, but when I determined to write these recollections I resolved, not to inflict on the public an autobiography, except in so far as it might be necessary, to make

**James Ashley's Autobiography**

James Ashley felt the only way to abolish slavery was to amend the Constitution, because the Emancipation Proclamation was a wartime act, and slavery could return once the war ended. In 1863, he proposed the first amendment to ban the institution, and that language was used to write the 13th Amendment. He helped to lead the effort to get the amendment passed in 1865. After his congressional career ended, in 1896 he decided to write his memoirs. Unfortunately, a fire in his home destroyed his personal papers, and he never completed his memoirs. But what does exist describes his view of slavery and why he worked so hard to end it.

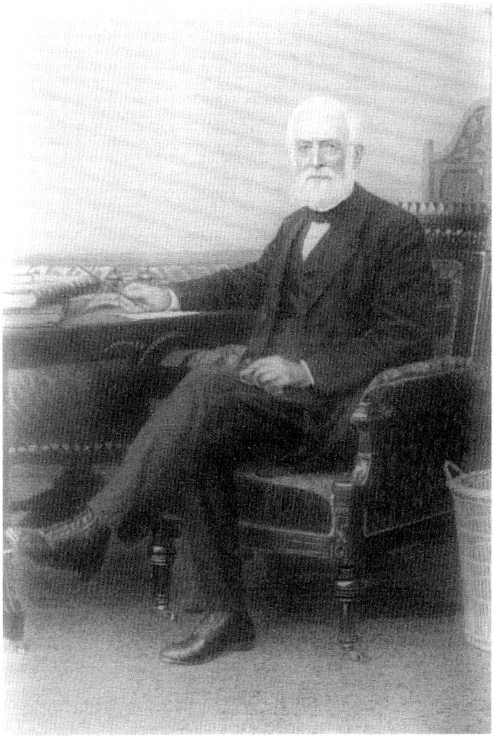

### Richard Mott

Richard Mott was born a Quaker in New York in 1804. Too poor to attend school, he began working as a store clerk at the age of 14. He became involved in banking at the age of 20.

In 1836, Mott came to Toledo, where he quickly assumed a prominent place in business circles as an early investor in the Erie and Kalamazoo Railroad. Because of his status in the community, he was elected to city council, and in 1845 was elected Toledo's mayor. He served two terms.

Mott's Quaker background made him a strong abolitionist and a believer in equality for all. He was an early supporter of women's suffrage, and his brother James was married to Lucretia Mott. In 1868, Richard met with Elizabeth Cady Stanton and Susan B. Anthony when they visited Toledo, and he provided financial support to their cause. He even gave the local Toledo Woman's Suffrage Association meeting space. He died in 1888, but he influenced his daughter to continue his efforts on behalf of women's rights.

### Anna Mott

Anna Mott was born in New York one year before her family moved to Toledo. She was a strict Quaker who opposed slavery and supported equal rights and women's suffrage.

In 1869, Mott was one of the organizers of the Toledo Woman's Suffrage Association. She was acquainted with the leaders of the national movement, including her aunt Lucretia Mott. Anna Mott also helped to found the Toledo Humane Society in 1884 to protect children in harm's way. She supported the Protestant Orphan Home, the Red Cross, and the Federation of Women's Clubs. In 1876, she and some of her friends created a literary club called the New Century Club. Upon her death in 1902, she left her sizeable fortune to many local charitable organizations. The Toledo-Lucas County Public Library named one of its branches in her honor. (Courtesy of the Toledo-Lucas County Public Library.)

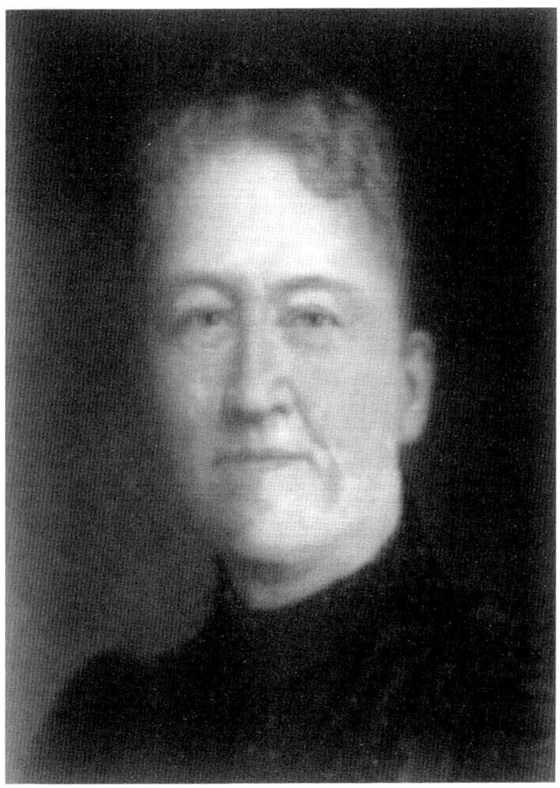

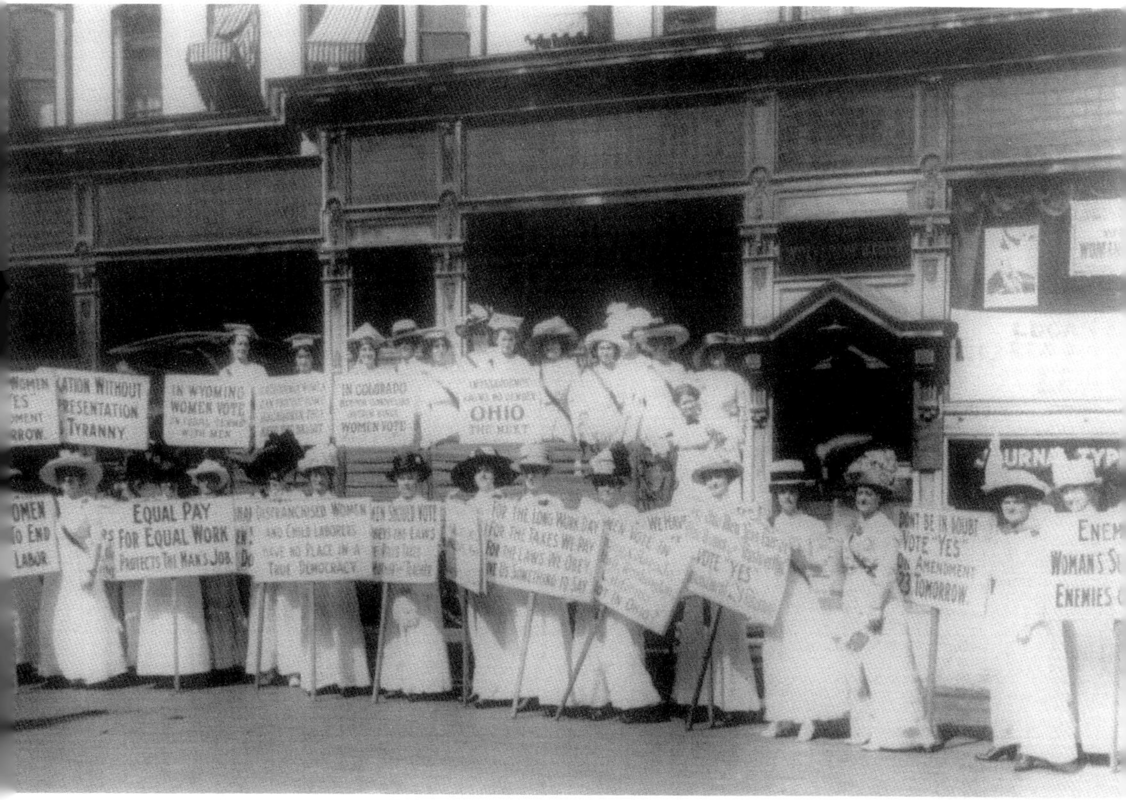


**Toledo Woman's Suffrage Association**
The Toledo Woman's Suffrage Association was a national leader in the movement to gain women the right to vote. (Courtesy of the Toledo-Lucas County Public Library.)

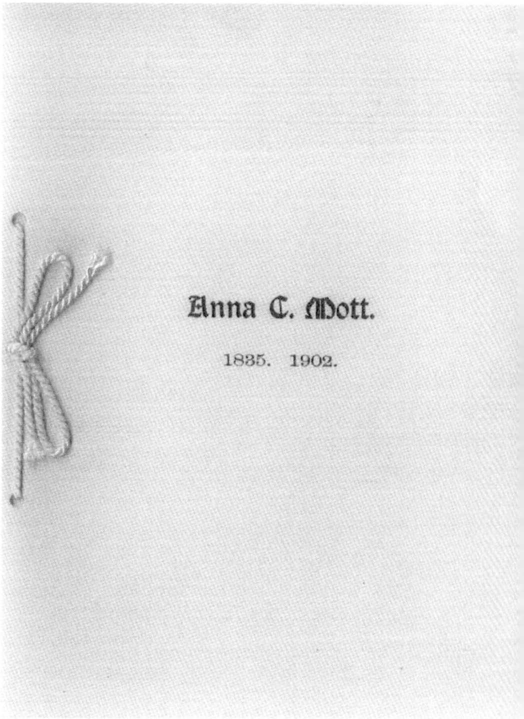
Anna C. Mott.

1835. 1902.

**Funeral Oration for Anna Mott, May 1, 1901**
Mott was described at her funeral as "She who was like sunshine in all the shadows and dark hours of this world; always ready to lighten the burden of others; loyal to those about her. Just, generous, kindly, faithful, tender, sympathetic, what noble trait did she not possess?"

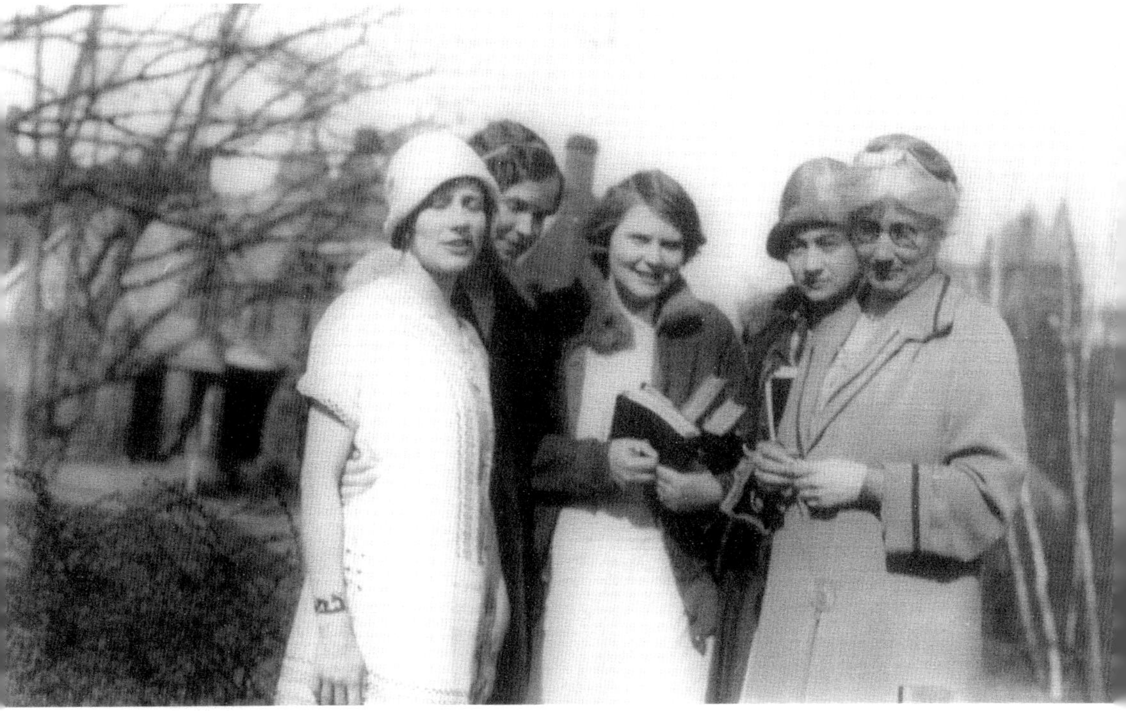

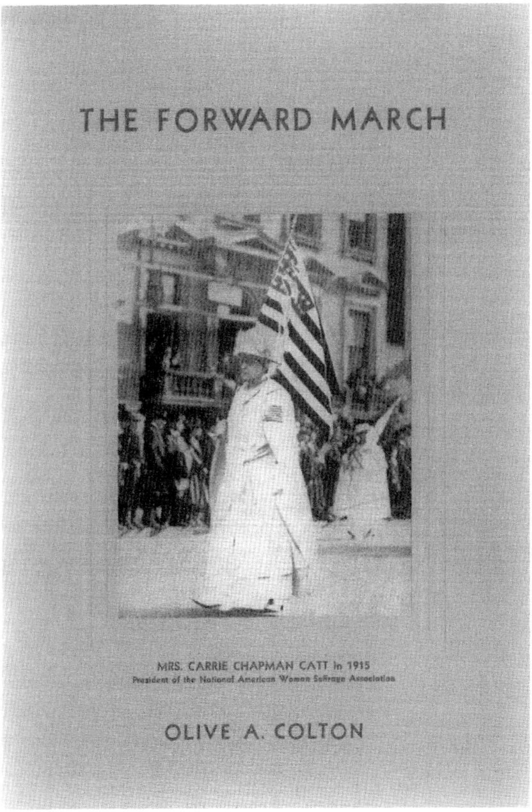


### Olive A. Colton

In 1896, Olive Colton (pictured above center) was one of the first women to cast a vote when she voted for school-board candidates, which was allowed under Ohio law. She wondered at the time "if I would be struck dead for doing such a brazen thing."

Born in 1874 into a wealthy Toledo family, where her father was president of a Lake Erie shipping company, Colton attended the elite Smead School for Girls. At an early age she became an activist for women's causes. In 1904, women helped elect Pauline Steinem to the Toledo school board. Steinem joined with Colton and other suffragettes, including Sarah Bissell, Anna Mott, and Sarah Williams, to form the Toledo Woman's Suffrage Association. When they finally won full voting rights, the organization became the Toledo League of Women Voters, and Colton was a founding member. She also campaigned successfully in 1919 for a state minimum-wage law. She died in 1972 at the age of 98.

### Scott Nearing

At a time when many Americans feared socialism, Scott Nearing, a professor of economics, was an outspoken critic of the free-market system. His advocacy for equality for women, against racial discrimination, and for a minimum wage was considered radical. In 1915, he was fired from the University of Pennsylvania but quickly hired in 1916 by the University of Toledo as professor of economics and dean of the college of arts and sciences.

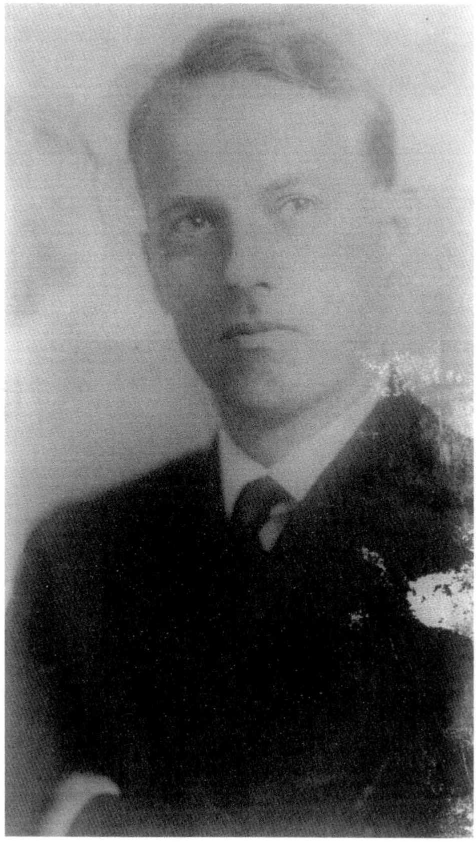

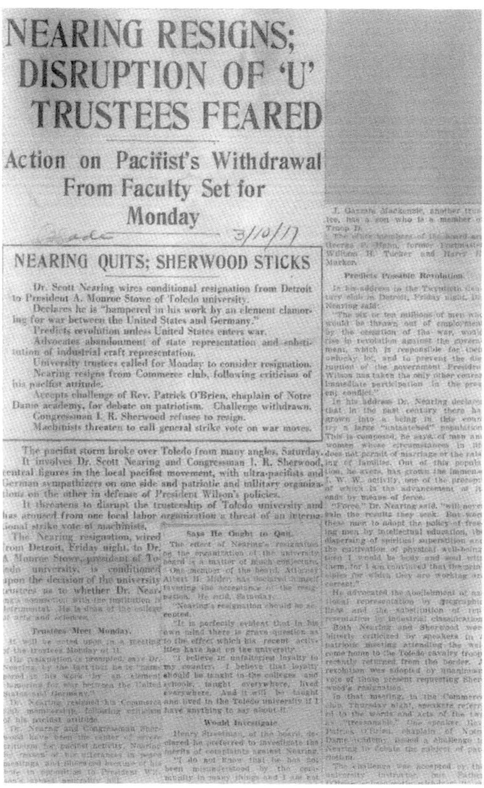

NEARING RESIGNS; DISRUPTION OF 'U' TRUSTEES FEARED

Action on Pacifist's Withdrawal From Faculty Set for Monday

3/10/17

NEARING QUITS; SHERWOOD STICKS

Dr. Scott Nearing wires conditional resignation from Detroit to President A. Monroe Stowe of Toledo university.

Declares he is "hampered in his work by an element clamoring for war between the United States and Germany."

Predicts revolution unless United States enters war.

Advocates abandonment of state representation and substitution of industrial craft representation.

University trustees called for Monday to consider resignation.

Nearing resigns from Commerce club, following criticism of his pacifist attitude.

Accepts challenge of Rev. Patrick O'Brien, chaplain of Notre Dame academy, for debate on patriotism. Challenge withdrawn.

Congressman I. R. Sherwood refuses to resign.

Machinists threaten to call general strike vote on war moves.

The pacifist storm broke over Toledo from many angles, Saturday.

It involves Dr. Scott Nearing and Congressman I. R. Sherwood, central figures in the local pacifist movement, with ultra-pacifists and German sympathizers on one side and patriotic and military organizations on the other in defense of President Wilson's policies.

It threatens to disrupt the trusteeship of Toledo university and has aroused from one local labor organization a threat of an international strike vote of machinists.

### Nearing's Dismissal from the University of Toledo, 1917

In lectures before community groups in Toledo, Nearing spoke out for the equitable division of the products of labor, better housing for the working class, and for the United States to stay out of world wars. As a result, political and business groups began calling for Nearing's dismissal. Many Toledoans decried the socialism being taught at the university. Nearing resigned, but the trustees dismissed him in 1917 rather than accept his resignation. Nearing's academic career at UT lasted just a little over one year, and it was his last academic job. He moved to rural Vermont, where he became a prolific author and advocate for the back-to-the-land movement. He died in 1983 at the age of 99.

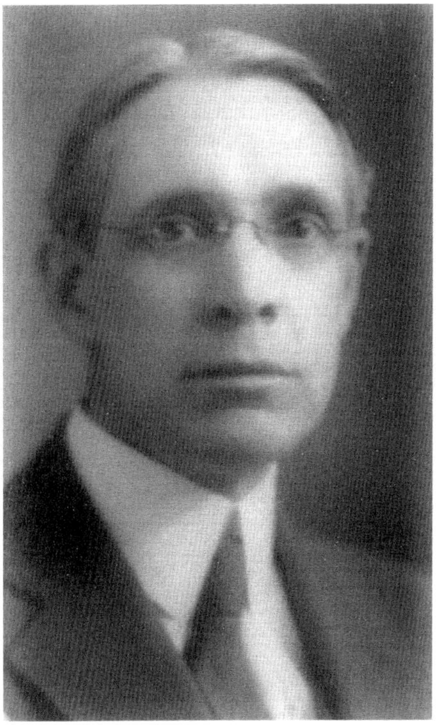

### Dr. Nathan Worth Brown

Dr. Nathan Brown was an early cardiologist in Toledo and a pioneer in the treatment of heart disease. Born to missionary parents in Japan in 1877, he received a bachelor of science degree from Denison University and a doctor of medicine degree from Western Reserve University. He studied under cardiologist Sir James Mackenzie in London.

In 1906, Brown became an instructor at the Toledo Medical College. He served in the Army during World War I as a major in the medical corps. After the war, Brown returned to Toledo and became a cardiologist at Toledo Hospital, where he used the first Mackenzie polygraph machine in the city to record pulses and respiration. The machine was eventually replaced with the electrocardiograph machine. He lectured and published often and established the Toledo Heart Center at Toledo Hospital, where he oversaw the development of the cardiac catheterization and angiographic programs prior to his death in 1962.

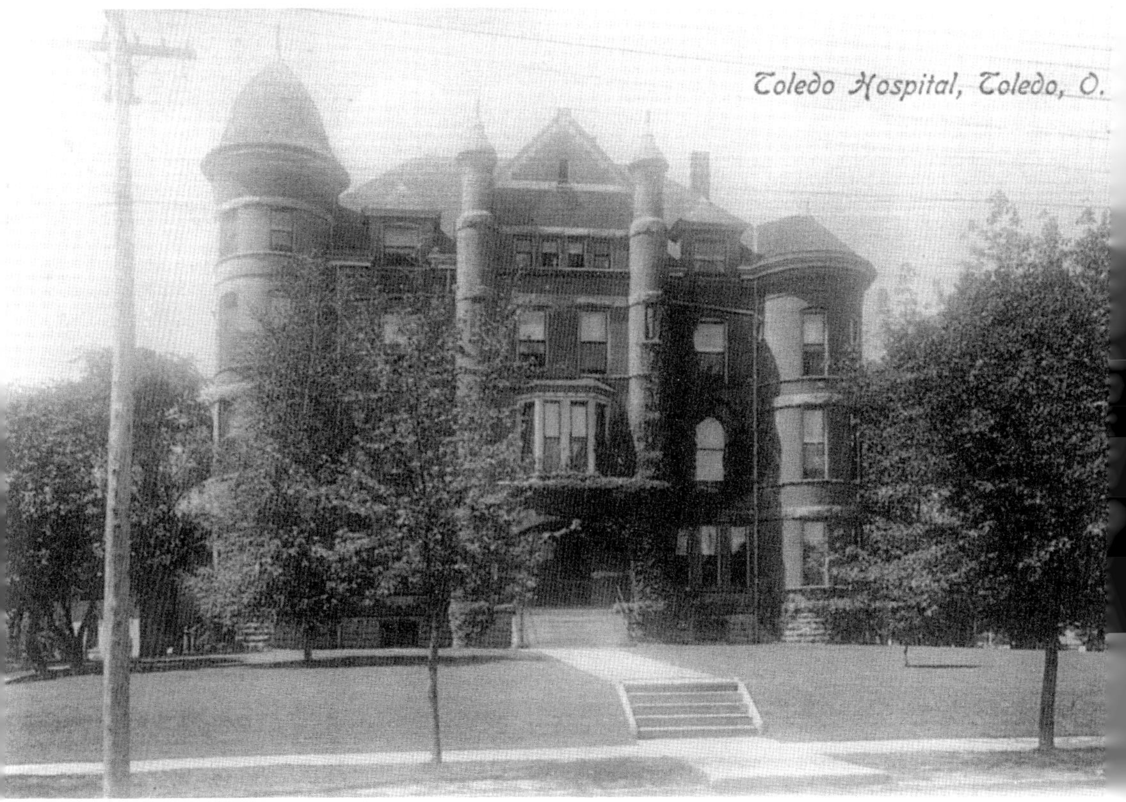

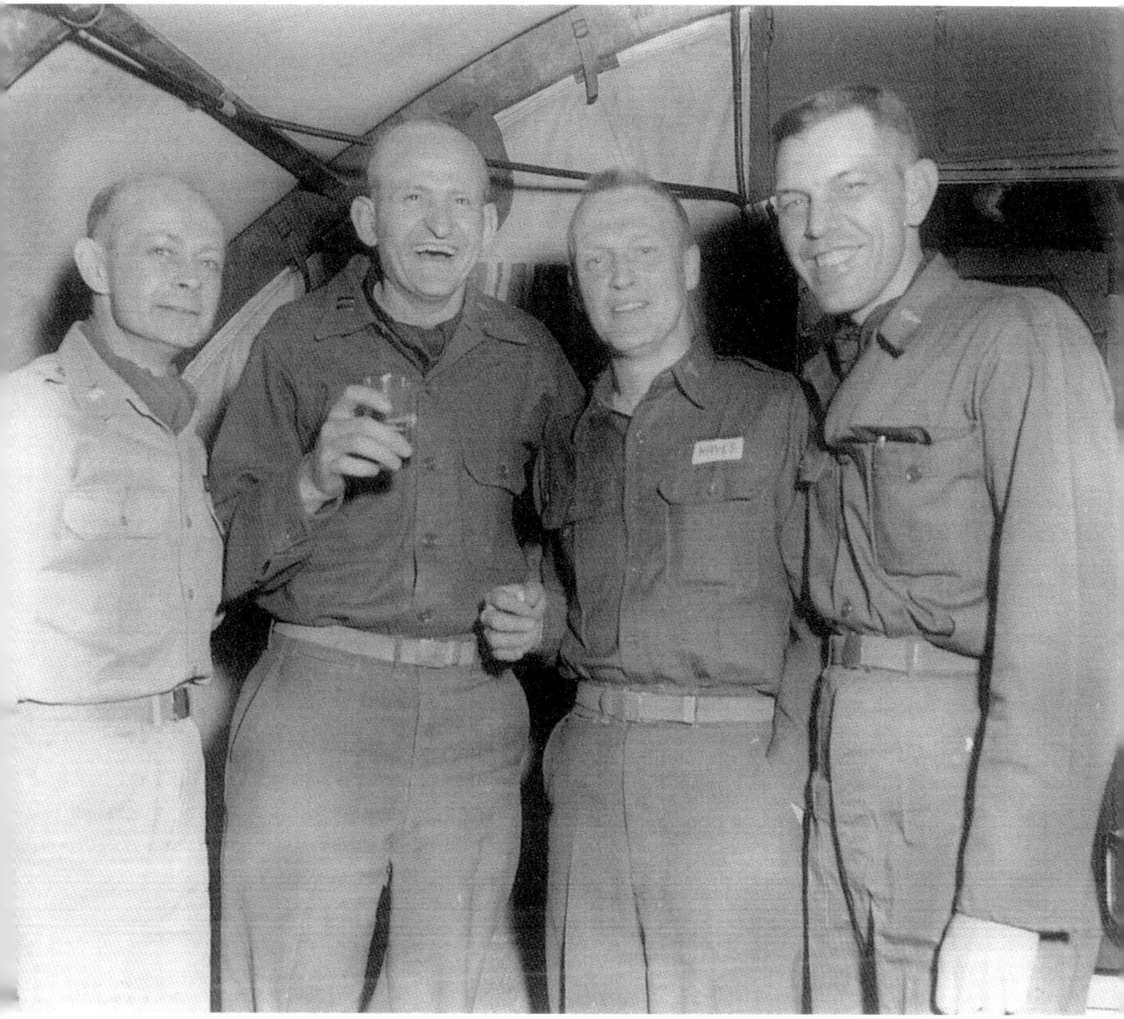

**John Howard**

John Howard's pioneering work influenced how the country developed its emergency medical system and how soldiers with traumatic injuries were treated in the Korean War.

Howard (second from left) received his medical degree from the University of Pennsylvania School of Medicine in 1944. During the Korean War, he served as a captain in the US Army Medical Corps, where he was assigned to one of the MASH units. The surgical hospitals treated soldiers wounded near the front lines, stabilizing them before they were evacuated to regular hospitals. He often had to improvise under the circumstances. During this time, he developed an artificial kidney machine, invented special arterial clamps that allowed the doctors to save mangled limbs, and administered blood stored in bags rather than bottles. He was awarded the Legion of Merit for this work, the highest award given by the Army for service and achievement.

In 1974, Dr. Howard was recruited to join the faculty of the Medical College of Ohio. He played an instrumental role in establishing the Regional Emergency Medical Services of Northwest Ohio. His work to organize this system, as well as one in Philadelphia, influenced similar systems in many other cities.

## Paul Block Jr.

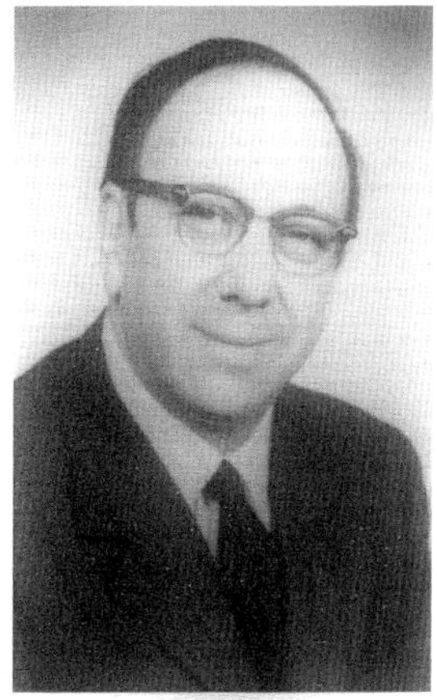

Paul Block Jr. pioneered the development of Toledo's downtown from 1945 until the time of his death in 1987. He also championed the creation of a medical college in the city.

In 1942, Block, who had been trained as a research chemist and held a doctorate in organic chemistry from Yale, took over as publisher of the *Toledo Blade* after his father's death. In his new position, he became concerned about the postwar economy of Toledo. Inspired by the "Futurama" exhibit at the 1939 New York World's Fair, Block contracted with its creator, Norman Bel Geddes, to design a similar exhibit that might imagine Toledo at the beginning of the 21st century. From the opening of the "Toledo Tomorrow" exhibit in 1945, Block became one of the most vocal proponents of the development of city's downtown.

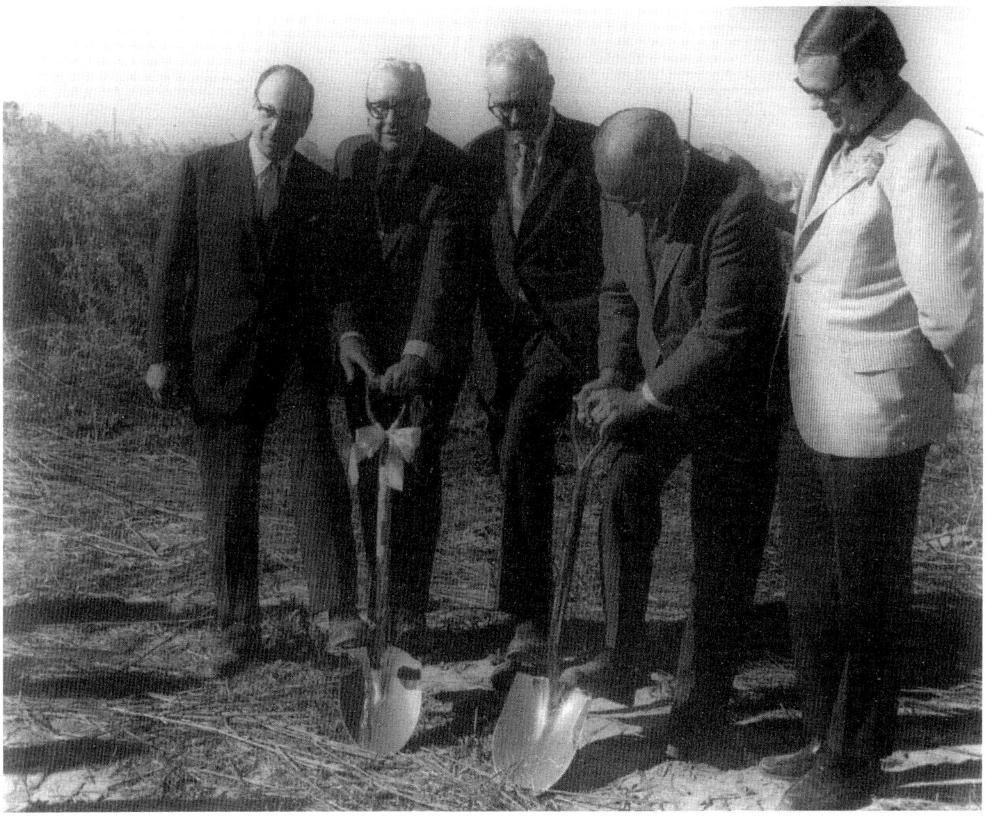

**Paul Block and Gov. James Rhodes at the Medical College of Ohio Dedication**

In the early 1960s, Block (left) pushed for the establishment of the Medical College of Ohio. Like downtown redevelopment, the medical college remained a passion of his throughout his life. In the 1980s, Block worked with government and industry leaders to develop a sweeping plan for the redevelopment of Toledo's decaying downtown as chairman of the Toledo Development Corporation. Not all of Block's plans ran smoothly, however, and he was criticized for his effort to try to get the historic St. Paul's Lutheran Church to move in order to accommodate the construction of a state office building on its site. He also battled with Owens-Illinois over the company's plans to build a hotel on Toledo's riverfront. Block died in 1987 at the age of 75.

### Norman Bel Geddes

Born Norman Melanction Geddes in 1893 in Adrian, Michigan, he took the surname Bel Geddes after marrying Helen Belle Schneider of Toledo in 1916. Bel Geddes would have a major influence on the development of Toledo's downtown.

He began his career as a theatrical designer. In the 1920s, his interest moved to industrial design, and he sought ways to make consumer products more efficient and aesthetically pleasing. He was a consultant to the 1933 Chicago World's Fair and afterward published the book *Horizons*, which prominently featured design work he had completed for the Toledo Scale company. But his most famous design was for General Motors' "Futurama" exhibit at the 1939 New York World's Fair. The 36,000-square-foot exhibit envisioned a landscape of superhighways, skyscrapers, suburbs, and airports. "Futurama" became the most popular exhibit at the fair and established Bel Geddes as a leading urban planner.

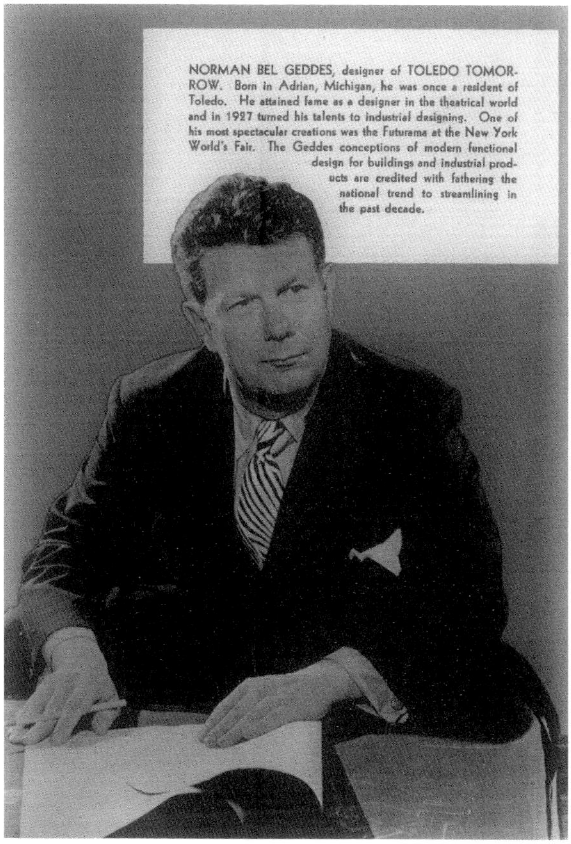


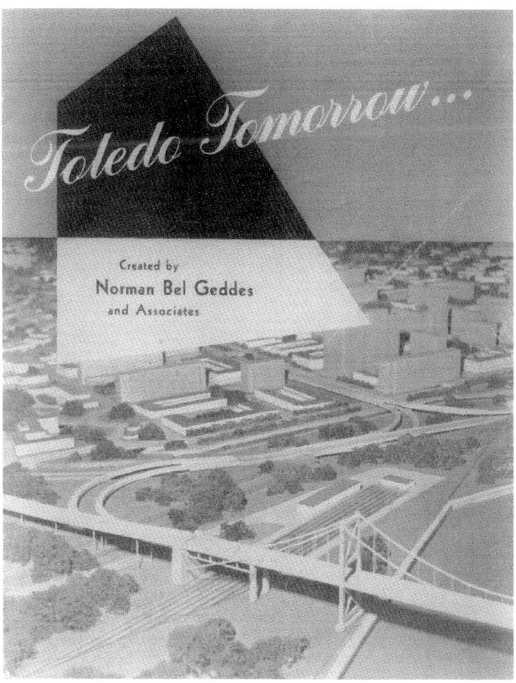


### "Toledo Tomorrow" Brochure, 1945

At the close of World War II, Paul Block Jr., publisher of the *Toledo Blade*, hired Bel Geddes to construct an exhibit similar to *Futurama* in Toledo. "Toledo Tomorrow" opened in 1945 in the science museum at the Toledo Zoo, where it quickly captured the city's imagination. The exhibit showed Toledo with multiple airports, express highways, pleasant residential communities built on cul-de-sacs, and parks. While the design had little influence on Toledo's actual development, "Toledo Tomorrow" fueled the imagination of Bel Geddes's patron, Paul Block Jr. Block would spend much of his life working to develop downtown Toledo into a world-class city.

Bel Geddes died in 1958.

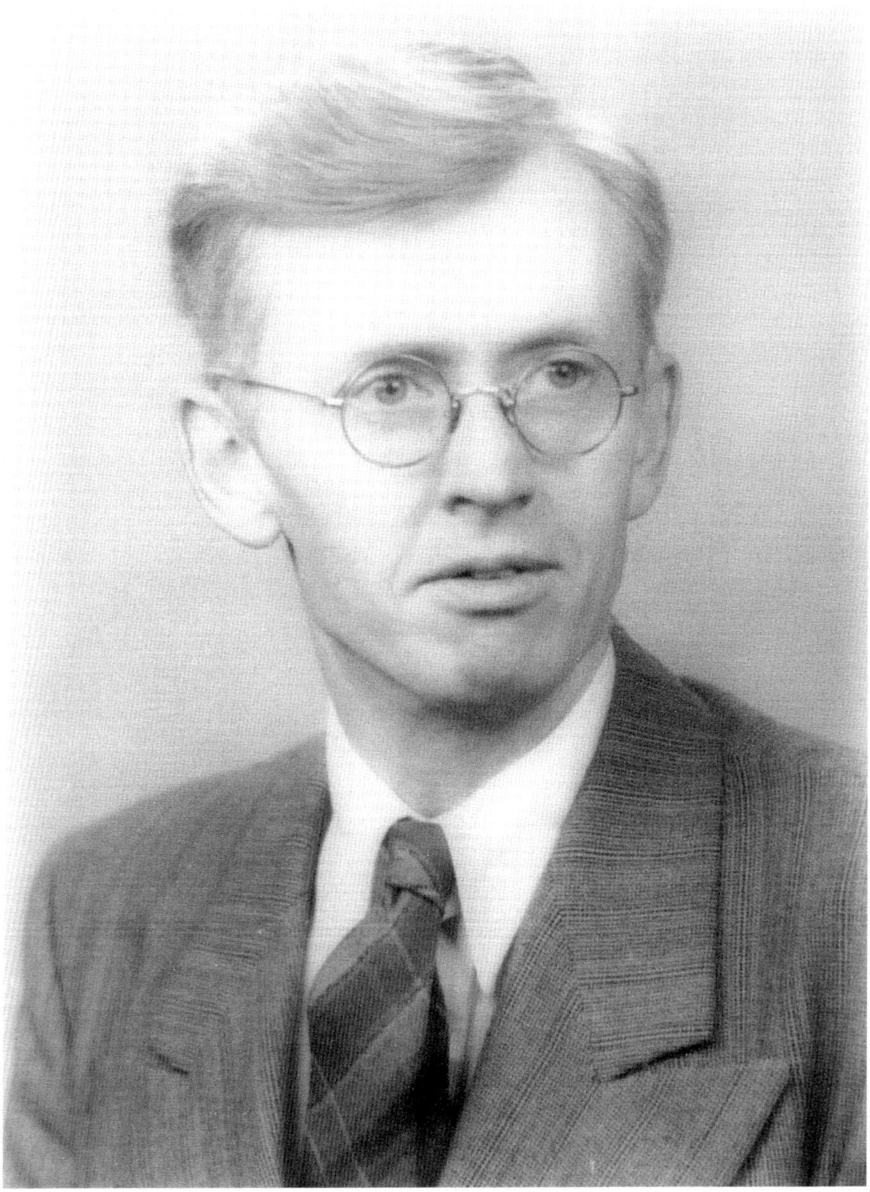

Randolph C. Downes

Randolph C. Downes made history by writing about it. He was one of the first serious historians to focus on Northwest Ohio, and during his career he authored 13 books, many about the region.

Downes was born in 1901 in Connecticut. He graduated from Dartmouth and the University of Wisconsin and received a doctorate in history from Ohio State University in 1929. During the Depression, he worked for the Writers Project of the Works Progress Administration.

In 1946, Downes joined the faculty of the University of Toledo's Department of History with a dual appointment as director of the Historical Society of Northwest Ohio (later called the Maumee Valley Historical Society). He edited the organization's journal, *Northwest Ohio Quarterly*.

During his first decade in Toledo, Downes devoted his research to the history of Northwest Ohio, and much of our understanding of that history today is due to Downes's scholarship.

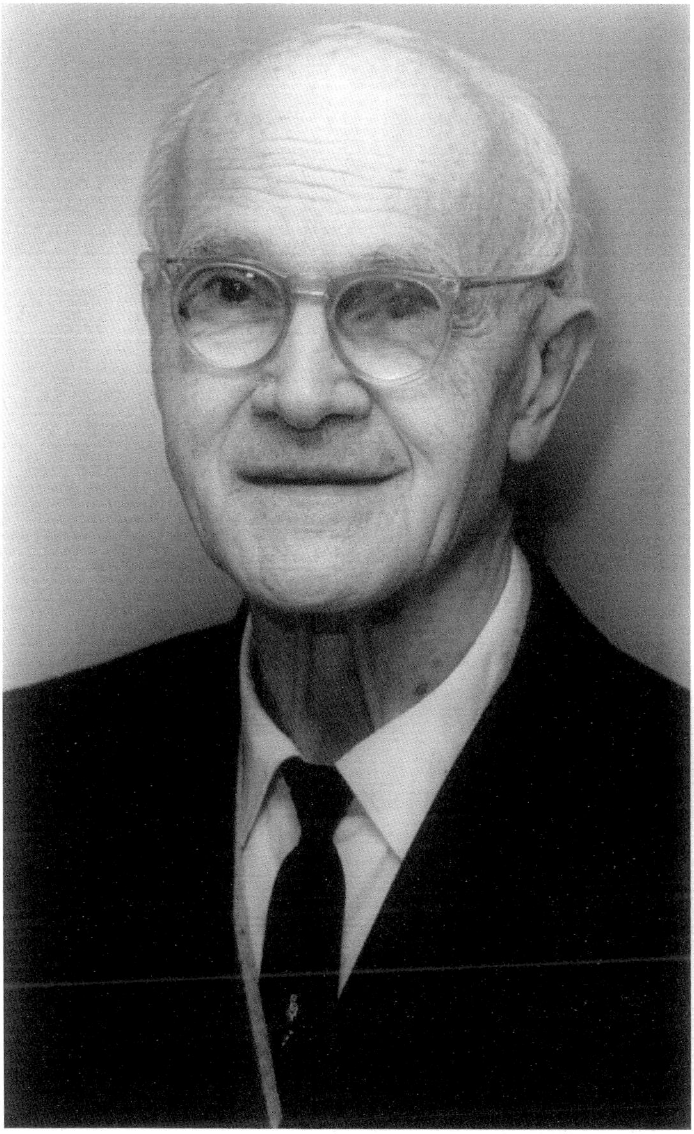

Wilhelm Eitel

Wilhelm Eitel was a pioneer in silicate science research, a field that helped to make possible much of modern technology.

Born in Germany in 1891, he received his doctorate in chemistry in 1912 and taught at several German universities. During World War I, he served as a pilot in the German army and was one of the first to recognize the military application of aerial photography. In 1926, he founded the Kaiser Wilhelm Institute for Silicate Research (now the Max Planck Institute), serving as its director until Germany's defeat in 1945. At the end of the war, Eitel was secreted out of Germany as part of Operation Paperclip, a government program to relocate scientists living behind the Iron Curtain to the United States, where they could contribute to postwar research. Eitel served as a scientist for the Navy until 1952, when he came to the University of Toledo and established the Silicate Research Institute. The institute became internationally known for its research in silicates, and Eitel's multivolume book on silicate science became the standard reference work in the field.

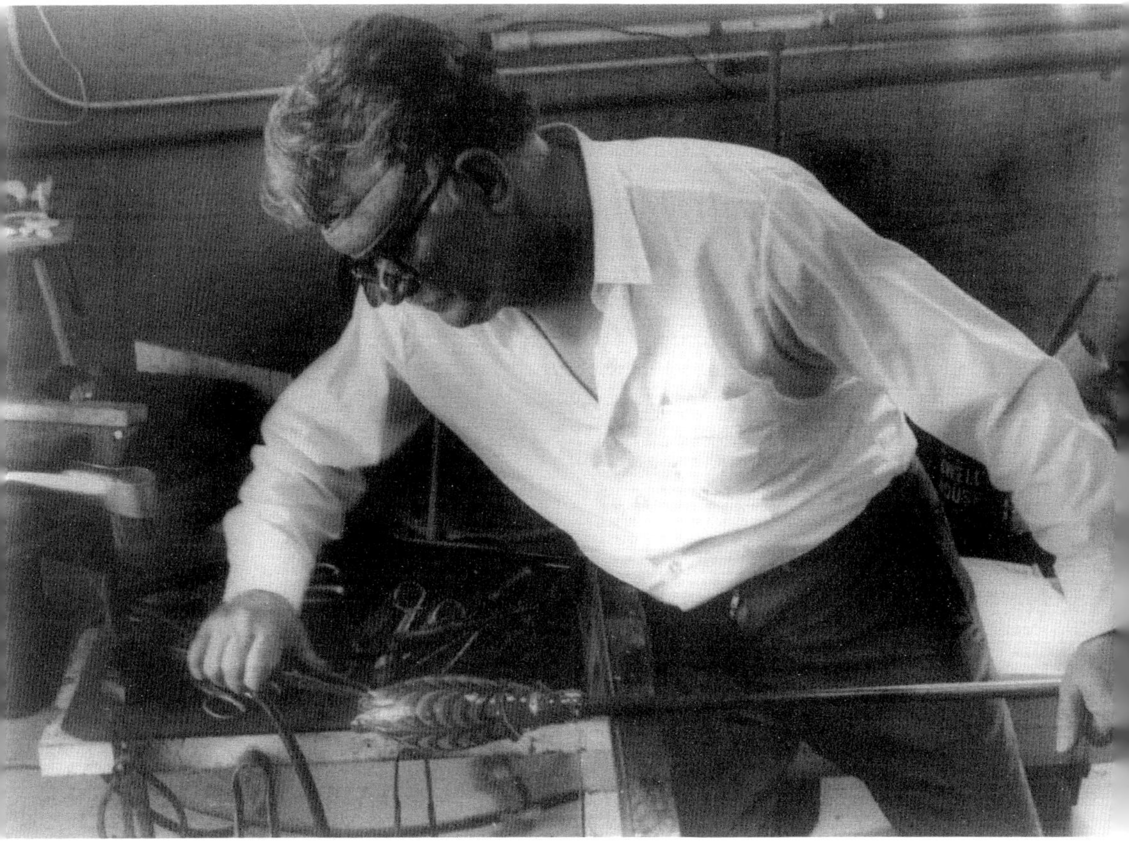

### Dominick Labino

Dominick Labino was a pioneer in glassmaking, both in industry and in art.

Born in 1910, Labino started working for the Owens-Illinois Glass Company in the 1930s, where he ran a small experimental lab and learned how to blow glass. From O-I, he moved to Glass Fiber, Inc., which merged with Libbey-Owens-Ford, where he was vice president for research. During his time in industry, he held 60 patents on glassmaking processes. He invented the pure silica fiber that was used in insulating the tiles that covered NASA spacecraft, including the space shuttles. The tiles were essential in protecting the spacecraft from burning up on reentry into Earth's atmosphere.

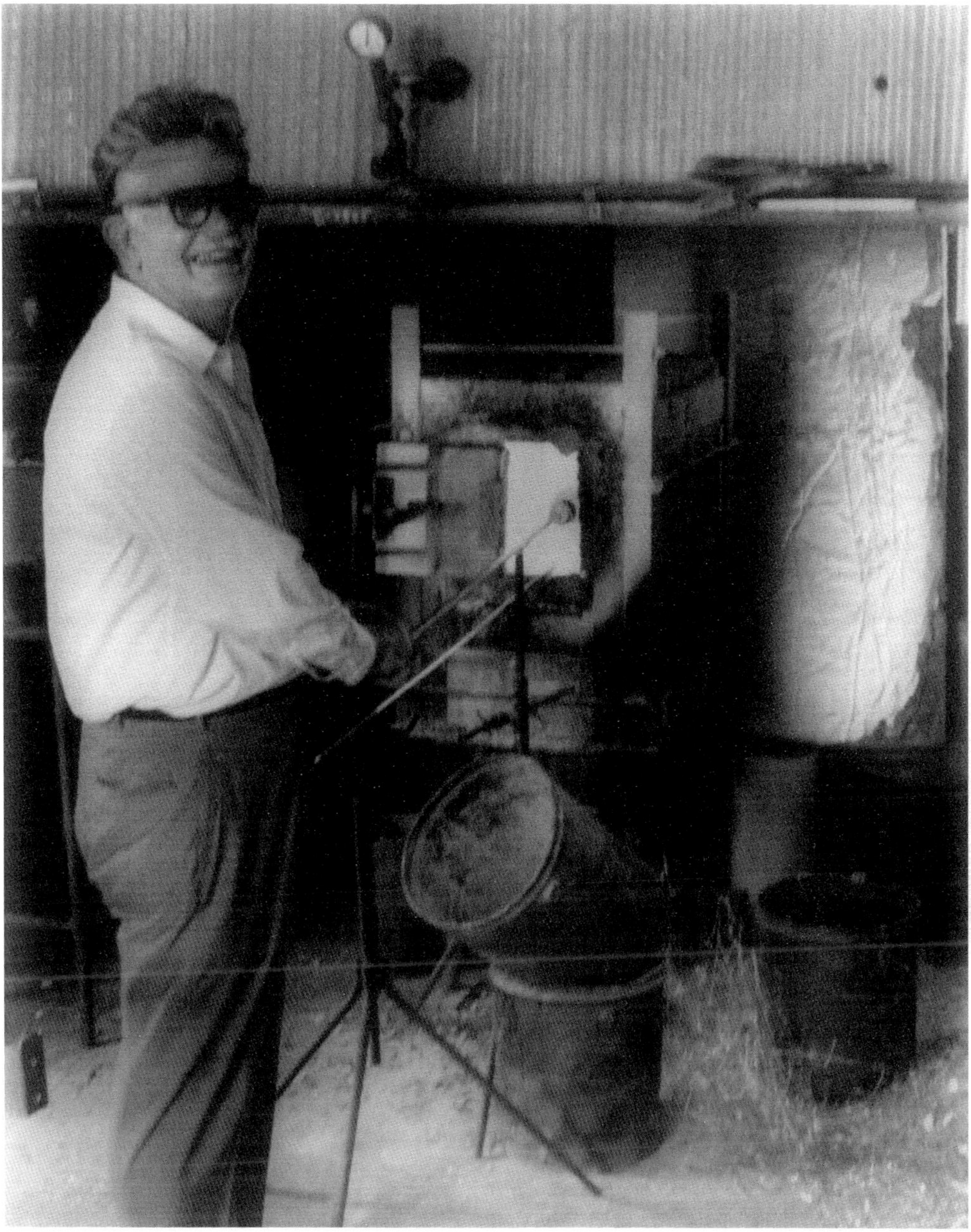

**Innovator in Glass Art**
In 1962, he and Harvey Littleton conducted workshops at the Toledo Museum of Art on glassblowing, where they hoped to take the skill from industry into art. The two are considered the founders of the Studio Glass Movement, which developed methods for artists to create unique pieces working in small glassblowing studios. Labino became a renowned glass artist, and his artistic works are displayed in over 60 museums around the world. While many glass artists were uninterested in the technical aspects of glass production, Labino believed it was essential to know about glass technology to be an accomplished artist. Dominick Labino died in 1987 in Grand Rapids, Ohio, where he had built a glass studio to practice his craft years before.

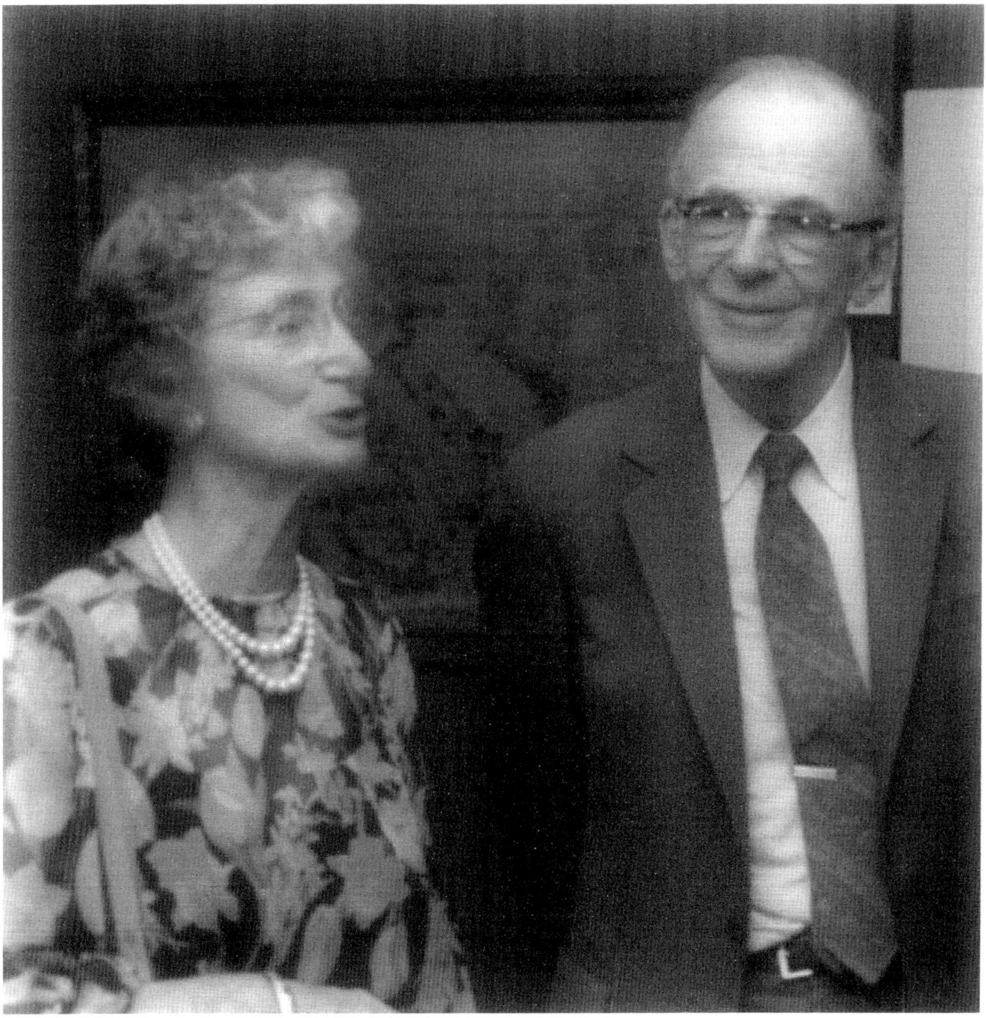

**Lyman Spitzer Jr.**

Lyman Spitzer Jr. was a pioneer in the study of astrophysics and is considered the father of the Hubble Space Telescope.

Spitzer was born in Toledo in 1914. He earned a bachelor's degree in physics from Yale in 1935. At Princeton, he studied astrophysics under Henry Norris Russell, one of the leading figures in American astronomy. During World War II, Spitzer conducted underwater sound research that helped to lead to the development of sonar. In 1947, he returned to Princeton as the chair of the astrophysical sciences department.

Spitzer's research focused on interstellar matter, the clouds of dust and gas between galaxies. In 1968, he published what became a classic book in the field, *Diffuse Matter in Space*.

Early in his studies, he recognized that a telescope stationed in space would have many advantages, and he first proposed such a telescope in 1946. In 1990, after Spitzer's years of technical and political guidance of the project, NASA launched the Hubble Space Telescope, one of its most successful projects in its history. In 1997, when he died, Spitzer was still working on analyzing data gathered by the Hubble. He is pictured here with his wife, Doreen Canaday Spitzer, in 1987.

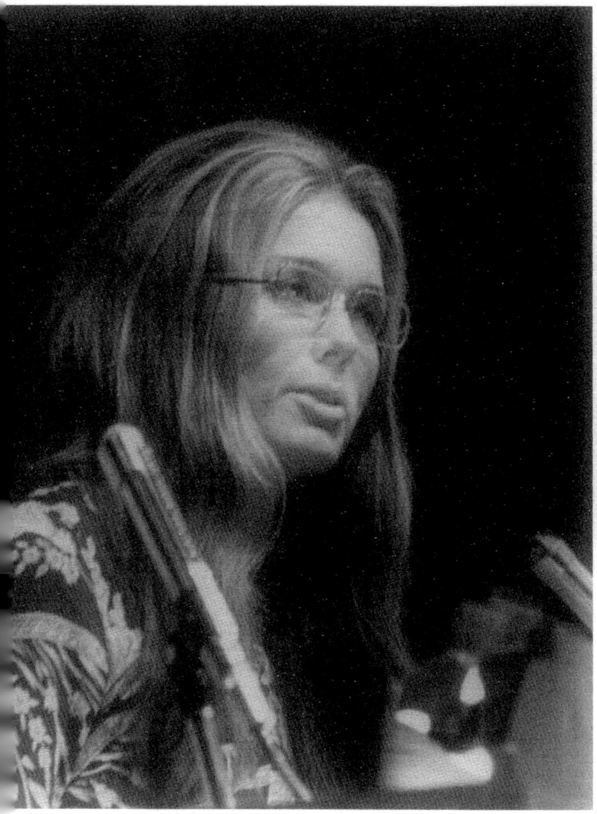

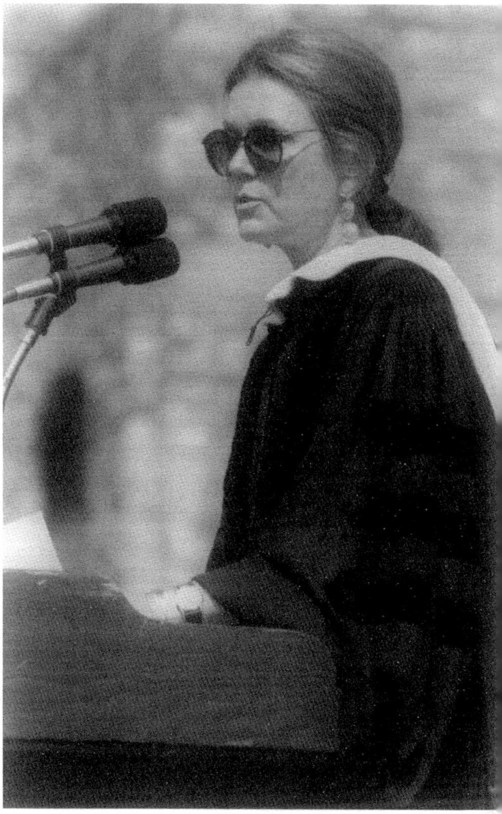

Gloria Steinem

Gloria Steinem is a pioneer in the fight for women's rights and equality. She is regarded as one of the most important feminists of modern times.

Steinem was born in Toledo in 1934. Her parents, Leo and Ruth Nuneviller Steinem, met while both attended the University of Toledo, where Leo founded the student newspaper. At the age of 34, Gloria's mother experienced a mental breakdown that left her incapacitated. When Gloria was 10, her parents divorced, and she remained in Toledo with her mother. Steinem attended Waite High School and graduated from Smith College.

Steinem began a career in journalism, writing for *Esquire* and *New York* magazines. One of her most famous articles was about working as a Playboy Bunny. It was one of her first pieces that focused on feminist themes. She became more politically active and in 1971 formed the National Women's Political Caucus to fight for women's issues, particularly passage of the Equal Rights Amendment. In 1972, she cofounded *Ms.* magazine.

Gloria Steinem continues to speak out on women's issues. While she has written of her childhood in Toledo as a painful time, she has often returned to the area to speak at special events, including receiving an honorary degree from her parents' alma mater in June 1993.

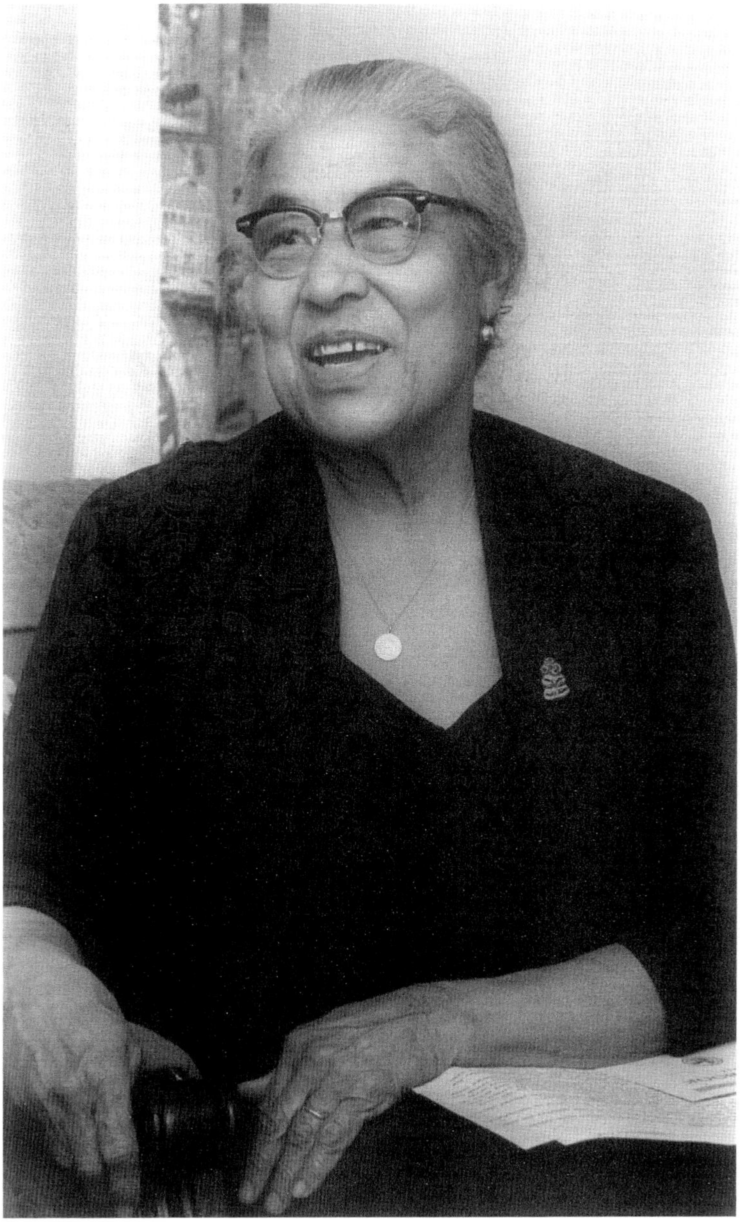

**Ella P. Stewart**

Ella P. Stewart was born in 1893 and dreamt of becoming a teacher. She attended Storer College, the only school in the region that accepted African Americans. But she did not complete her teacher's training, instead marrying and giving birth to a daughter. After her daughter died, she began working in a pharmacy as a bookkeeper and decided to become a pharmacist herself.

When she applied to the University of Pittsburgh, she was told that she would not be admitted because of her race, but she persisted. Stewart graduated in 1916, becoming one of the first African American female pharmacists in the country. In 1922, she and her husband, who was also a pharmacist, purchased a building in Toledo on Indiana Avenue because there were no black-owned pharmacies in the city.

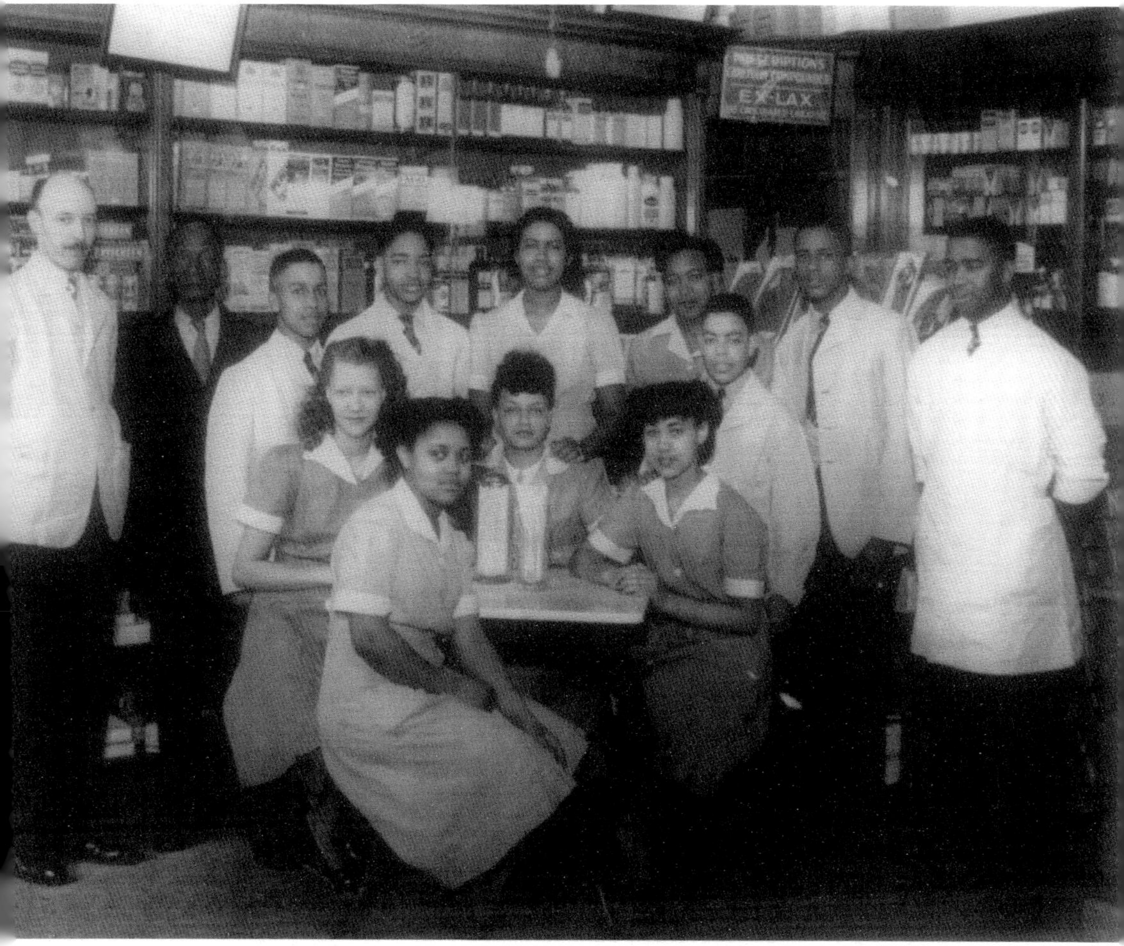


**Stewart's Pharmacy**

Stewart's Pharmacy became a center for the African American community in Toledo, and Ella became a community leader. From 1948 to 1952, she was president of the National Association of Colored Women, lobbying for causes such as anti-lynching and anti–poll tax legislation. In 1952, she was a delegate to the International Conference of Women of the World, promoting peace and understanding with Asian women, and later the United Nations appointed her a commissioner for the UN Education, Scientific, and Cultural Organization, where she traveled around the world speaking out for peace and against discrimination. Stewart's work was also recognized when a Toledo public elementary school was named in her honor. She died in 1987. (Courtesy of the Toledo-Lucas County Public Library.)

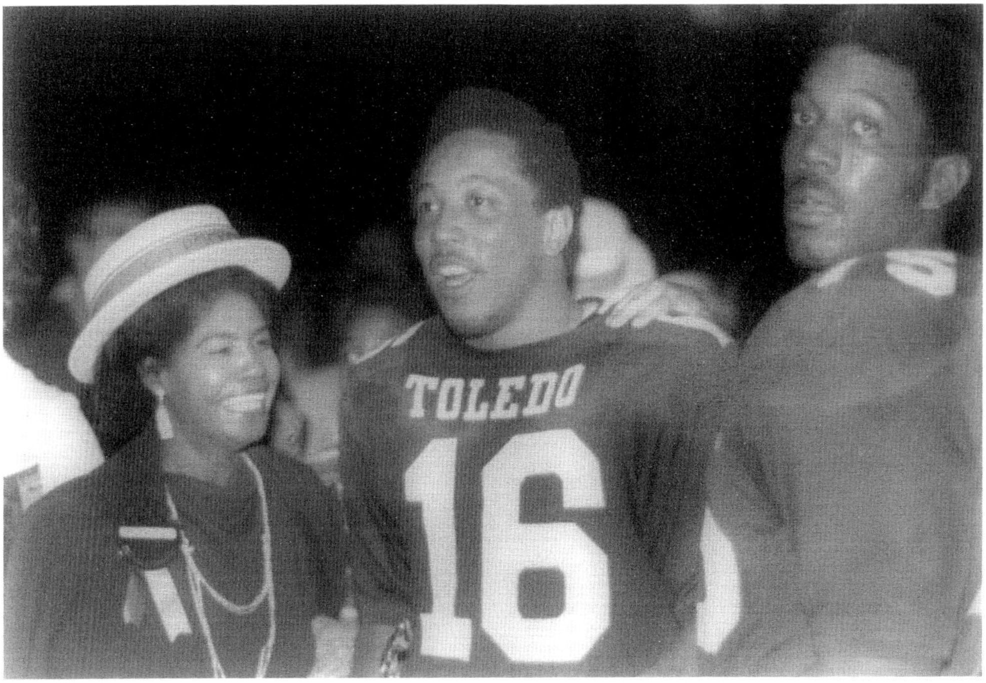


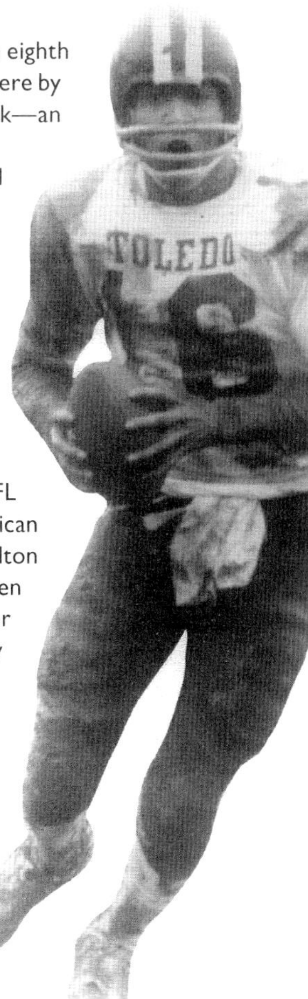


Chuck Ealey

Chuck Ealey was born in Portsmouth, Ohio, in 1950. His mother had only an eighth grade education, but she supported Ealey's desire to go to college. He got there by playing football for Notre Dame High School in Portsmouth as a quarterback—an unusual position for an African American player in the 1960s.

But when it came time to be recruited for college, several expressed interest, but not as quarterback. African Americans were not quarterbacks. But one, Frank Lauterbur of the University of Toledo, not only recruited Ealey, but told him he could play the coveted position he so wanted.

Between 1969 and 1971, Chuck Ealey led the UT Rockets to a 35-game winning streak. Several of the games were close—Ealey would find himself losing with just a few seconds left in the game, but he always pulled it out. In 1971, he was eighth in the balloting for the Heisman Trophy, an incredible accomplishment for a player from a small public university in Ohio not known as a football powerhouse.

But once again, Ealey's accomplishments seemed to be ignored. A few NFL teams expressed interest in drafting him—but not as quarterback. African Americans were not quarterbacks. Ealey was finally drafted by the Hamilton (Ontario) Tri-Cats of the Canadian Football League, where he had seven successful seasons playing the position that no one in the NFL would consider him for. Today, no one thinks it unusual that an African American can play quarterback. Chuck Ealey helped to make that change in attitude possible.

# CHAPTER TWO

# Business and Industry

When Jesup W. Scott published a pamphlet in 1868 with the grandiose title "Toledo: Future Great City of the World," there seemed little chance that the city would live up to his expectations. In fact, it lagged behind most other cities in Ohio at the time. While the state was founded in 1803, few people settled in Northwest Ohio because of Native Americans and British hostility and the miserable environmental conditions of the region. The area was known as the Great Black Swamp, and not only was travel difficult, disease was rampant. Malaria, typhoid, and cholera were common, and earned Toledo the nickname "Graveyard of the Midwest."

Eventually, the Native Americans and British were driven out after the War of 1812. The land was drained through the building of canals, which became the primary impetus for founding Toledo in 1837. And Jesup Scott's vision drove city leaders to constantly look for business and industry leaders who could be enticed to move to the city to help make Scott's dream come true. They succeeded—with the glass industry, with bicycle and automotive-related companies, with a company that produced scales, and with agriculture-related companies.

The men—and, for the most part, they were men—who risked their life savings and their reputations to build businesses in Toledo left their mark. Unfortunately, some of these industries have moved on or evolved, and their influence on the city is no more. The city became, in the 1970s, not the "Future Great City of the World," but instead a symbol of the rustbelt and a punchline for jokes in the song "Saturday Night in Toledo, Ohio." As songwriter Randy Sparks's infamous lyrics stated, "Saturday night in Toledo, Ohio, is like being nowhere at all."

But even though some of the businesses and industries are a part of the city's past, and not its future, residents can still see today the important marks left by the individuals who founded them. And many continue today to shape the economic future. Toledo may never be the Future Great City of the World, but it is today a pleasant place to live, work, and play thanks to its business leaders and their employees.

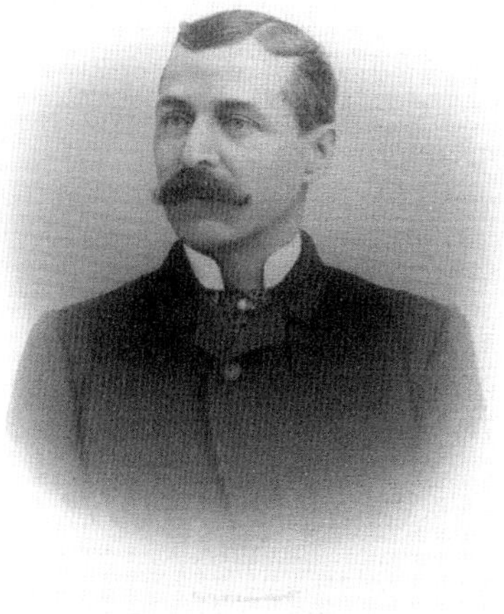

**Peter Gendron**

Peter Gendron did not invent the wheel, but he invented improvements, and the company he founded still exists today. Gendron was born in 1844. While a young man, he manufactured and repaired wagons. In 1865, he moved to Toledo. At the Toledo Novelty Works he developed the idea of a wheel with wire spokes, which he first attached to children's wagons.

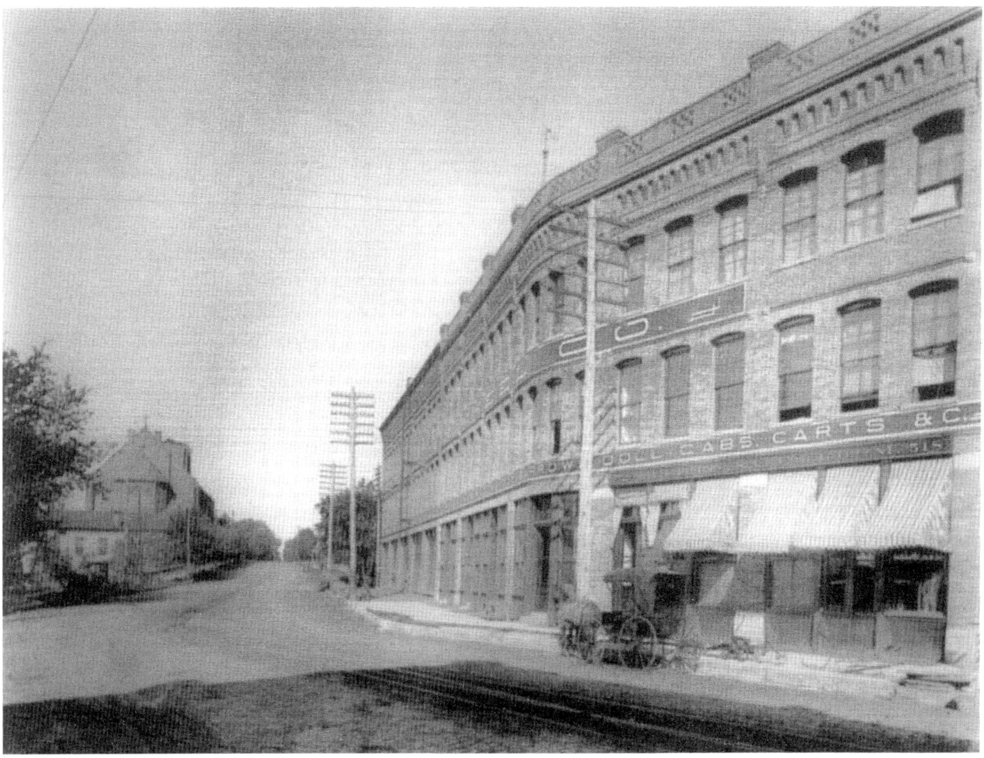


**The Gendron Wheel Company**

In 1877, Peter Gendron started his own company to make these wheels, but it failed. In 1880, he founded the Gendron Wheel Company. In 1882, Gendron patented a lighter and more durable version of his wire-spoked wheel in which the spokes crossed from one side of the wheel to the other over other spokes. The wheel was placed on velocipedes, baby carriages, and bicycles. Gendron continued to experiment with his wheel design and secured 72 patents on his inventions. His wheels were also added to wheelchairs that the company manufactured. Gendron died in 1910, but his company continued. In 1941, it moved to Perrysburg, in 1959 to Archbold, and is presently headquartered in Bryan, Ohio. It continues to sell wheelchairs today.

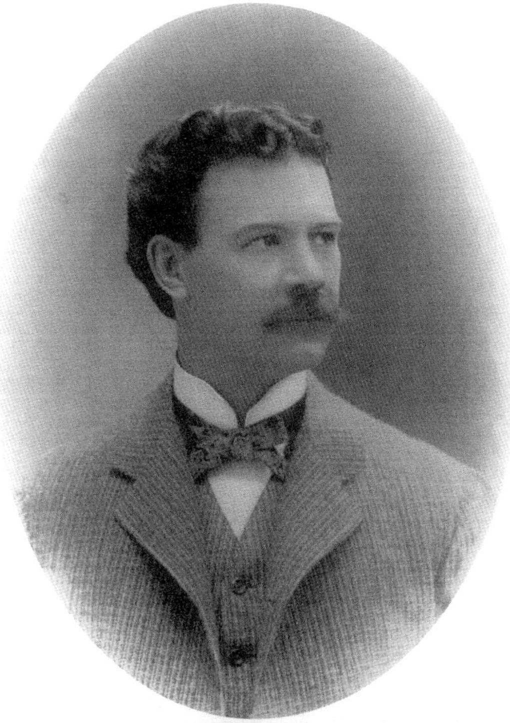

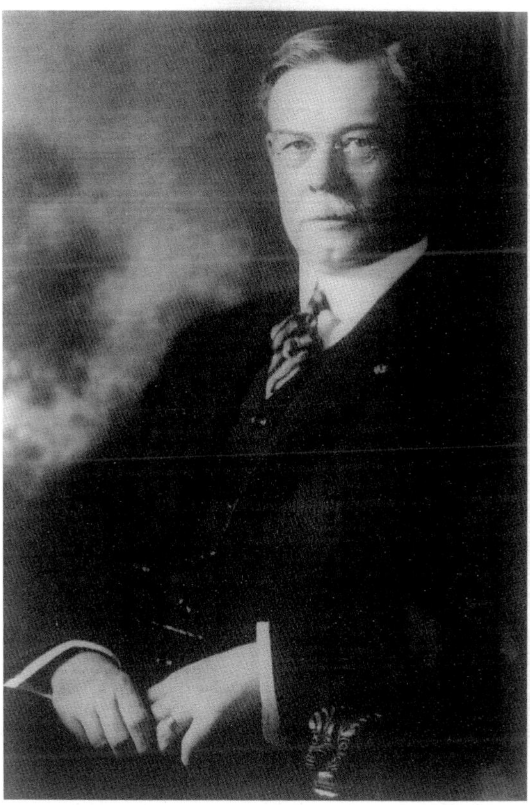

**Robinson Locke**

Robinson Locke was the son of *Toledo Blade* editor and satirist David Ross Locke. When he was 29 years old, he took over the paper after his father's death. He had a fondness for the arts, becoming the paper's theater and music critic. He said, "Take away music, painting, drama, sculpture, and architecture, and all the material glory of the world would not be compensation."

He was one of the founding members of the Toledo Museum of Art in 1901; the first president of the Toledo Symphony Orchestra League, founded in 1897; and one of the founding members of the Northwest Ohio Historical Society, founded in 1918.

Under Locke's direction, the *Blade*'s circulation grew from 10,000 to 90,000. Locke's national reputation was built through his work as a theater critic. When he died in New York City in 1920, he had accumulated a collection of theater memorabilia that was donated to Lincoln Center, which today is preserved by the New York Public Library.

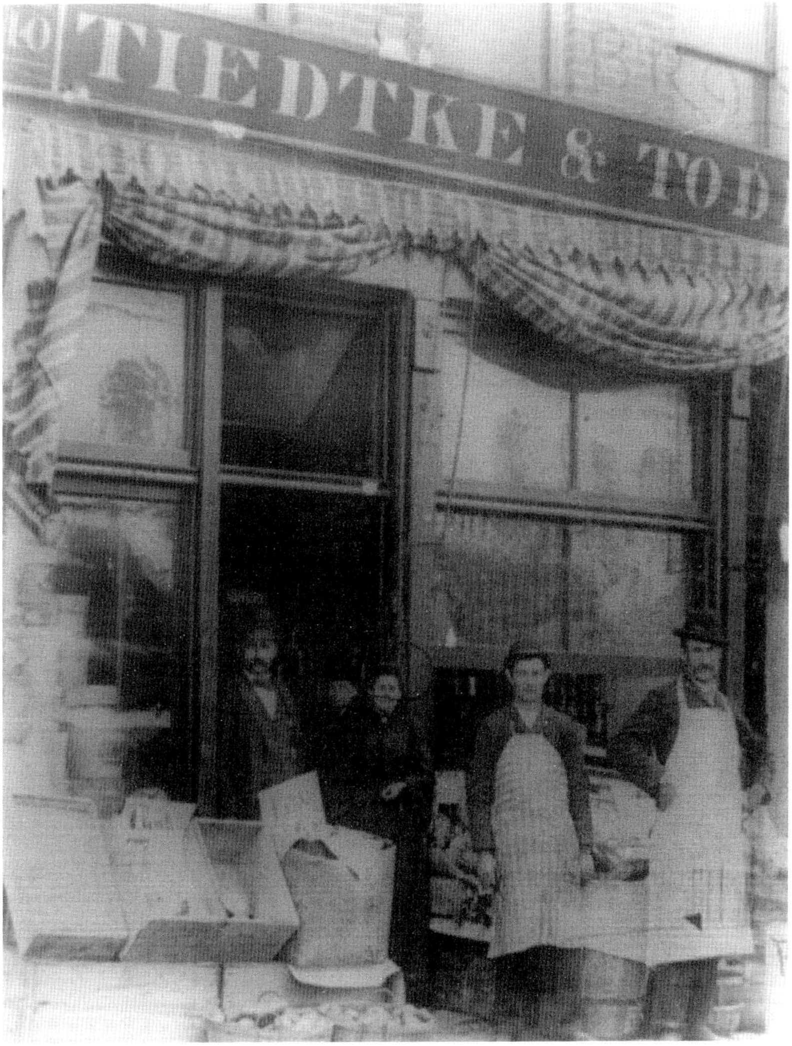


**Charles and Ernest Tiedtke** (ABOVE AND OPPOSITE PAGE)
Charles and Ernest Tiedtke were born near East Toledo. In 1893, they saved up $350 and opened a grocery store in the downtown. As the company grew, the brothers purchased a tugboat, which would meet freighters out on the lake and take their orders. Once the ships were tied up at the docks, the tug returned with their order. Later, the brothers extended their delivery service to land customers with a fleet of horse-drawn wagons, which reluctantly gave way to motorized trucks.

The Tiedtkes moved into a larger store on Water Street at the corner of Summit Street in 1910. They made shopping an event—they roasted their own coffee, offered freshly baked breads, sold fresh fish and meats, and expanded into general merchandise. Tiedtke's came to be known around the country, and even Gertrude Stein, who visited Toledo in 1935, remarked that she was impressed with the store. At times the store resembled a circus more than a retailer. At Christmas, children from the local orphanage were invited into the store and given $2 to spend on whatever they wished.

Tiedtke's became a part of the fabric of the city. Charles Tiedtke died in 1928 at the age of 63, and Ernest died in 1950 at the age of 78. The store was sold to a Columbus firm in 1925, to a chain in 1961, and closed in 1972. Three years later, it was destroyed in a spectacular fire. (Courtesy of the Toledo-Lucas County Public Library.)

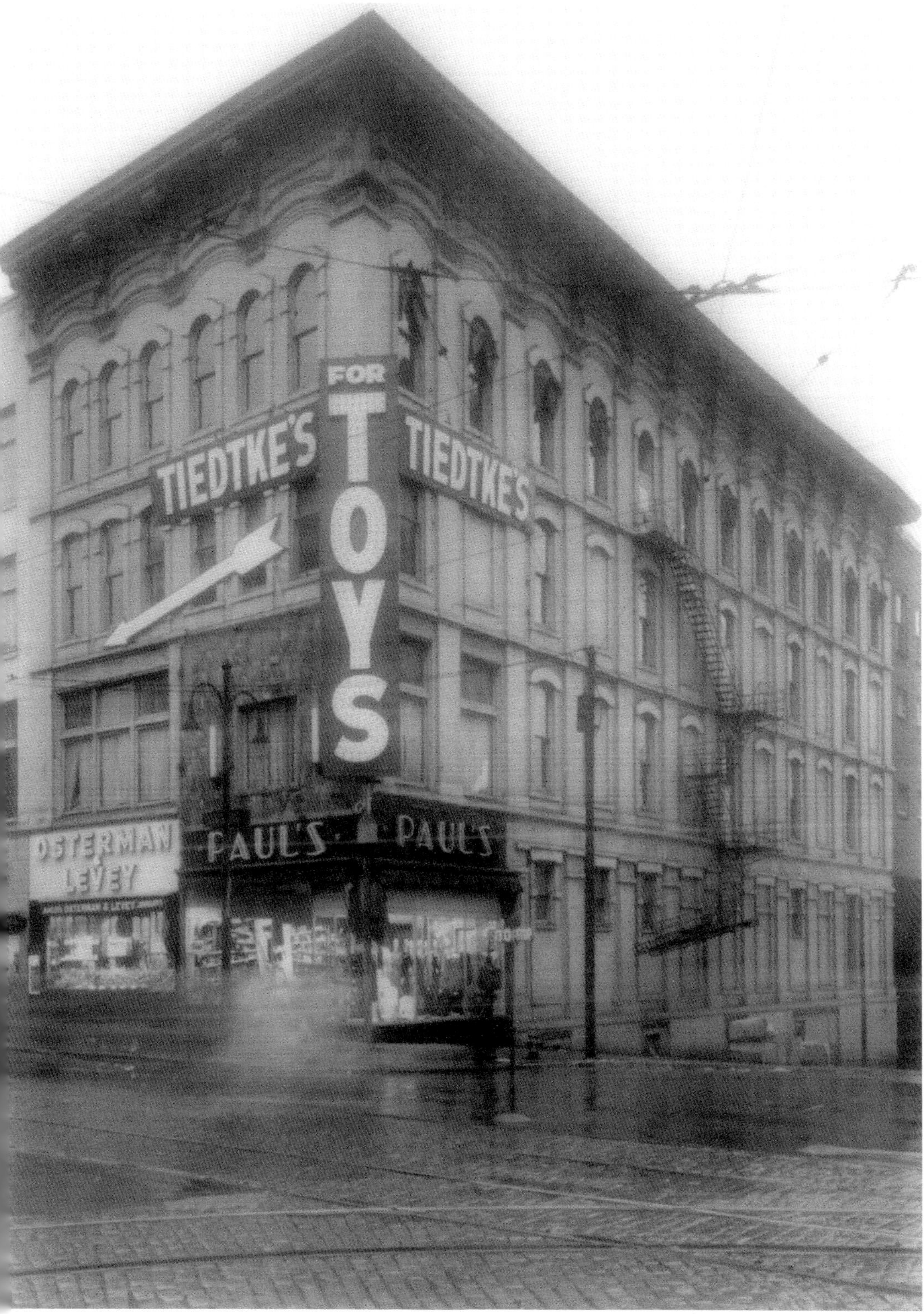
FOR
TOYS
TIEDTKE'S
TIEDTKE'S
OSTERMAN
LEVEY
PAUL'S
PAUL'S

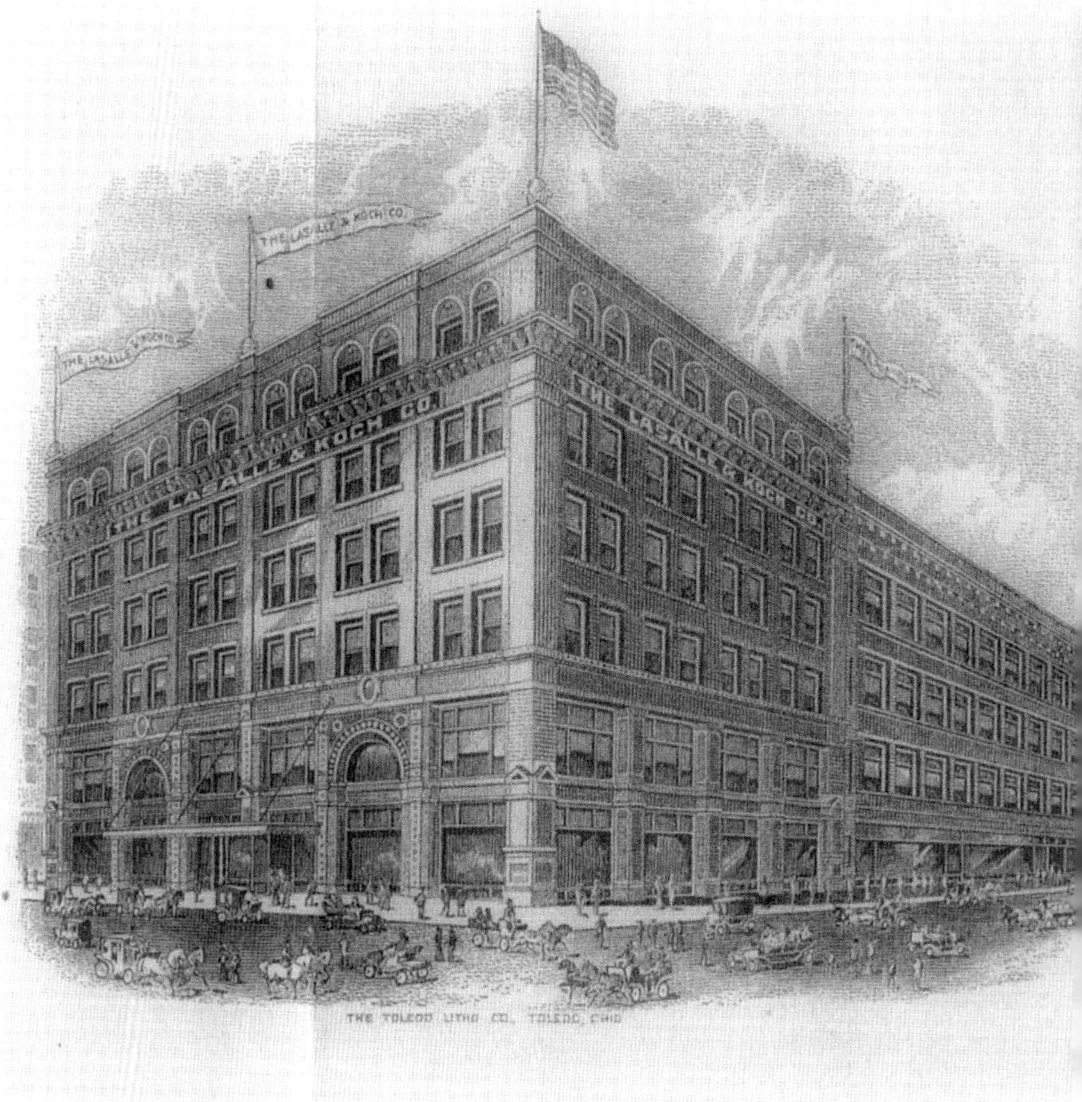


### Lasalle & Koch

The Lasalle & Koch department store began as a partnership between Jacob Lasalle and Joseph Koch. It continued after their deaths under their two sons Alfred Koch and Sol Lasalle. The roots of the company date back to 1865, when Jacob Lasalle and Joseph Epstein opened a dry-goods store in downtown Toledo. In 1876, a competing store operated by Joseph Koch and A.S. Cohn opened down the street. The two stores merged in 1880 and took the name Lasalle & Koch. Lasalle & Koch recognized the increasing prosperity of Toledo and focused their goods on the upper class. In 1917, it moved into a new building at Huron and Adams Streets, and in 1927 it added three additional floors.

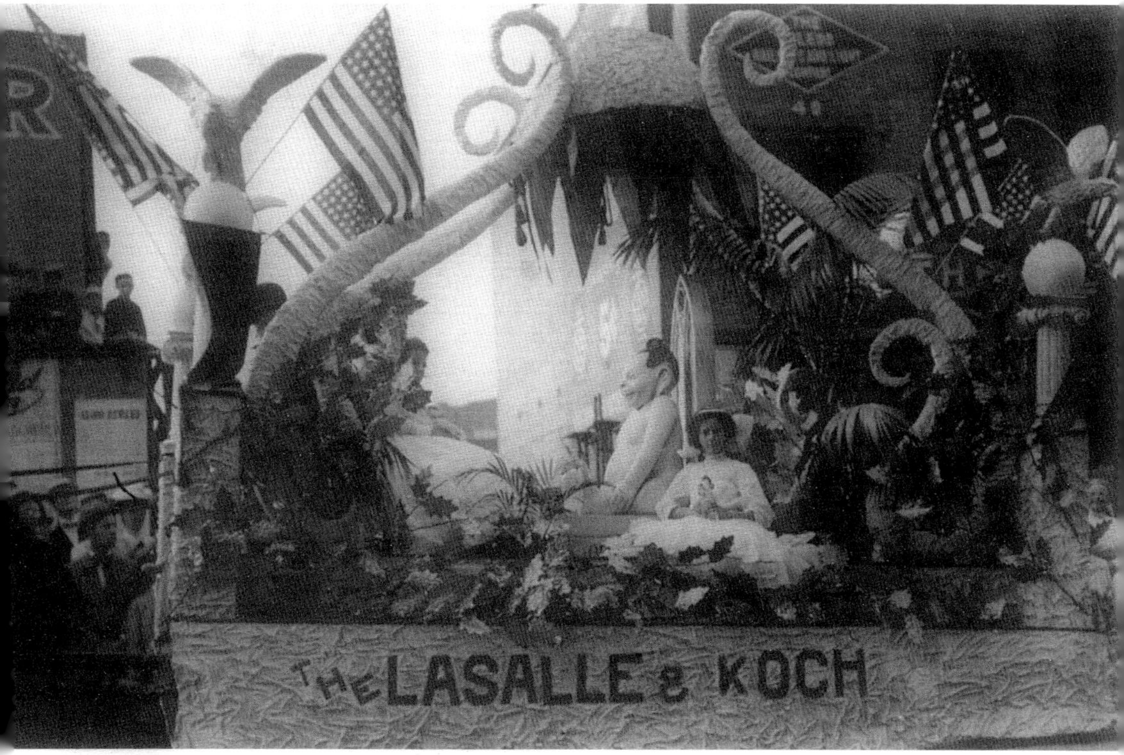


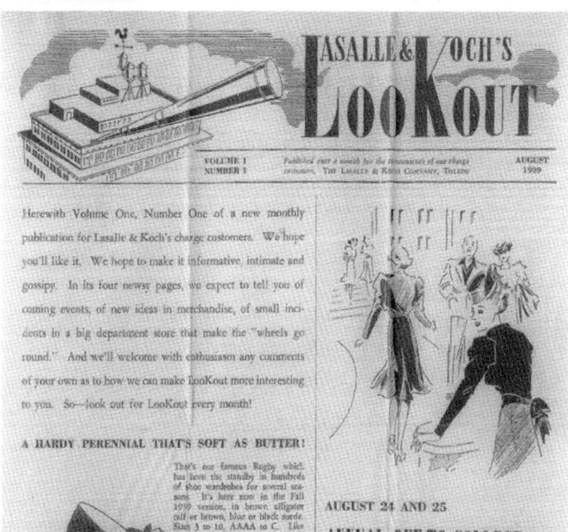

LASALLE & KOCH'S

LOOKOUT

VOLUME 1
NUMBER 1

*Published once a month for the convenience of our charge customers.* THE LASALLE & KOCH COMPANY, TOLEDO

AUGUST
1939

Herewith Volume One, Number One of a new monthly publication for Lasalle & Koch's charge customers. We hope you'll like it. We hope to make it informative, intimate and gossipy. In its four newsy pages, we expect to tell you of coming events, of new ideas in merchandise, of small incidents in a big department store that make the "wheels go round." And we'll welcome with enthusiasm any comments of your own as to how we can make LooKout more interesting to you. So—look out for LooKout every month!

A HARDY PERENNIAL THAT'S SOFT AS BUTTER!

That's our famous Rugby which has been the standby in hundreds of shoe wardrobes for several seasons. It's here now in the Fall 1939 version, in brown alligator calf or brown, blue or black suede. Sizes 3 to 10, AAAA to C. Like so many good things, exclusive with us in Toledo and it's still a low, low $6.50. *Second Floor*

AUGUST EVENTS

July 31-Aug. 6: "The Desert Song." *Zoo Amphitheater*
Aug. 2, 9, 16, 23 and 30: Bring your husband down between 7 and 9 on these evenings to our Furniture Floor—full of August Sale buys!
Aug. 1: "Time Off for the Cook" at 2:00 *Homemakers' Center, 6th Floor*
Aug. 7-13: "The Chocolate Soldier" *Zoo Amphitheater*
Aug. 8: "Easy Dishes for Busy Days" at 2:00 *Homemakers' Center, 6 Floor*
Aug. 15: "Fashions in Food" at 2:00 *Homemakers' Center, 6th Floor*
Aug. 22: "Cool Cooking for Comfort" at 2:00 *Homemakers' Center, 6th Floor*
Aug. 24 and 25: Annual College Show and Luncheon *8th Floor*

AUGUST 24 AND 25

ANNUAL OFF-TO-COLLEGE STYLE SHOW AND LUNCHEON

Ziegfeld was famous for his "Follies," Billy Rose is noted for his "Aquacade," and Lasalle & Koch's is celebrated all over Northwestern Ohio for its annual Off-To-College Style Show. So again, our College Sketch Book turns its pages with college girls showing the best in classics and the newest fads for campus and dates, while college men provide "atmosphere."

All the clothes you see will have the official Okay of our College Board, consisting of four college girls and four college men. There will be music, college hostesses, plenty of excitement. To satisfy the crowds, we're going to stage this gala affair for two days in the air-conditioned French Room and Auditorium, Eighth Floor.

A delicious luncheon, at 75c, will be served at 12:30. Please make your reservations early. Incidentally, all reservations will be closed two days prior to the shows because of the necessity of making accurate floor plans, and reservations will not be held after 1:00 on both days of the shows. We'll be seeing you!

Lasalle & Koch Float at Toledo's Wamba Parade, 1909

The King Wamba Parade was a huge event in Toledo in 1909, honoring the 17th-century king of Spain. Many of the local businesses had elaborate floats in the parade, including Lasalle & Koch. Jacob Lasalle died in 1921, and in 1924 Alfred Koch partnered with R.H. Macy of New York. In 1933, Alfred Koch died, and Macy became the sole owner, although the store kept its local name until 1982. In the 1960s, Lasalle's expanded into the suburbs. The downtown store closed in 1984.

Newsletter of Lasalle & Koch, 1939

Lasalle & Koch's monthly store newsletter was used to promote events and sales. The issue included advertisements for $58 fur coats and $78 living room furniture groups.

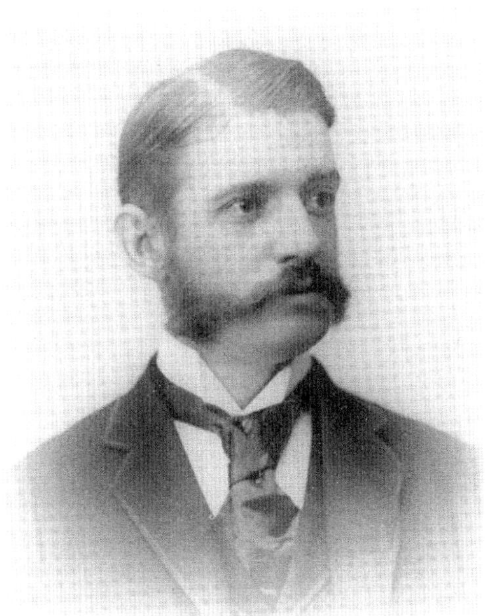

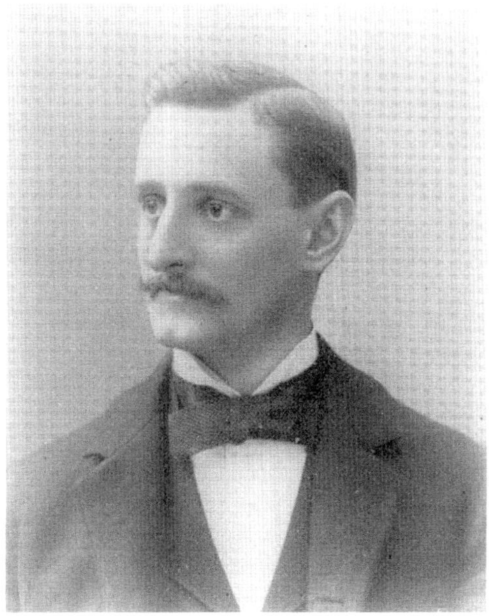

Julius Lamson and John D.R. Lamson

John and Julius Lamson were born in Elbridge, New York, in the 1850s. Julius came to Toledo with their brother Edgar in the 1870s and began working in retail. Julius worked for the predecessor of Lasalle & Koch but sought to found his own store, which became possible through the generosity of this wealthy father-in-law. In 1885, Julius asked his brother John to come to Toledo to operate the dry-goods store, which opened on October 6 of that year as the Lamson Brothers Company on Summit Street.

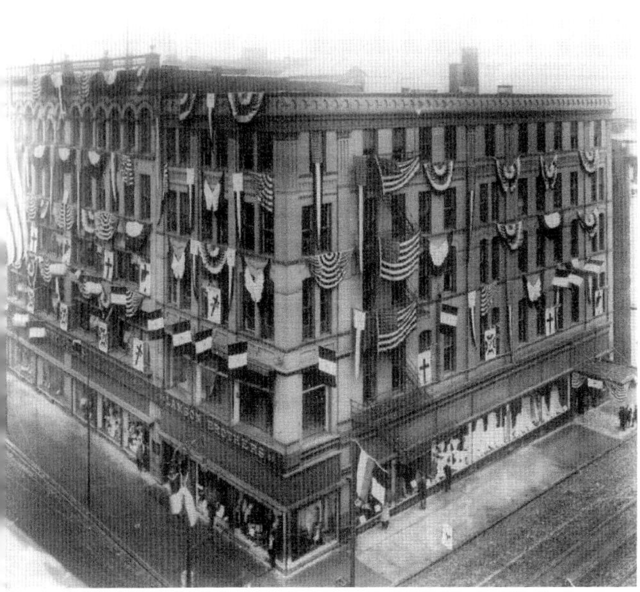

Lamson's Department Store

The store quickly expanded, mostly due to its reputation for honesty in business. John D.R. died at the young age of 56, and Julius was joined in the business by his son-in-law Sydney Vinnedge. The store outgrew the six buildings it occupied on Summit Street by the late 1920s and in 1928 broke ground for a new store at the corner of Huron Street and Jefferson Avenue at a cost of $3 million. Lamson's focused on upscale merchandise and expanded into the suburbs in the 1960s and 1970s, opening stores in Parkway Plaza in Maumee (1961), Franklin Park Mall (1971), and Southwyck Mall (1972). In 1976, the store was forced into bankruptcy, and all of its stores closed. (Courtesy of the Toledo-Lucas County Public Library.)

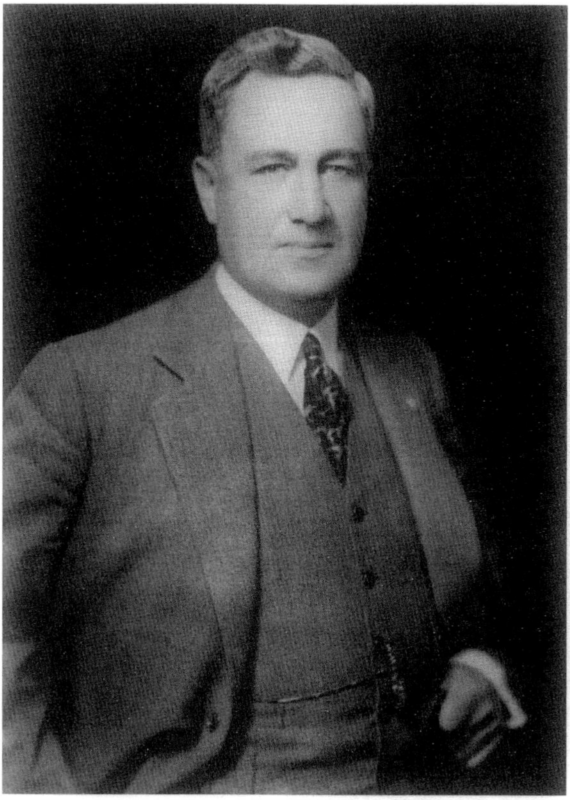

## Henry Page

Henry Page was born in England in 1879. In 1888, the family moved to the United States, settling in Dixon, Illinois. In 1896, Page established a dairy in Dixon, and in 1913 he founded the Page Dairy Company in Toledo. The company became one of the largest independent producers of dairy products in the Midwest.

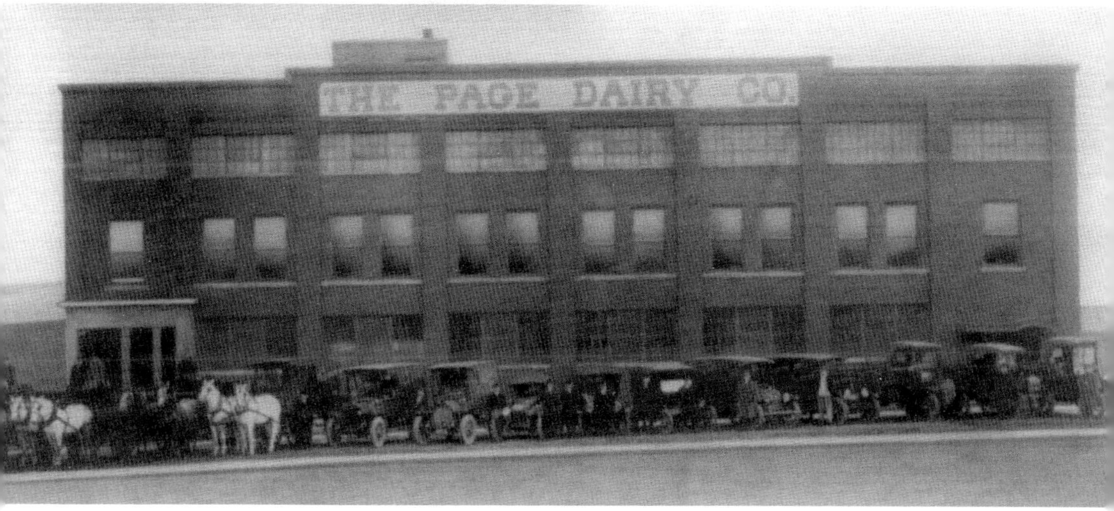


## The Page Dairy Company

In addition to his business, Henry Page was also known for his support of civic affairs. During the Depression, the dairy provided desperately needed milk to children through the local schools, a program that continued for over 20 years. Page also chaired the food council of Lucas County during World War II and continued to provide milk and dairy products to the needy. The stadium at DeVilbiss High School was named in recognition of his contributions to the community. Henry Page died in 1950, and the company was taken over by his sons.

### Isaac D. Smead

Isaac Smead was born in Massachusetts in 1849. He became a proponent of the need for fresh air in buildings. At the time, most buildings were heated in ways that were not healthy. While working for a company that sold a heating system developed by Henry Ruttan, Smead worked to improve the system. In 1882, he established Isaac D. Smead and Co. in Toledo. Smead held 13 patents related to furnaces and ventilation systems by 1886.

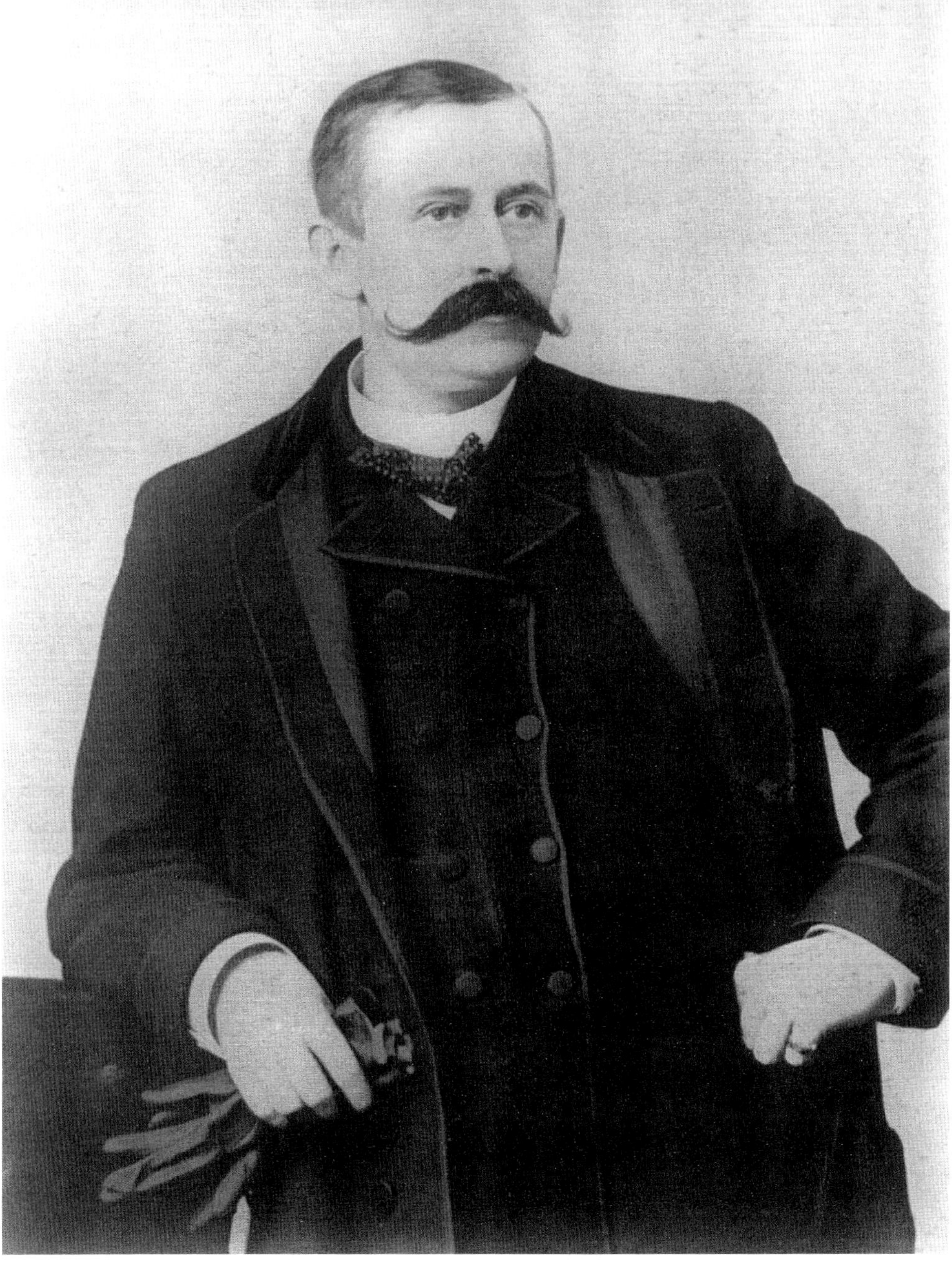

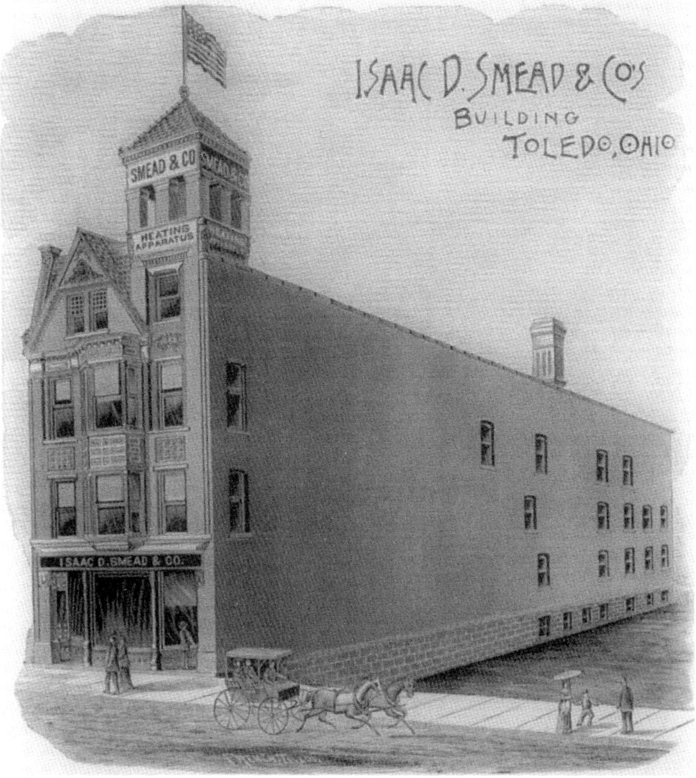


**Isaac D. Smead and Company**
In 1886, Smead published a book of plans from many schools and other public buildings that utilized what was then known as the Ruttan-Smead System. Despite his numerous contracts, in 1889 Smead was forced to declare bankruptcy with almost $1 million in debts. At the time of the filing, his case was the largest bankruptcy ever filed.

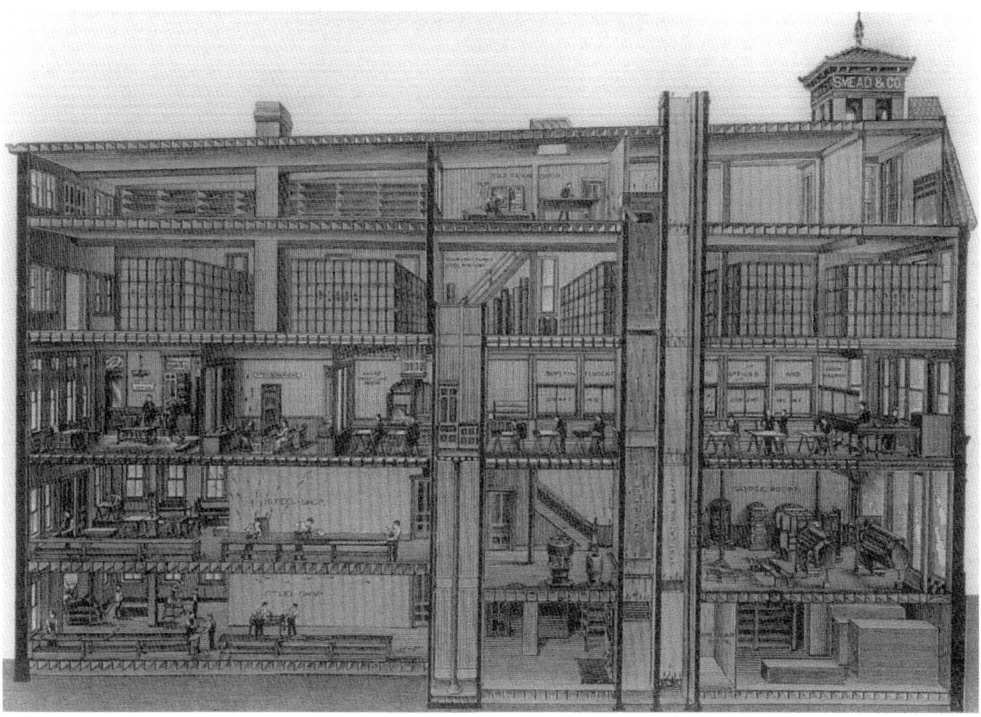

## Edward Ford

With his father, Capt. John Ford, Edward Ford helped to found the plate glass industry in the United States.

Edward's father had been involved in many kinds of businesses in the years before the Civil War, including building riverboats used by the Union army.

After the war, the riverboat business declined, and the older Ford embarked on a new venture, making plate glass. But plate glass had never been made in the United States, and neither Ford nor his son Edward (born in 1843) knew much about it. After a small factory failed, the Fords decided that the only profitable way to make plate glass was to open a large factory. They did so near Pittsburgh, Pennsylvania, and the called their company Pittsburgh Plate Glass (PPG).

After a falling out with their partner, the Fords left PPG and started a company in Michigan that supplied glass-making chemicals. But Edward Ford wanted to produce glass, so he bought land along the Maumee River, and in 1898 he founded the Edward Ford Plate Glass Company. He also founded the town of Rossford, a combination of his name and that of his wife, Caroline Ross.

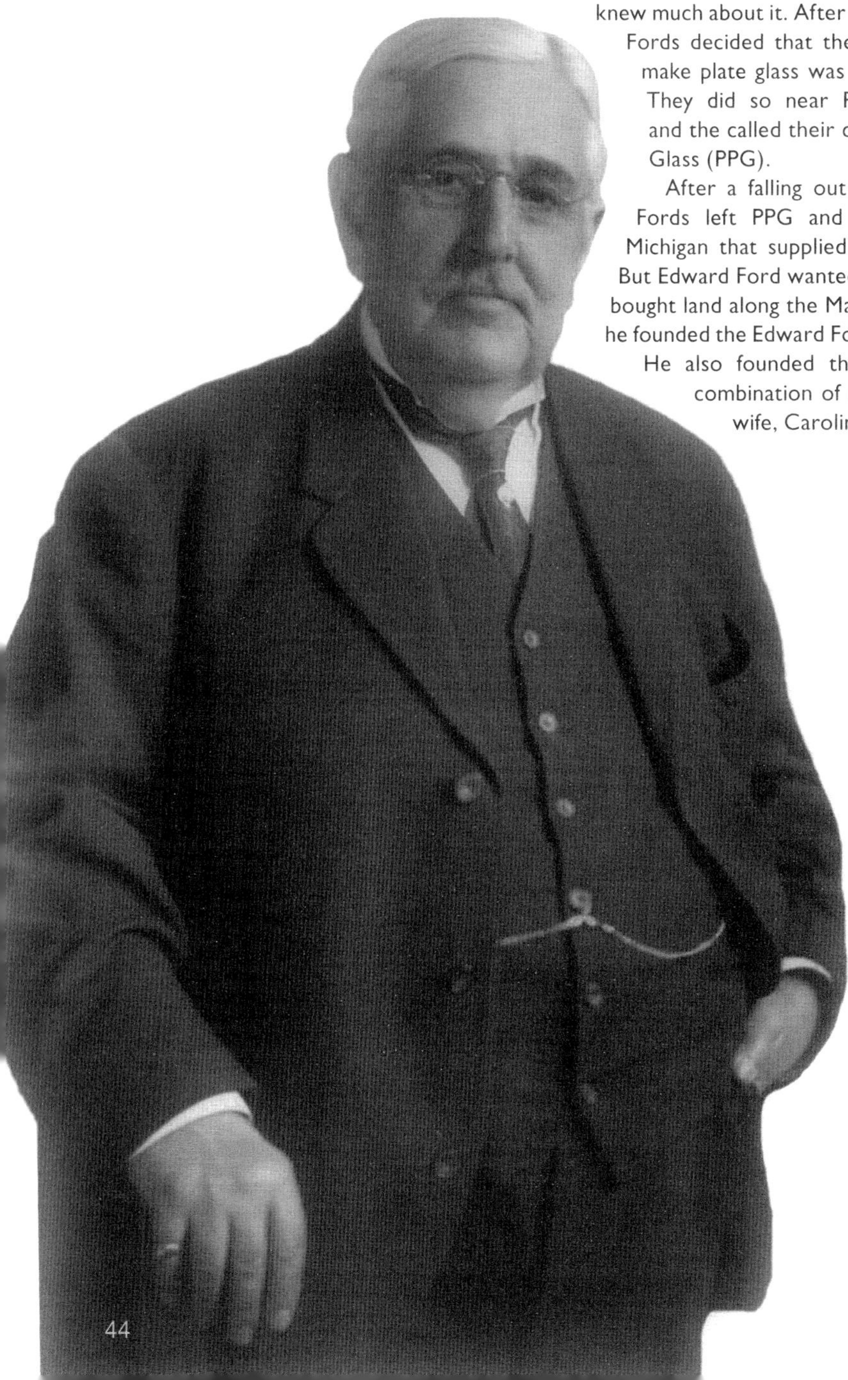

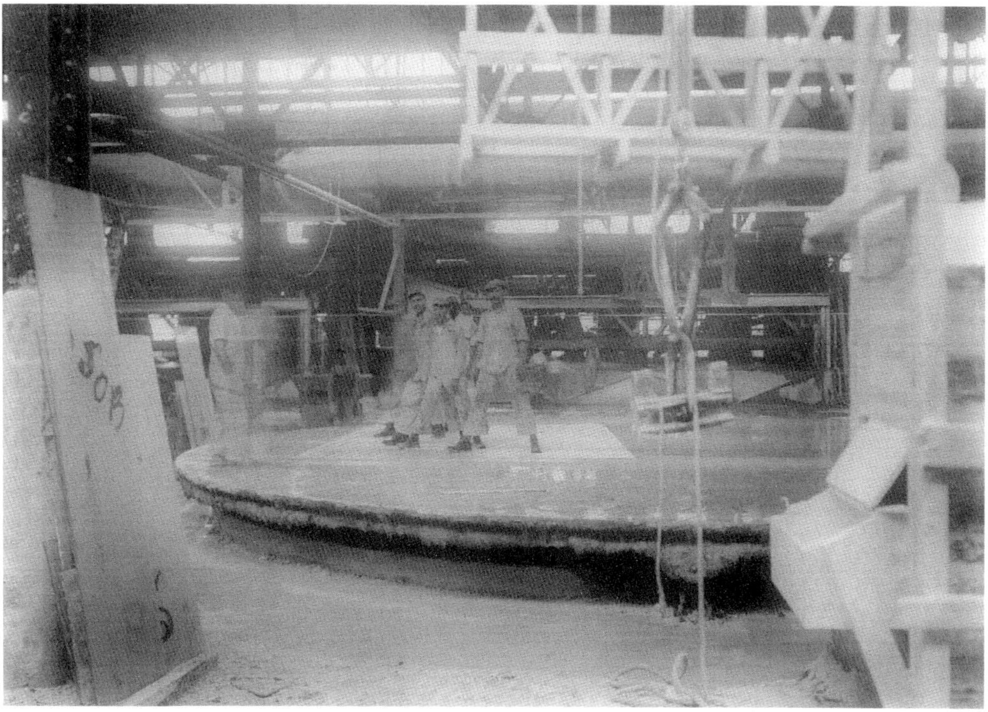

**Edward Ford Plate Glass Company**

The company produced plate glass by pouring molten glass onto large molds, then grinding and polishing it until it was smooth and distortion-free. The company was led by Edward Ford until his death in 1920. In 1929, it merged with the Libbey-Owens Sheet Glass Company to create Libbey-Owens-Ford, Inc.

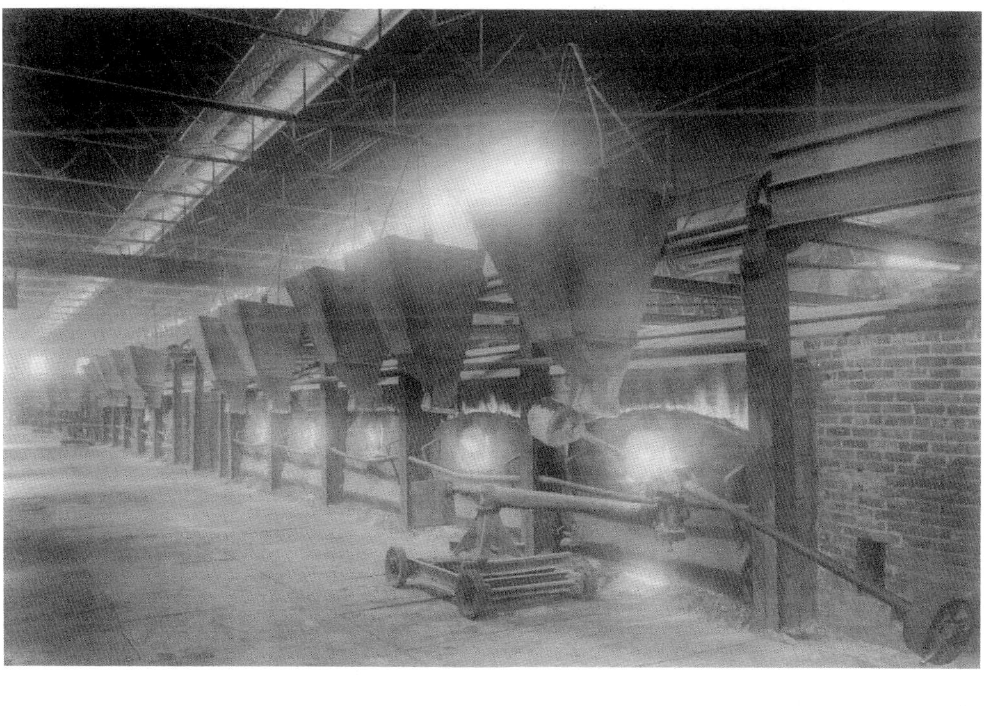

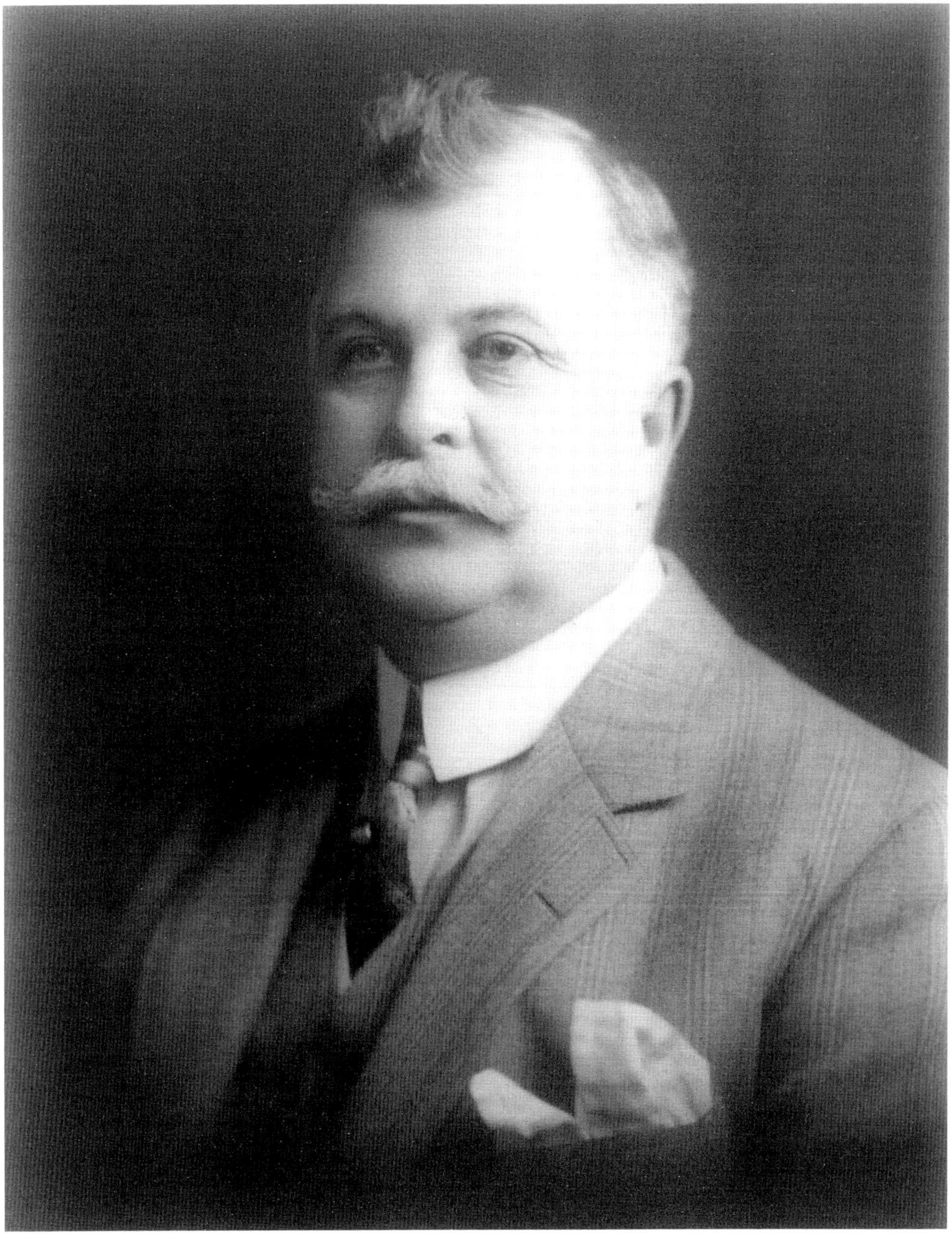

**Edward Drummond Libbey**

In 1888, Edward Drummond Libbey moved his New England Glass Company from Cambridge, Massachusetts, to Toledo. The company, established in 1818, was going through difficult times in Massachusetts due to escalating labor and fuel costs. Toledo gave Libbey land for a new factory and a promise of cheap and plentiful natural gas.

But the company struggled in its early years. Many of the workers returned home, and the natural gas boom went bust. But Libbey persevered, and with the help of a successful exhibition at the 1893 World's Columbian Exposition, the newly named Libbey Glass Company became a national brand.

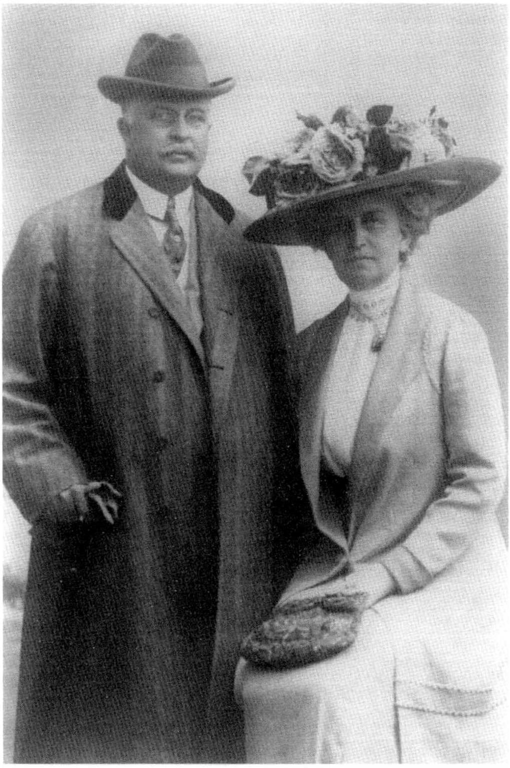

**Edward D. Libbey and Florence Scott Libbey**
In June 1890, Libbey married Florence Scott from one of Toledo's most prominent families. Florence brought to the marriage a deep love of art. With her encouragement, in 1901 Libbey and others founded the Toledo Museum of Art.

**The Toledo Museum of Art**
In 1912, the museum moved into this beautiful Neoclassical building that was constructed on land owned by Florence's father. The couple traveled the globe buying art for the new museum. Libbey died in 1925, leaving his fortune to the museum and to many Toledo charities.

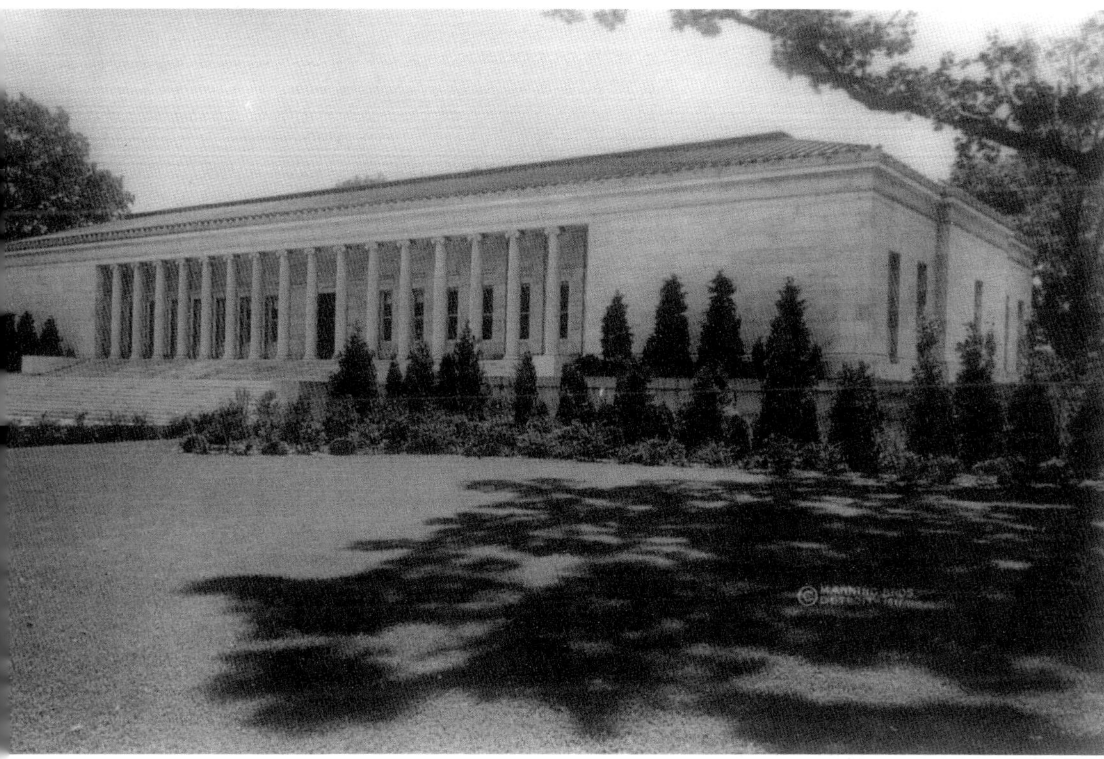

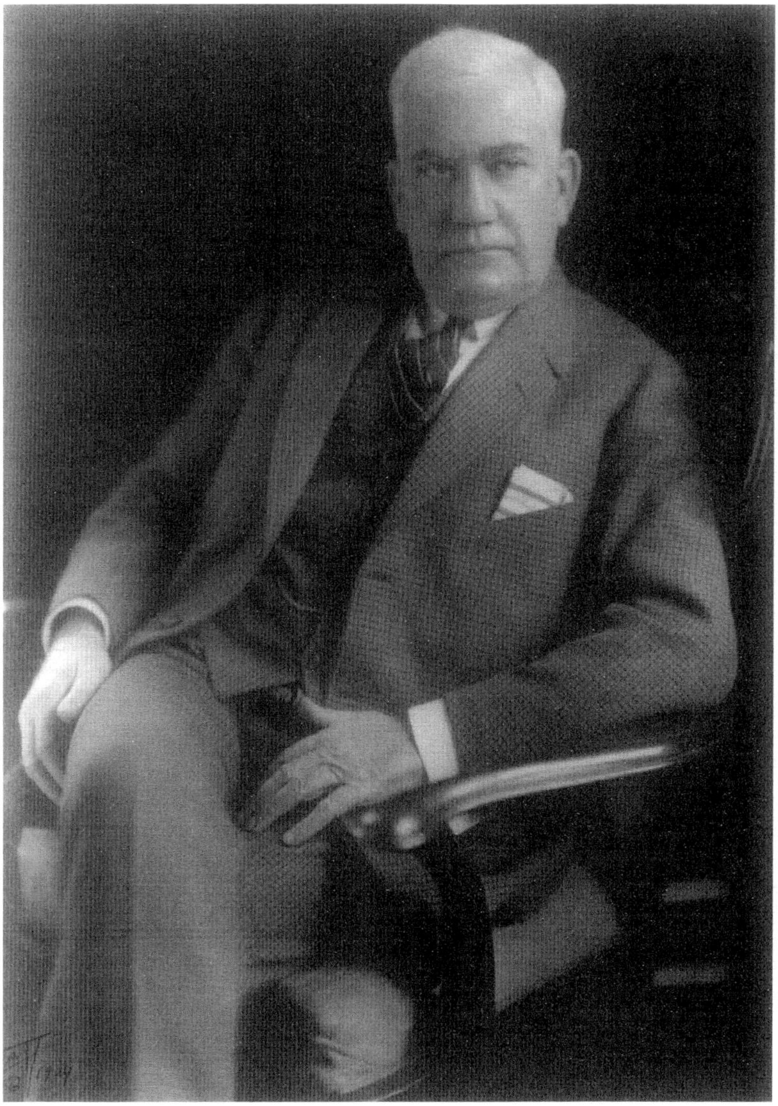

**Michael J. Owens**

When many of Edward Drummond Libbey's skilled glass workers left Toledo to return to Massachusetts in 1889, Libbey traveled to West Virginia for replacements. There he found an Irish immigrant who had been working in glass factories since he was 10 years old, Michael J. Owens. Owens's first job had been shoveling coal into the glass furnaces, which he did for 10 hours a day. He graduated to become a "blower's dog," helping skilled blowers make bottles by hand. The demeaning, dangerous, and demanding work would later inspire Owens to invent a machine to automatically produce bottles without the need for child labor. His invention of the Owens Bottle Machine in 1903 is credited with ending the use of child labor in the industry. He also helped to create the Libbey-Owens Sheet Glass Company in 1916.

Unlike Libbey, who was well educated and refined, Owens had little formal education and a quick temper. But as supervisor of Libbey's factory, he helped to make it successful. He was perhaps more comfortable among the workers than among the educated and wealthy set, even after becoming the president of his own company. Owens died in 1923.

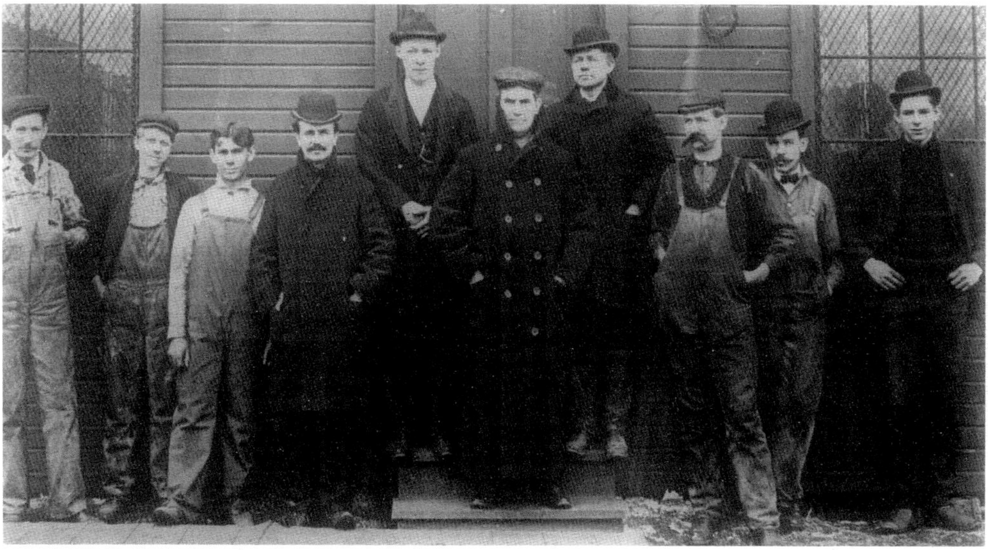

Michael Owens

Michael Owens (center) is seen here with workers at Libbey Glass.

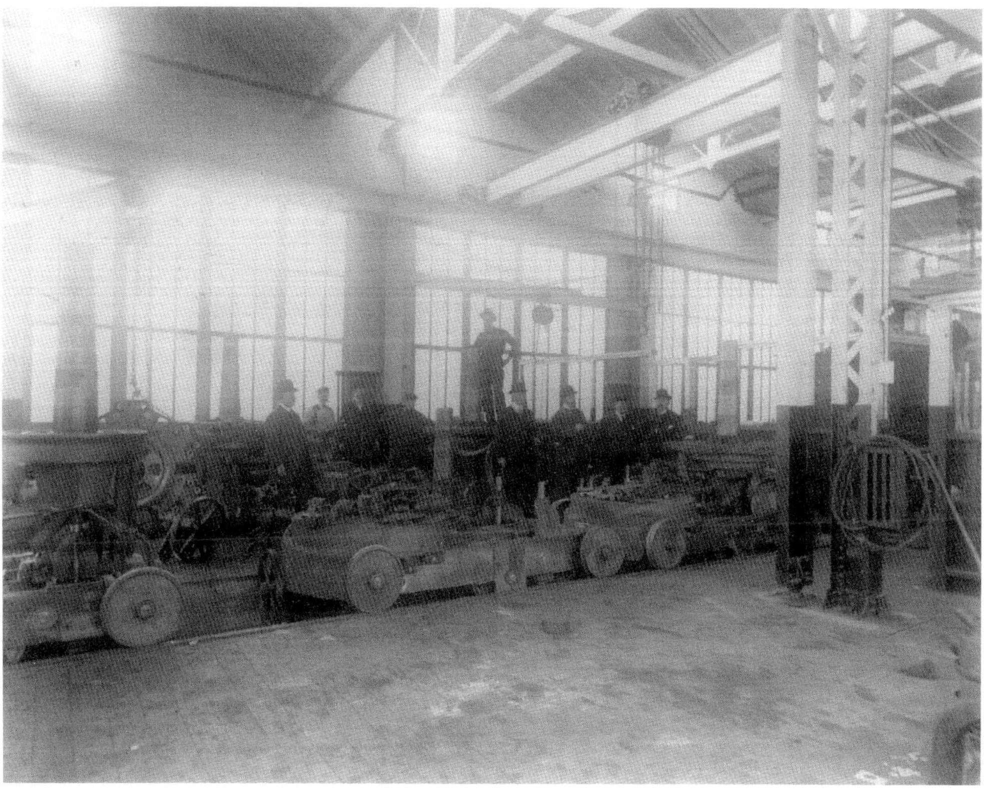

Michael Owens and His Automatic Bottle Machine, 1906

Owens, second from left, is pictured here in Manchester, England, demonstrating his new bottle machine.

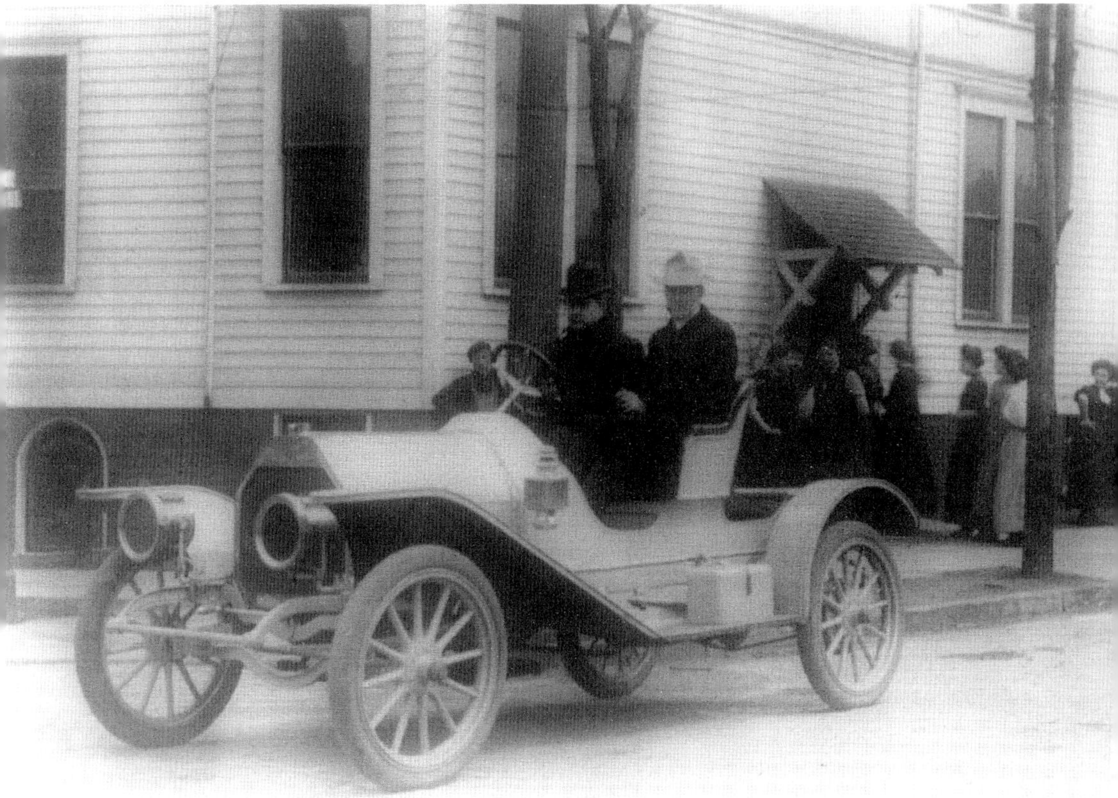

### Thomas A. DeVilbiss

Thomas DeVilbiss took an idea invented by his father—the throat-spray atomizer—and turned it into a paint-spraying machine.

DeVilbiss was born in 1878 in Indiana, and the family soon moved to Toledo, where his father, Dr. Allen DeVilbiss, was a specialist in diseases of the nose and throat. Dr. DeVilbiss sought an effective, comfortable way to apply medicine to his patients' throats. By attaching a ball to a piece of rubber hose, he invented the atomizer.

After two years of studying to become a doctor, Thomas DeVilbiss decided to become a businessman. After working for his brother's company, the Toledo Computing Scale Co. (which became Toledo Scale), he began to experiment with other uses for the atomizer, including as a paint sprayer. He developed a fan-shaped sprayer for use in the growing automobile industry. His idea was so successful that he built a large new factory on Detroit Avenue in Toledo. He is pictured seated in the car, right.

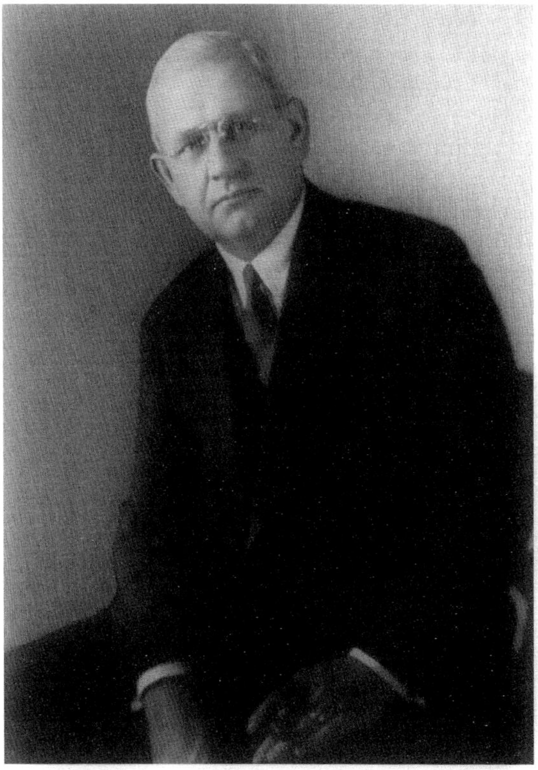

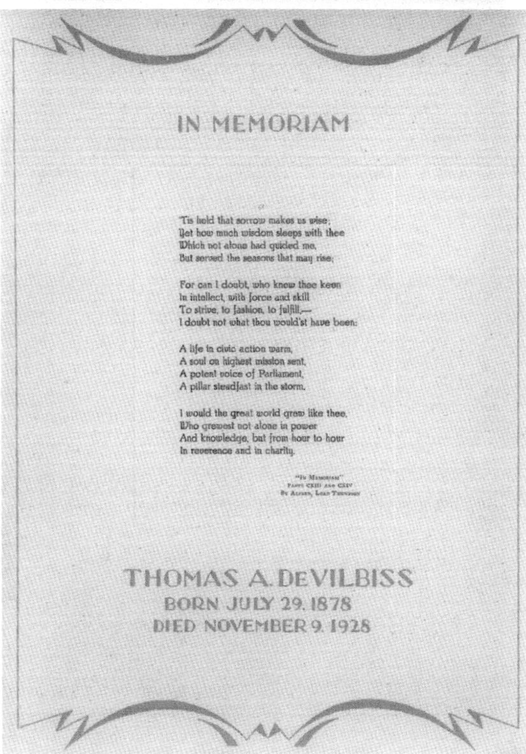

IN MEMORIAM

'Tis held that sorrow makes us wise;
Yet how much wisdom sleeps with thee
Which not alone had guided me,
But served the seasons that may rise;

For can I doubt, who knew thee keen
In intellect, with force and skill
To strive, to fashion, to fulfill,—
I doubt not what thou would'st have been:

A life in civic action warm,
A soul on highest mission sent,
A potent voice of Parliament,
A pillar steadfast in the storm.

I would the great world grew like thee,
Who grewest not alone in power
And knowledge, but from hour to hour
In reverence and in charity.

"In Memoriam"
Parts CXIII and CXIV
By Alfred, Lord Tennyson

THOMAS A. DEVILBISS
BORN JULY 29, 1878
DIED NOVEMBER 9, 1928

### Active in Civic Engagement

Thomas DeVilbiss was also committed to civic engagement. He was elected to the Toledo Board of Education in 1915 and led the fundraising campaigns for Scott and Waite High Schools. DeVilbiss High School was named in recognition of his service. He was a leader of the boards of the Toledo Council of Boy Scouts, the Community Chest, the Toledo Museum of Art, the Toledo Rotary, and the Toledo Chamber of Commerce. Upon his death in 1928 at the age of 50, his estate donated nearly $300,000 to charitable organizations in the city.

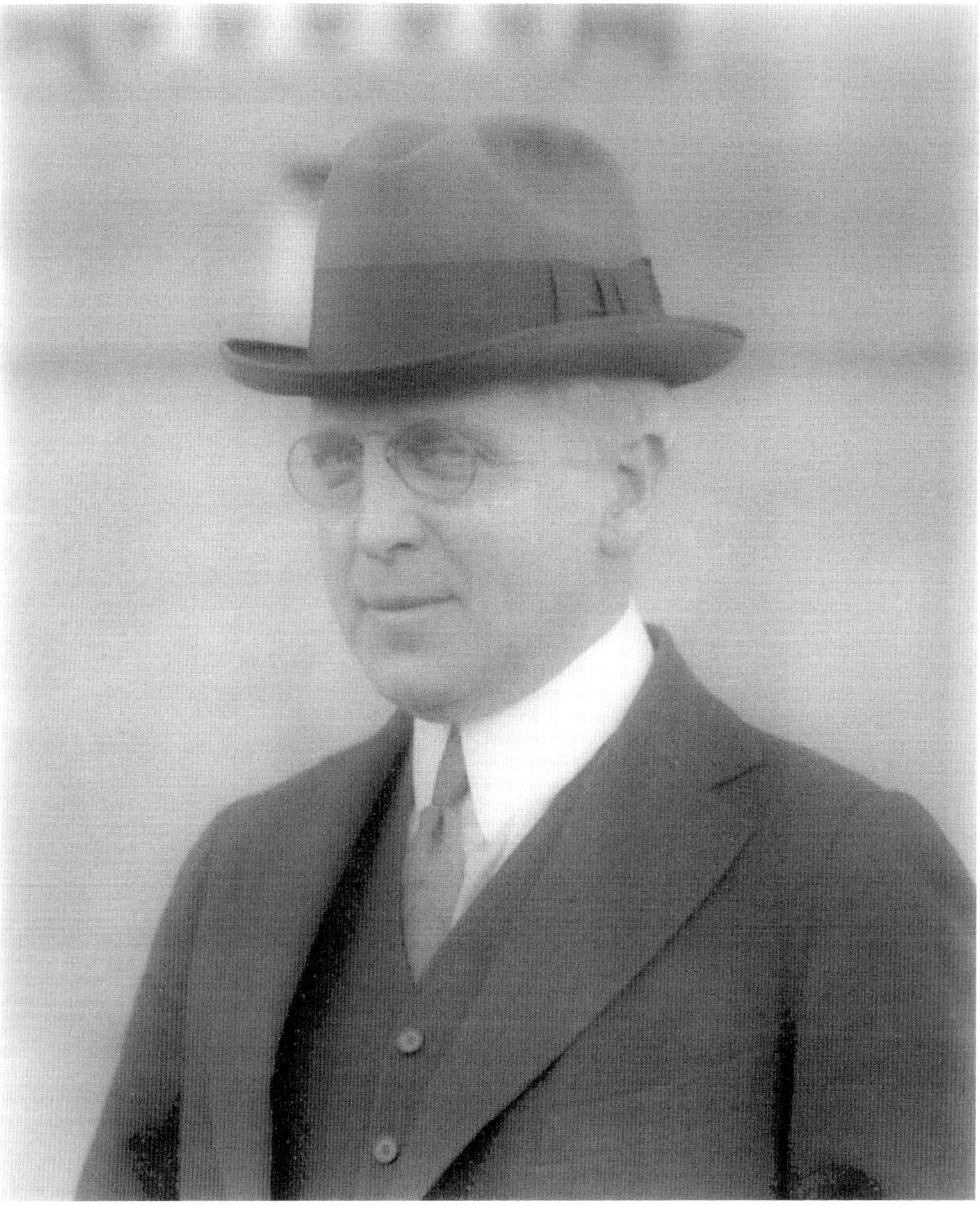

**John North Willys**

John Willys was born in upstate New York in 1873. While young, he started selling Overland automobiles at a dealership in Elmira, New York. A supply problem led Willys to purchase the Overland Company, then located in Indiana, in 1907. In 1909, he bought the former Pope manufacturing plant in Toledo and began producing Overland vehicles there. In 1912, the name was changed to the Willys-Overland Motor Company. (Courtesy of the Toledo-Lucas County Public Library.)

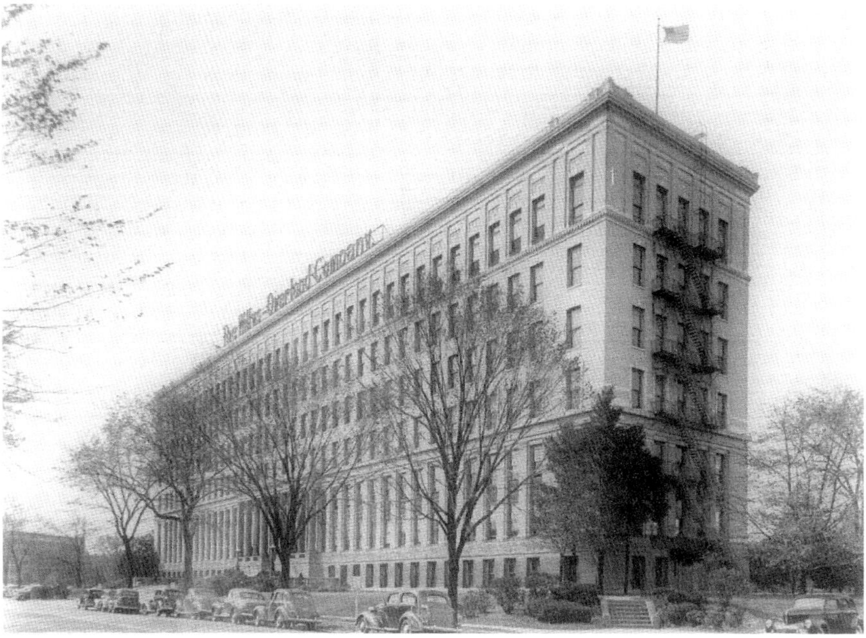


Willys-Overland Administration Building

For the next six years, the company bought up other automobile manufacturers to become the second-largest producer in the country, trailing only Ford. One-third of Toledo's workforce was employed by the company or its suppliers. The company also produced Willys-Knight cars and farm tractors and acquired control of the Duesenberg car company in 1919.

But Willys-Overland also experienced labor difficulties, with a major strike in 1919 shutting the plant down for several months. Willys had also gone into debt to purchase many of his subsidiary companies. The stock market crash of 1929 forced the sale of several companies and ended the production of the Whippet, Willys-Knight, and Stearns-Knight automobiles. The company went into receivership in 1933 and operated under bankruptcy protection until 1936. The following year, it was reorganized as Willys-Overland Motors. Willys died in 1935 in New York City.

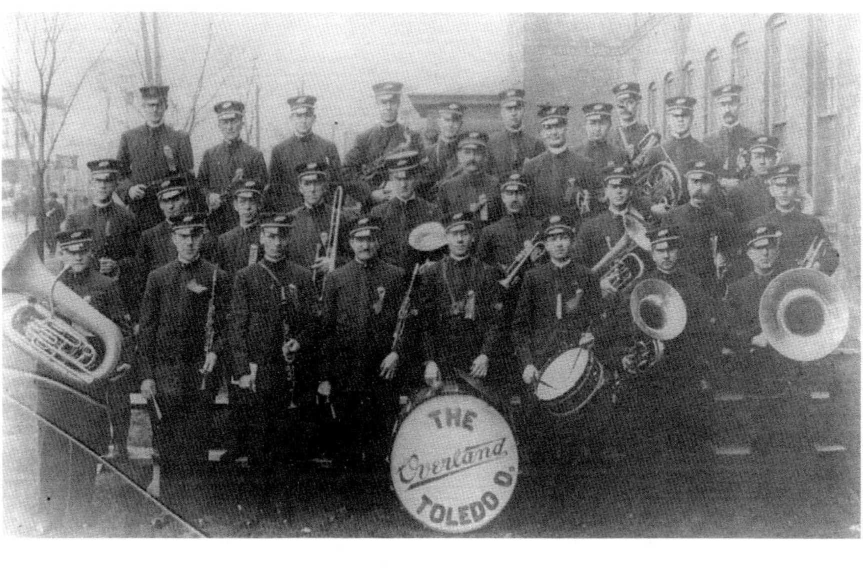

## Ward M. Canaday

Ward Canaday graduated from Harvard University in 1907. His first job was as advertising manager for the Hoosier Cabinet Company, where he developed the concept of consumer credit by allowing people to buy cabinets for $1 down and $1 a week. In 1916, he joined the Willys Overland Company as advertising manager and established the first automobile consumer credit corporation.

During World War I, when Willys Overland was experiencing financial difficulties, Canaday spun off the advertising department as the US Advertising Corporation. In 1932, Willys Overland was forced into receivership, and Canaday reorganized the company and took over as chairman.

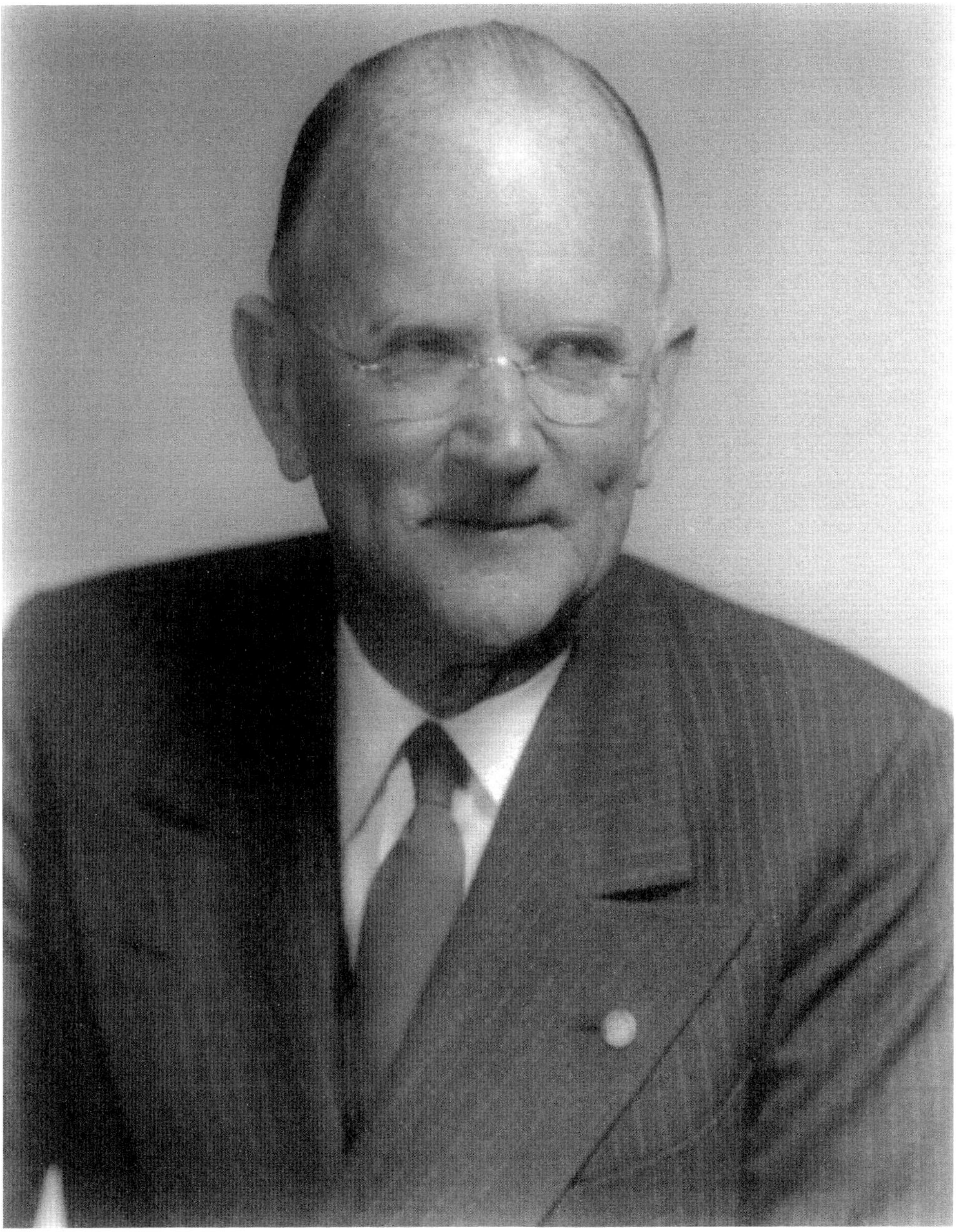

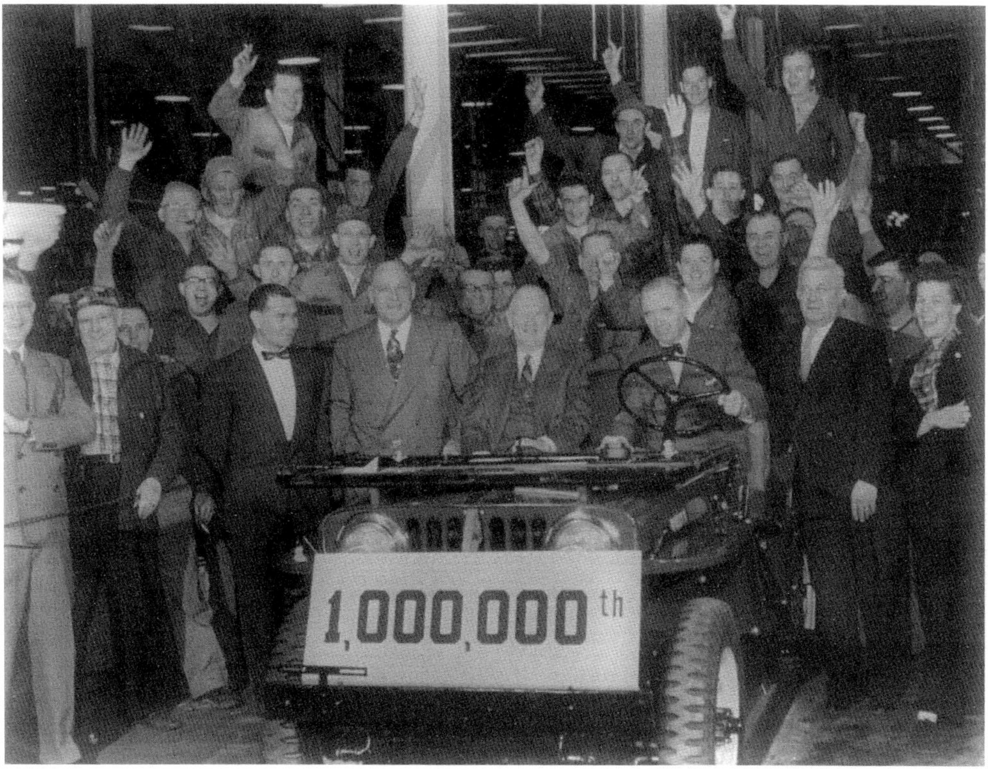


**Ward Canaday and the Millionth Jeep**

When the War Department sought a lightweight general-purpose vehicle for World War II, Canaday led the development of what would become known as the Jeep. Today, he is often called the father of the Jeep. In 1953, Canaday sold the company to Kaiser Motors.

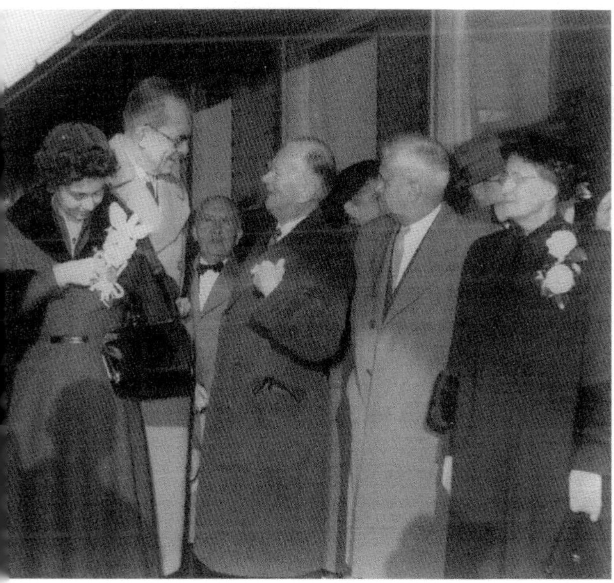

**Ward Canaday Greets the King and Queen of Greece**

The Canadays donated some of their considerable fortune to help restore ancient ruins in Athens, Greece. At the end of World War II, King Paul and Queen Frederica toured the United States to thank the country for its help during World War II. They included a stop in Toledo to visit Ward Canaday and his wife, Mariam. They are pictured greeting the Greek monarch on November 5, 1953.

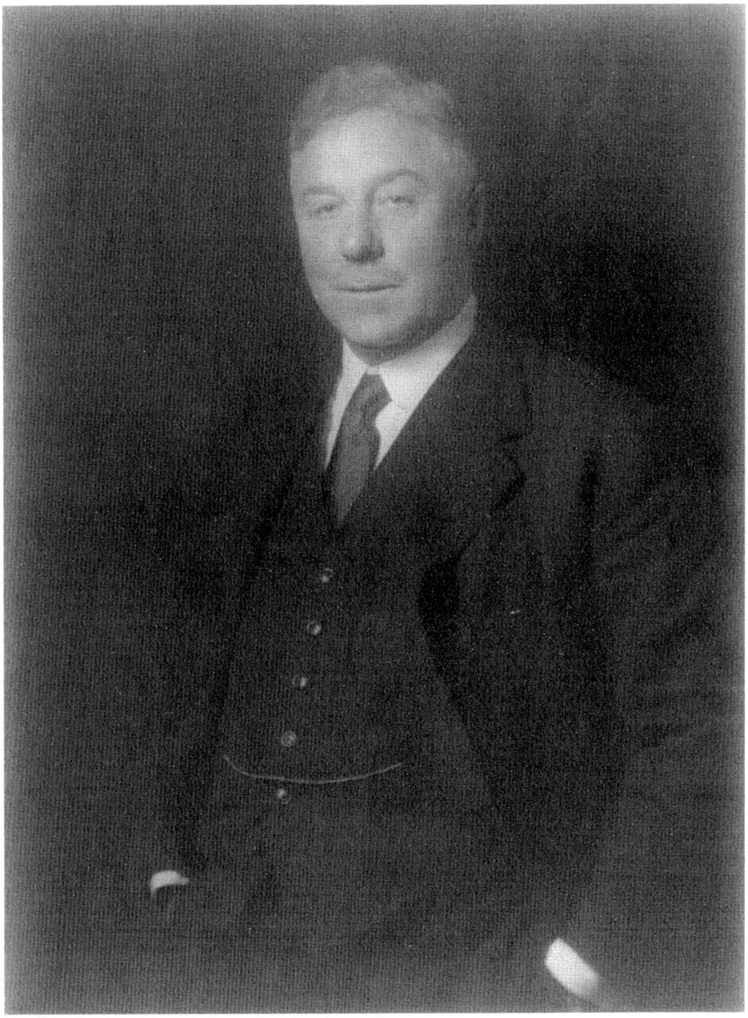

Charles A. Dana

Early-20th-century automobiles were unreliable because power was transmitted to the engine by means of two sprockets connected by a chain, much like a bicycle. The chain often broke because of the poor condition of early roads.

In 1902, while a student at Cornell, Clarence Spicer designed a car that replaced the chain with a universal joint. Spicer patented his invention and opened the Spicer Manufacturing Company in Ithaca, New York in 1904. The company grew rapidly, and by 1913 it supplied Cadillac, Chevrolet, and General Motors. But because competitors often violated Spicer's patents, the company was short of cash.

A young prosecuting attorney from New York named Charles Dana offered to loan the Spicer Manufacturing $15,000 for one year. By early 1914, Dana became a director and president. Clarence Spicer remained with the company, serving as vice president and chief engineer.

The Spicer Manufacturing Company helped design a military truck for World War I. By the end of the war, the company reported annual sales of $30 million. In 1929, the company moved to Toledo to be closer to Detroit, the center of car manufacturing.

Government contracts during World War II increased sales dramatically, and the company's workforce rose to 10,000. In 1946, Spicer Manufacturing Company changed its name to honor of the man responsible for rescuing it—Charles Dana. Dana died in 1975 at the age of 94.

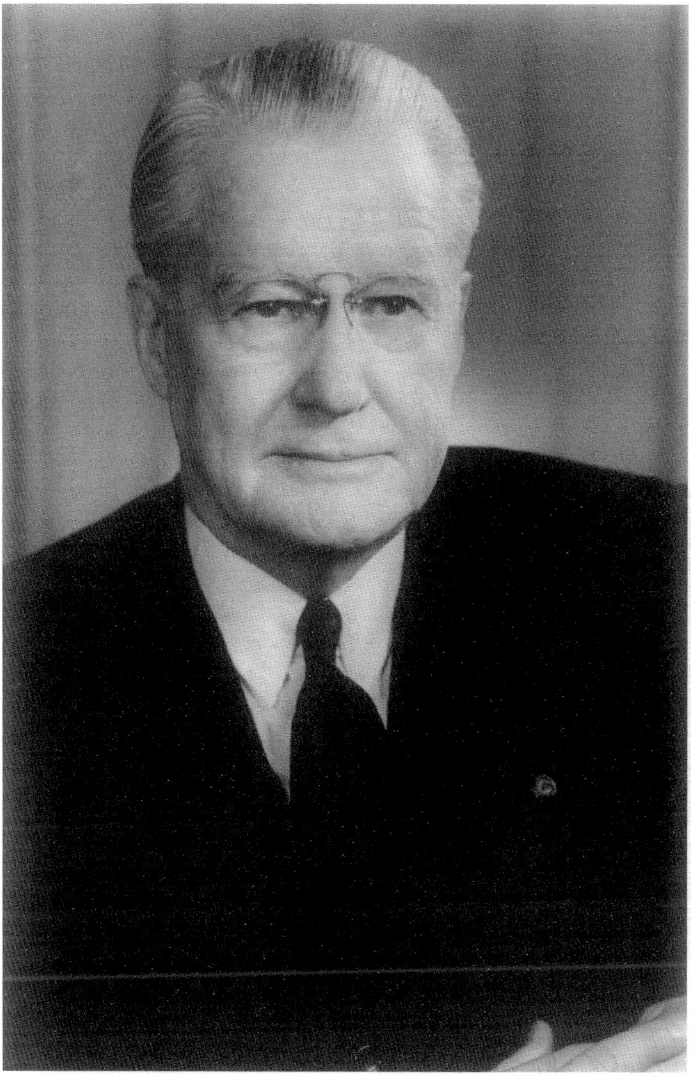

## John D. Biggers

John D. Biggers was not sure how his company, Libbey-Owens-Ford, was going to come up with $9.5 million in 1931 to purchase National Plate Glass and become the sole producer of windshields for General Motors, but he knew the offer would not come along again. The contract he negotiated with the owners of the Fisher Body Company suddenly made L-O-F the second largest plate glass company in the country, with 45 percent of the market share.

Biggers was born in 1888. In 1911, he moved to Toledo and was soon recruited to become assistant treasurer of the Owens Bottle Machine Company. In 1930, Biggers became president of the new Libbey-Owens-Ford Company. The following year, in the middle of the Great Depression, Biggers gambled nearly everything on the contract with General Motors, and the company continued as the sole supplier of windshields for GM until the 1960s.

At the request of Pres. Franklin D. Roosevelt, from 1937 to 1938 Biggers oversaw the first census of the unemployed in the country. In 1939, Biggers again served his country in England working on the Lend-Lease Program to provide military equipment to the British in their fight against the Nazis. He retired from L-O-F in 1960 after 30 years as president and died in 1973 at the age of 85.

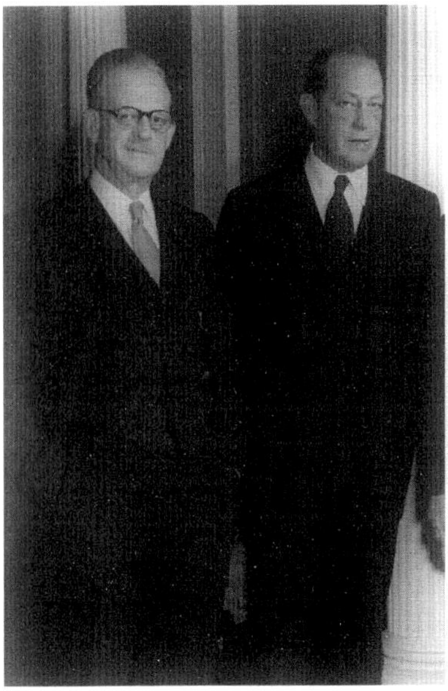

### J. Preston (left) and William Levis

The Levis family of Alton, Illinois, founded the Illinois Glass Company in 1873 to produce glass bottles. In 1910, the company purchased its first Owens automatic bottle machine. By 1915, nearly all of its bottles were made by machine, and Illinois Glass became the largest producer of bottles in the world.

William Levis, grandson of the company's founder, was born in 1890. After surviving World War I (and receiving the Distinguished Service Cross), he returned to Alton anxious to take over the Illinois Glass Company from his aging father and uncles. He did so in 1928 and brought his cousin John Preston into the company along with his friend Harold Boeschenstein. In 1929, the Illinois Glass Company merged with the Owens Bottle Company of Toledo to form Owens-Illinois.

Levis soon took control of O-I, and he continued to build the company. The company expanded rapidly when Prohibition ended and the market for liquor bottles returned. William Levis served his country again in 1941 and 1942 as assistant to the chairman of the War Production Board, which oversaw industry during World War II. After serving as president and chairman of the board of O-I, William Levis retired in 1950, and J. Preston, who had been serving as president, succeeded him as chairman of the board.

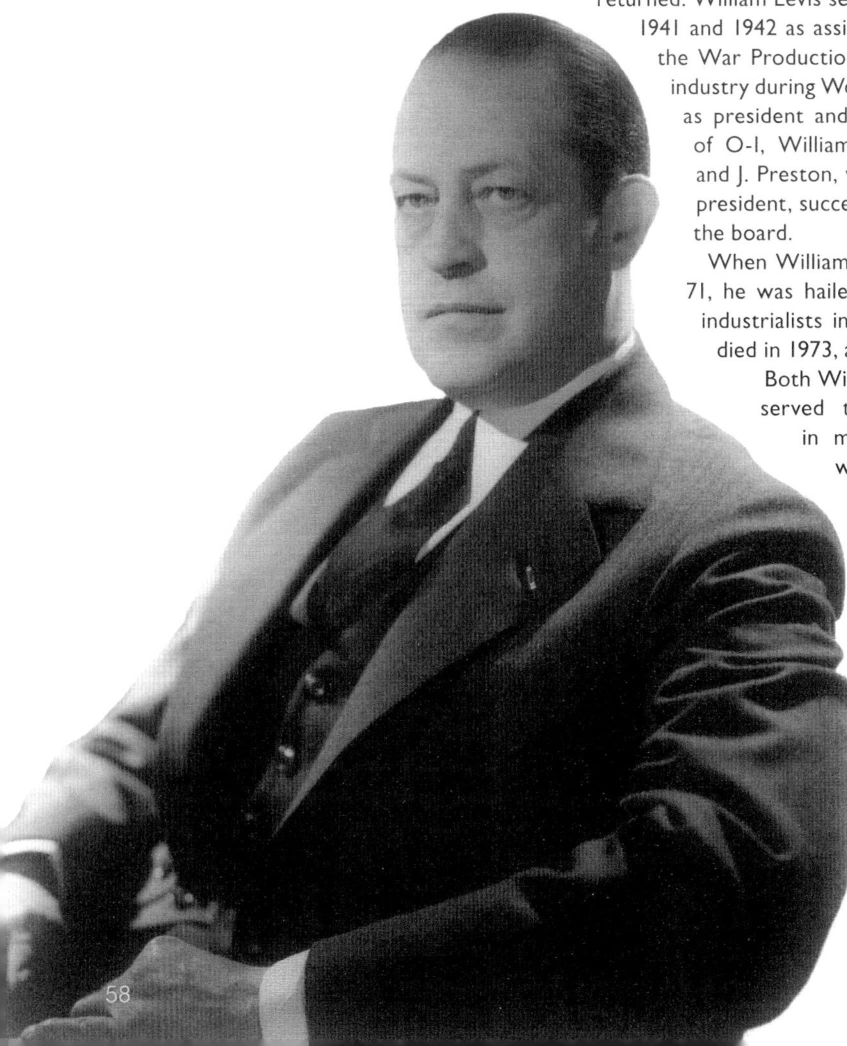

When William Levis died at the age of 71, he was hailed as one of the leading industrialists in the country. J. Preston died in 1973, also at the age of 71.

Both William and J. Preston Levis served the Toledo community in many capacities. William was instrumental in the creation of the Toledo Express Airport. J. Preston served on the board of trustees of the University of Toledo, the Medical College of Ohio, and Cornell University. He also served as president of the Toledo Museum of Art board.

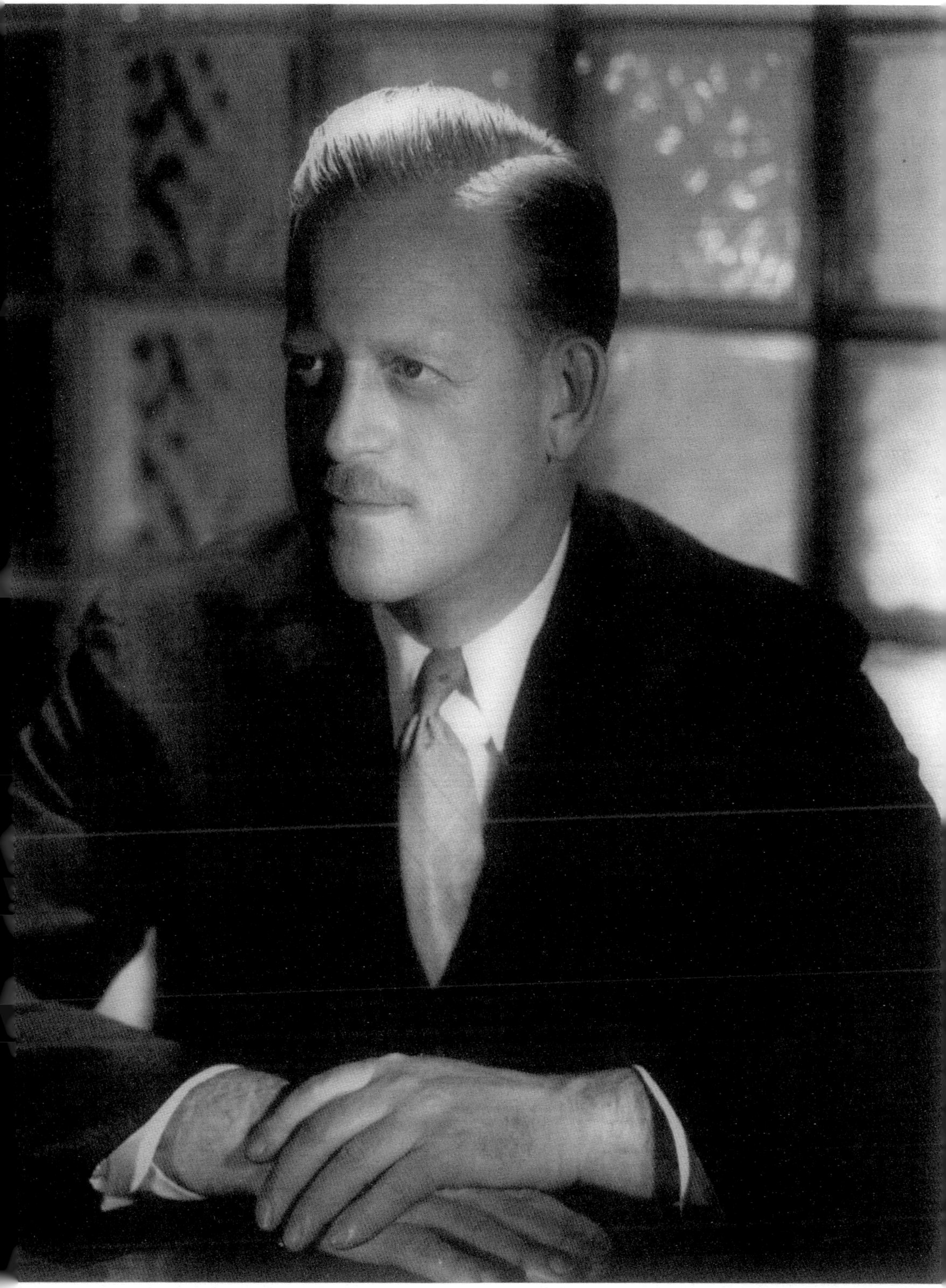

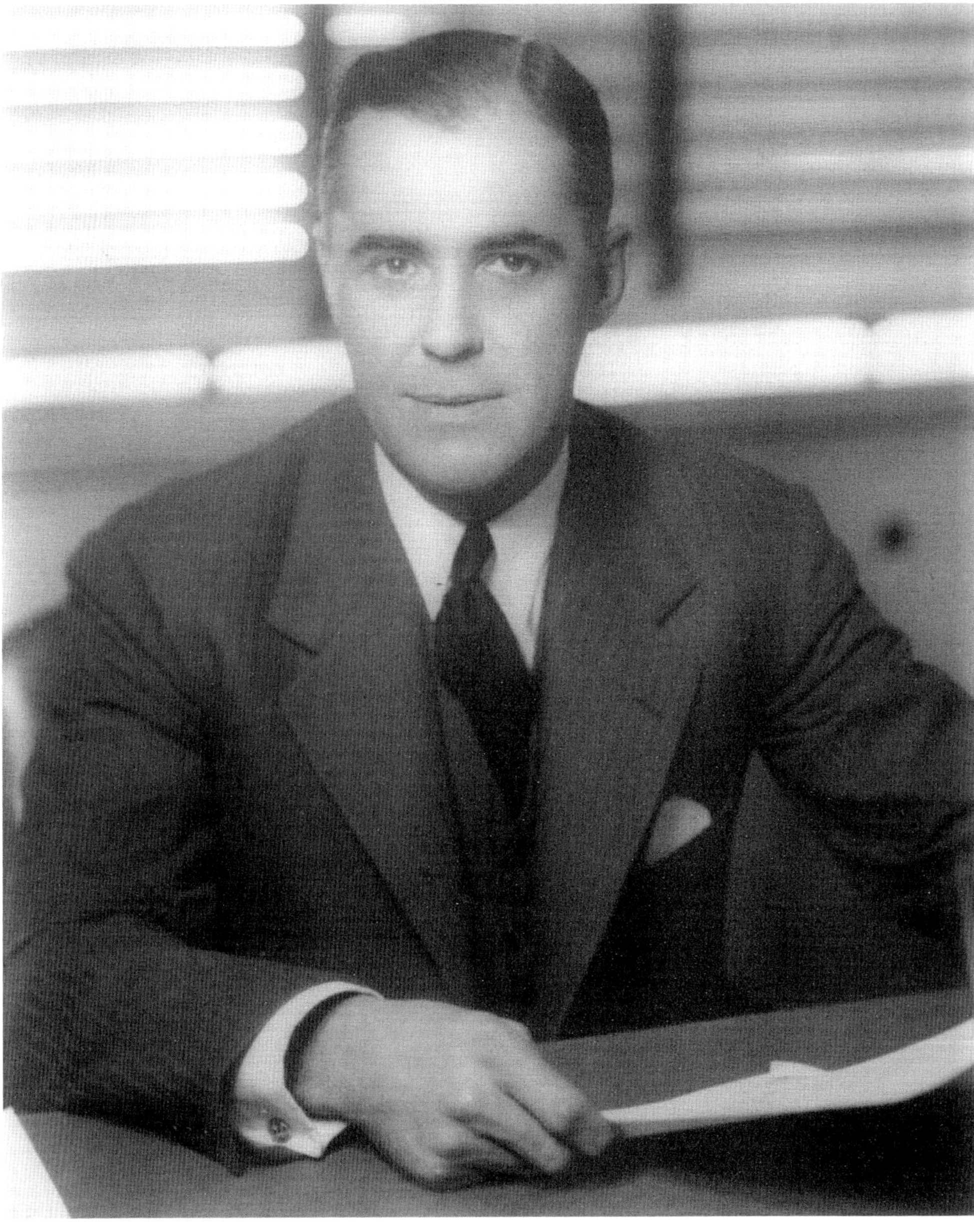

**Harold Boeschenstein**
Harold Boeschenstein was born in Edwardsville, Illinois, in 1896. In 1927, he began at the Illinois Glass Company working for his friend William Levis. When the company merged in 1929 with the Owens Bottle Company to create Owens-Illinois, Inc., Boeschenstein moved to Toledo to become vice president of the new company.

During Prohibition, O-I found itself without one of its largest markets—bottles for alcoholic beverages. The company diversified its product line with structural glass blocks. To weld the two halves of the blocks together, engineers used a thin ribbon of glass, and by accident, they discovered they could create fine strands of glass threads. In 1938, O-I spun off its fiberglass operations as Owens-Corning Fiberglas, and Boeshenstein became president of the new company, a position he retained until 1963.

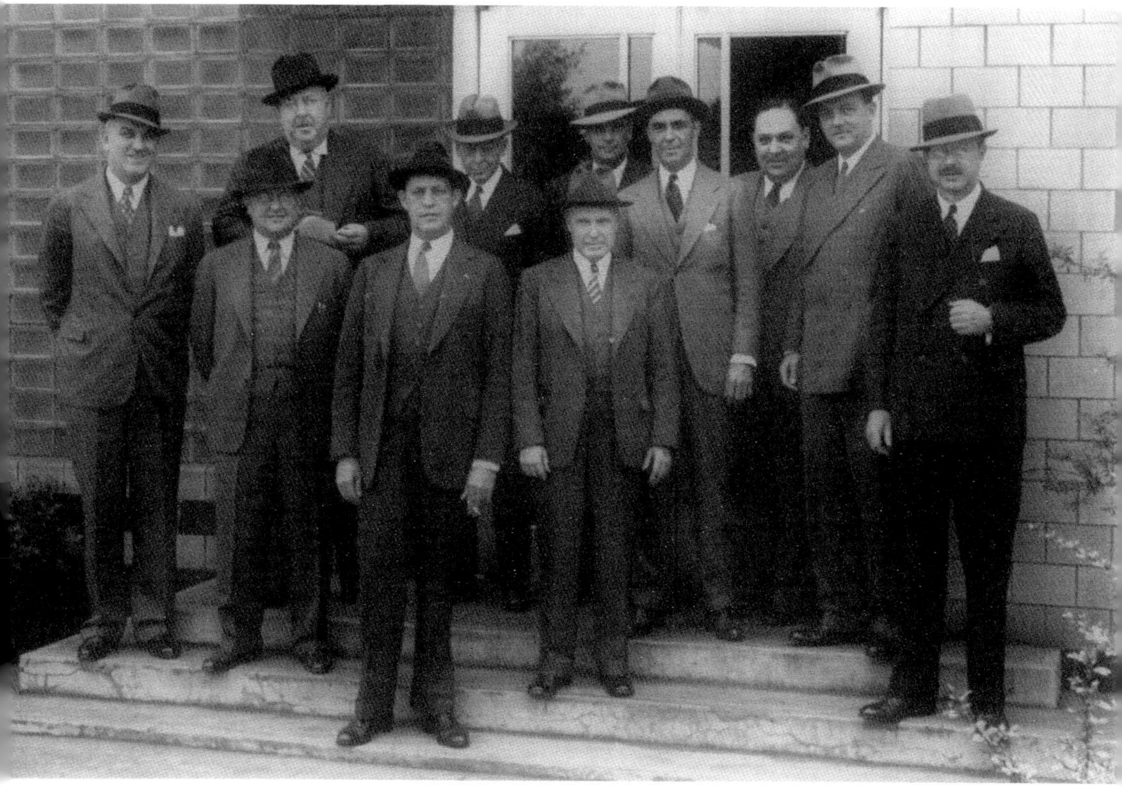

**Boeschenstein and the Board of Directors of Owens-Corning Fiberglas**
Pictured here in 1939 is the first meeting of the board of directors of the new company.

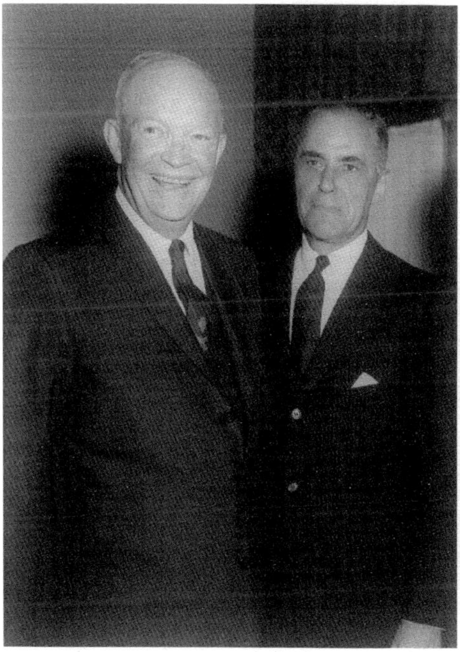

**Boeschenstein and Pres. Dwight D. Eisenhower**
During World War II, Boeschenstein served on the War Production Board, and after the war he collaborated with many national business-advisory boards. In 1958, he was appointed by Pres. Dwight D. Eisenhower to a committee that sought to establish trade with the Soviet Union, and he accompanied Vice Pres. Richard Nixon on Nixon's trip to the Soviet Union in 1959. Boeschenstein was friends with many political leaders, and in 2004 it was revealed that he had been secretly appointed by Eisenhower as one of six US businessmen who were to lead the government in the case of a nuclear attack. He was also a supporter of many charitable and cultural organizations, including the Toledo Museum of Art. He died in 1972.

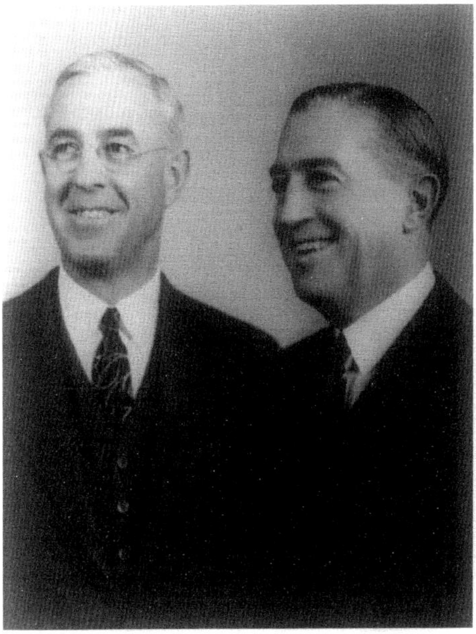

### Robert A. and Frank R. Stranahan

When Robert (pictured left) and Frank Stranahan arrived in Toledo from Boston in 1910, they brought with them the equipment for a new factory to make spark plugs—and $22,000 in debt. After graduating from Harvard in 1908 (in just 2.5 years), Robert persuaded his brother Frank to join him in the development of spark plugs for the new automotive industry. Robert designed a new gasket that improved the product. John Willys of Willys-Overland promised the Stranahan brothers a contract if they moved their company to Toledo. They established Champion Spark Plug on the second floor above a laundry near the Willys plant. (Courtesy of the Toledo-Lucas County Public Library.)

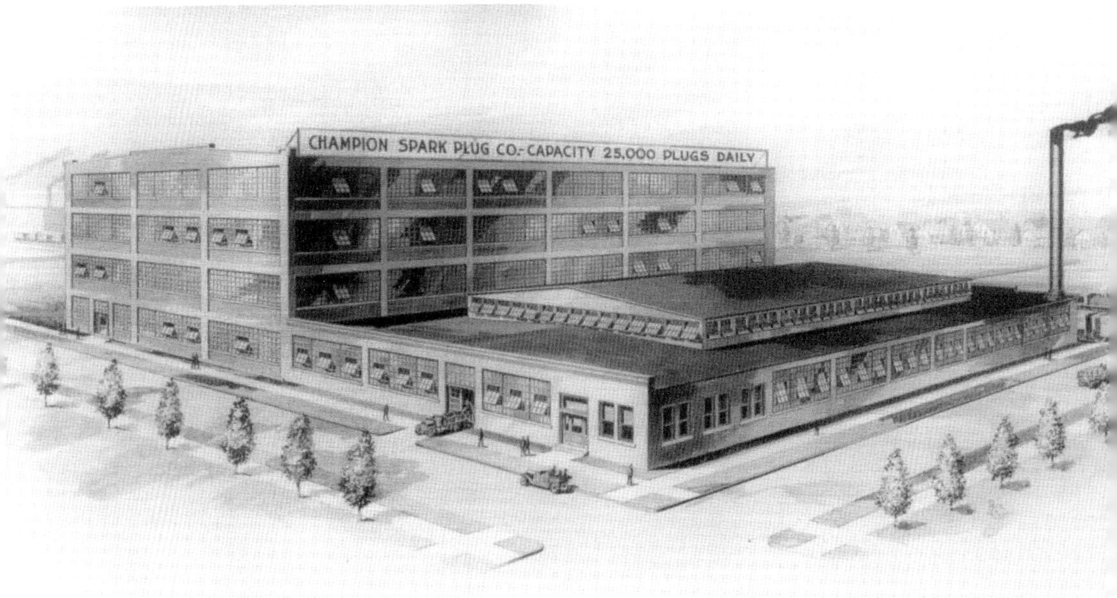


### The Champion Spark Plug Factory

The company continued to expand after getting a contract with Ford Motors, and by 1911 the company supplied 200,000 plugs to Ford. That would soon grow to 3.5 million annually. The company also expanded to supply spark plugs for aviation after Robert designed a long-lasting plug with a ceramic insulator, which led to the expansion of the US aerospace industry during World War II. The company's bow-tie logo became one of the most recognizable brands in the world.

In 1954, both Robert and Frank Stranahan retired from the company. Robert Jr. succeeded his father as president and ran the company for 35 years. The Stranahan family was also known for its philanthropy, funding many charitable causes in Toledo through its family foundation. The estate of Robert Stranahan Sr. is now the much-beloved Wildwood Preserve Metropark.

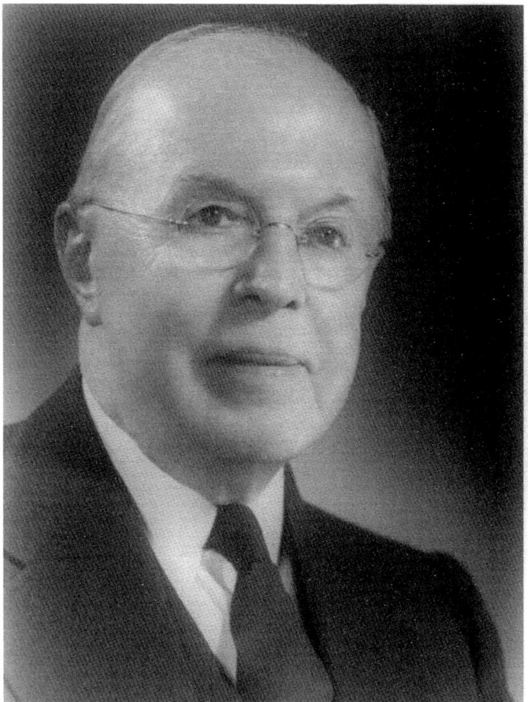

### William W. Knight Sr.

William W. Knight Sr. was often referred to as "Mr. Toledo." After graduating from Yale in 1899, he accepted a job in Toledo as a clerk for the Reynolds Grain Company. He invested his savings in the First National Bank, a "grain man's bank." In 1904, he married Edna Ford, daughter of the founder of the Ford Plate Glass Company. In 1918, he and other Toledo businessmen merged several banks to create the Toledo Trust Co.

He was best known civically for two efforts—the Toledo Hospital and the Toledo Metropolitan Parks. In 1921, Knight led the campaign to raise $1.5 million to build a new hospital, which opened in 1930. He served as the first chairman of the Metropolitan Parks Board in 1929, and during his leadership, the parks expanded to preserve over 4,000 acres of natural space. Knight died in 1968 at the age of 90.

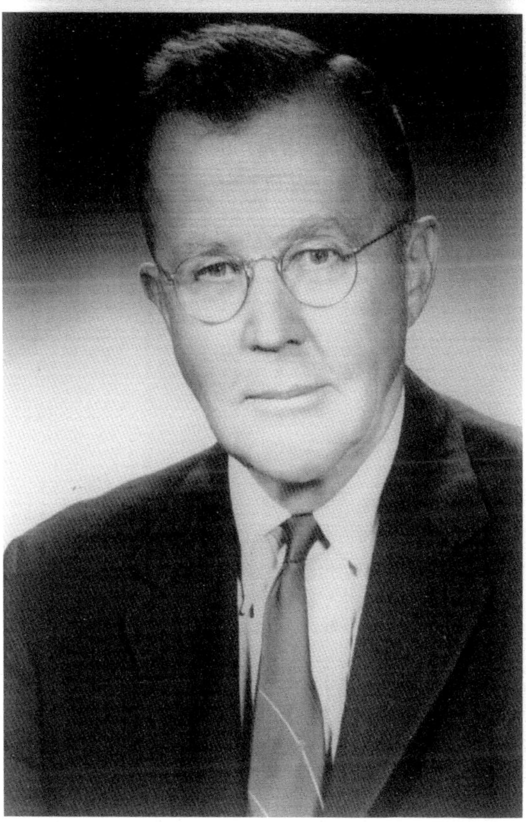

### William W. Knight Jr.

Like his father, William W. Knight Jr. was active in many civic affairs, but he was best known for his work to develop the Port of Toledo after the opening of the St. Lawrence Seaway.

Knight was born in Toledo in 1905. He earned degrees from Yale and Harvard and from 1929 to 1940 was director of the Wyandotte Chemical Company. After service in World War II, he joined Libbey-Owens-Ford and was later named president of the company's Plaskon Division. In 1953, he became president of the Nicholas Company.

He was named to the Toledo-Lucas County Port Authority board in 1955 and served as chairman for 18 years. He represented Congress at the dedication of the St. Lawrence Seaway in 1959 and in 1969 was appointed to the St. Lawrence Seaway Development Corporation's advisory board. William Jr. died in 1984.

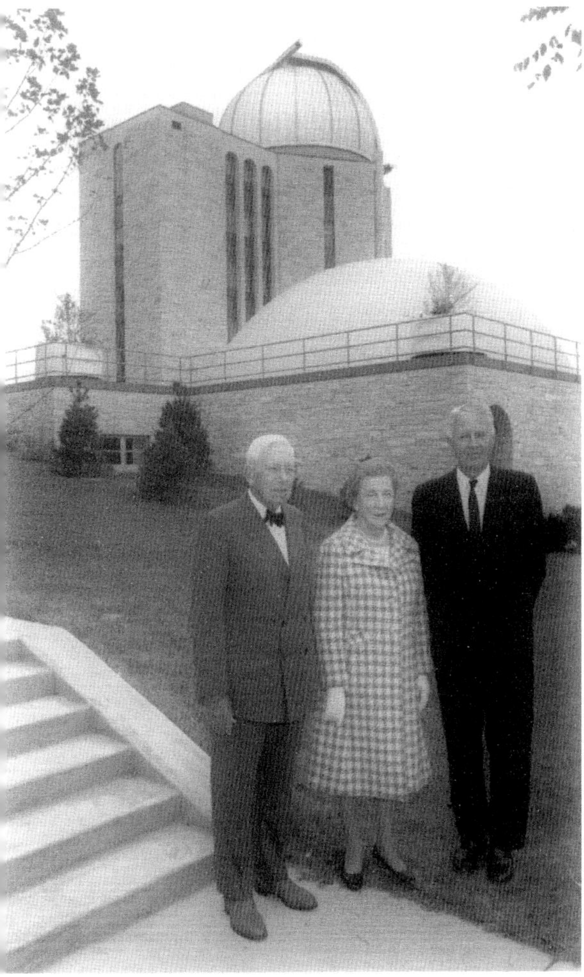

## George Ritter

In 1925, Toledo attorney George Ritter became counsel to John North Willys, the founder of Willys-Overland. When the company was forced into receivership following the stock market crash of 1929, Ritter and Ward M. Canaday reorganized the company as Willys-Overland Motors in 1936. Ritter served as a corporate executive until the firm was sold to Kaiser Motors in 1953.

But Ritter is best known for the philanthropic efforts. One investment of lasting impact began in the early 1960s when Ritter expressed an interest in astronomy to Dr. John Turin, head of the University of Toledo's physics department at the time. Turin and Dr. William S. Carlson, UT's president, convinced Ritter to donate money for the Ritter Observatory and Planetarium, which opened in 1967. The observatory boasted the largest telescope in the state, and the planetarium has been visited by thousands of students over nearly 50 years. Ritter also donated money to many college libraries and established scholarship funds to help students interested in studying law. He died in 1979. Ritter is pictured at left by the Ritter Planetarium in 1967.

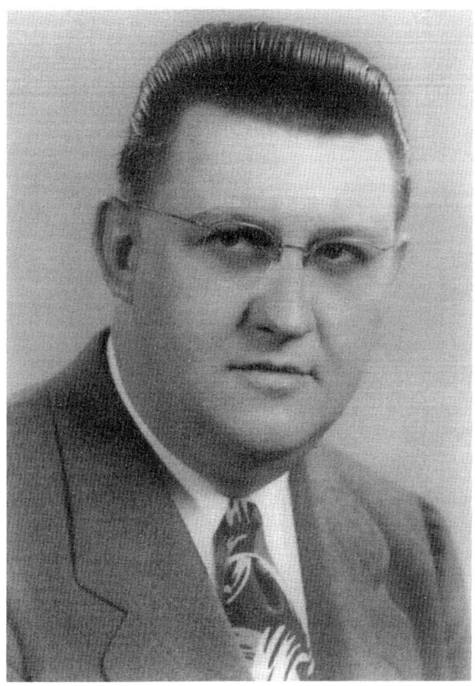

## Virgil Gladieux

Virgil Gladieux specialized in making food available whenever anyone wanted it, through vending machines that sold everything from sandwiches to candy bars and soda pop. Born in Indiana, Gladieux was one of 11 children. In 1923, he opened a grocery store with his brothers in his native Fort Wayne. In 1926, Virgil moved to Toledo, where he began working for a vending-machine company that evolved into the Buddies Lunch System, Inc. The company did industrial catering and box-lunch production and distribution for area factories. Later, he and his brother became the owners of the Canteen Services Company of Toledo.

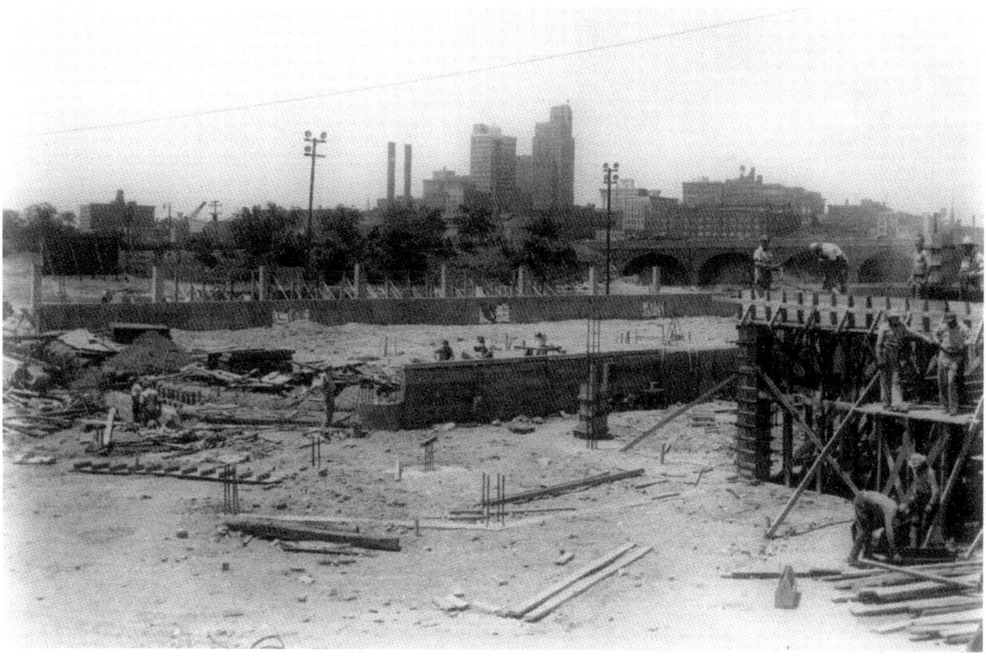

Toledo Sports Arena under Construction, 1947

Virgil Gladieux's experience in providing catering to large operations led him to become president of the Sports Arena, built in 1947. While primarily a hockey rink (where Toledo hockey teams the Mercurys, the Blades, the Hornets, the Goaldiggers, and the Storm played), the arena was also a popular concert, boxing, and wrestling venue. Performers as varied as Liberace, Peter Frampton, and John Denver played there. (Courtesy of Dan Saevig.)

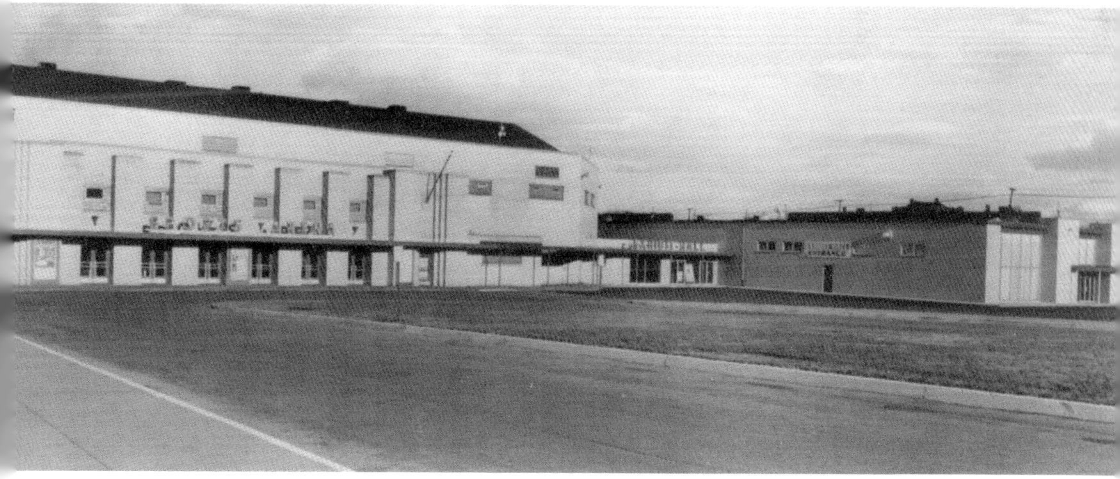

Toledo Sports Arena, c. 1960

The arena closed in 2007 and was demolished in August of that year. In the mid-1980s, Gladieux sold much of his business to the Marriott Corporation, although V/Gladieux Enterprises continued to provide food concessions at several large Toledo venues, including the SeaGate Convention Center and the Huntington Center. (Courtesy of the Toledo-Lucas County Public Library.)

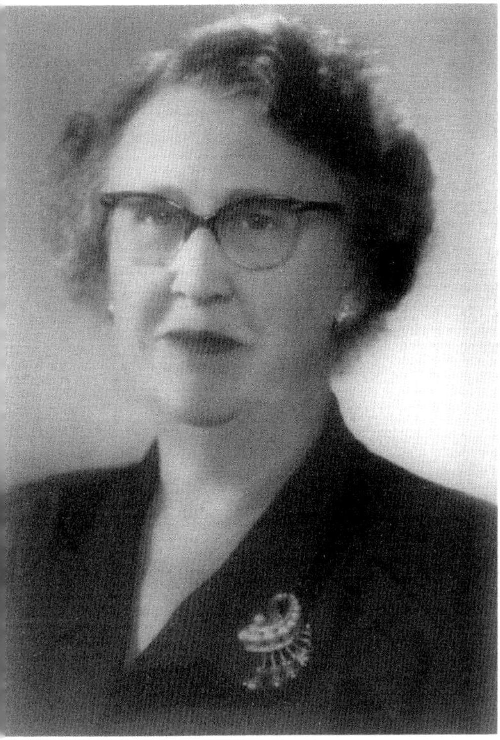

### Grace E. Smith

Grace Smith brought a new way of eating out to Toledo—the cafeteria.

While enrolled at Wooster College, she helped her father run a lunch counter in the town. She came to Toledo to work for the YWCA and helped to save the organization's restaurant as a place where young unescorted women could eat. In 1916, she opened the cafeteria on Madison Avenue downtown. People liked the chance to select from a large variety of items, and because the restaurant did not serve alcohol, it was a place where proper women felt comfortable.

Smith also impacted the restaurant business nationally. In 1921, she hired a home-economics teacher to take charge of the kitchen and standardize the recipes so that the food was always of good quality and consistency. This concept was revolutionary for its time. All of the food was cooked by women who were supervised by nutritionists. The techniques she used led to the restaurant's slogan: "Nationally Known for Good Food." She was the first woman president of the National Restaurant Association.

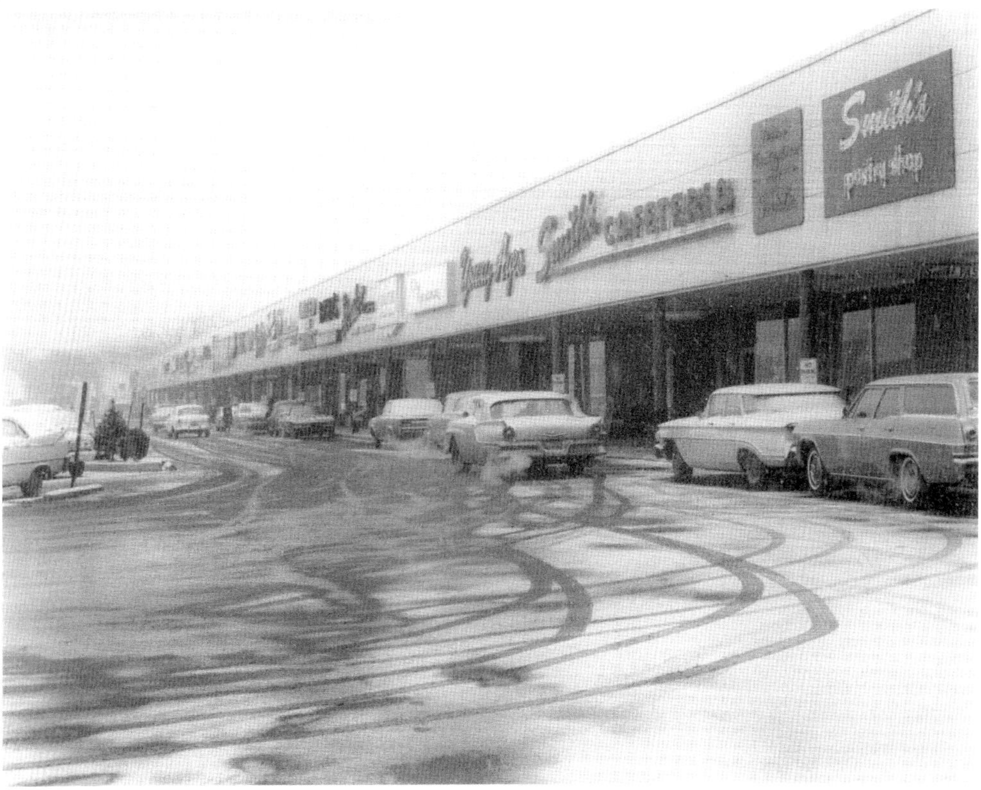

### Tony Packo

Tony Packo was not a politician, sports figure or actor, but today his name is associated with Toledo more than almost any other. Born Anthony Packo, in 1934 he opened a restaurant in the city's Hungarian neighborhood at Front and Consaul. He sold Hungarian food, including spicy hot dogs, and his café soon became popular with Toledoans. He had to expand the restaurant twice.

Tony Packo's became nationally famous in the 1980s when Jamie Farr, a Toledo native, mentioned his love for the hot dogs on the television show *M*A*S*H*, in which Farr played Corporal Klinger. In one episode, the fictional Klinger was able to get a shipment of the hot dogs delivered to Korea. The hot dogs and other products of the restaurant were soon so popular that the company began national distribution. Tony Packo's original restaurant continues to operate in East Toledo and at several other locations. In addition to its hot dogs, the company is known for displaying hot dog buns signed by famous people who have visited Toledo and the restaurant. Hundreds of them can be viewed hanging on the walls of the restaurants.

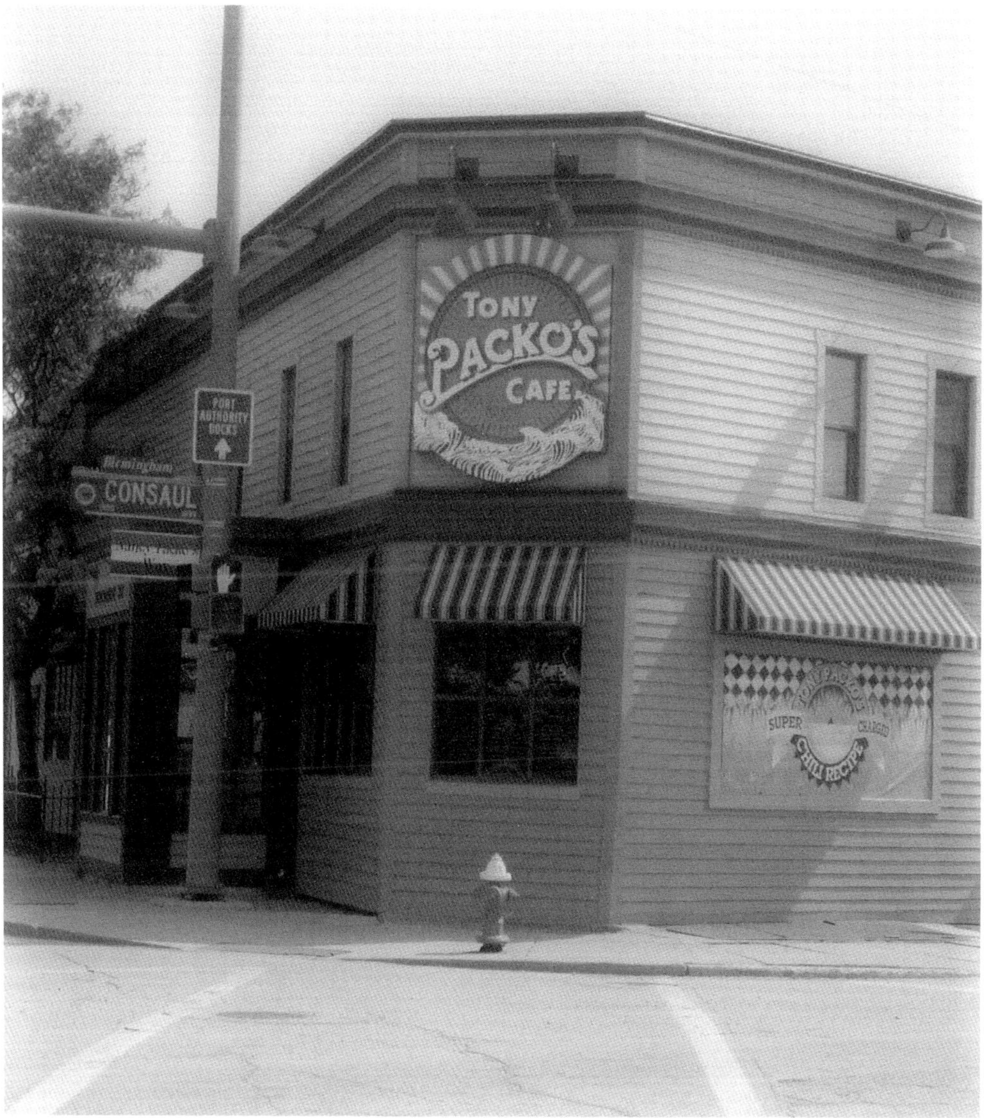

### Harold Munger Sr.

Many of Toledo's iconic buildings are examples of the work of architect Harold Munger Sr. Munger was born in Perrysburg in 1907 and received his architecture degree from Notre Dame, where he played football with Knute Rockne. One of his first jobs after college was overseeing the construction of several large public schools in Toledo, including Libbey and Woodward, and over the course of his career, Munger would have a hand in designing more than 150 school buildings. With Carl Britsch, he also designed many residential houses in Toledo, Perrysburg, and Ottawa Hills. During the Great Depression, Munger advocated for constructing low-income housing in Toledo and the establishment of the Lucas County Metropolitan Housing Authority. He was the chief architect for two large-scale, low-income housing projects—Brand Whitlock Homes and Charles F. Weiler Homes.

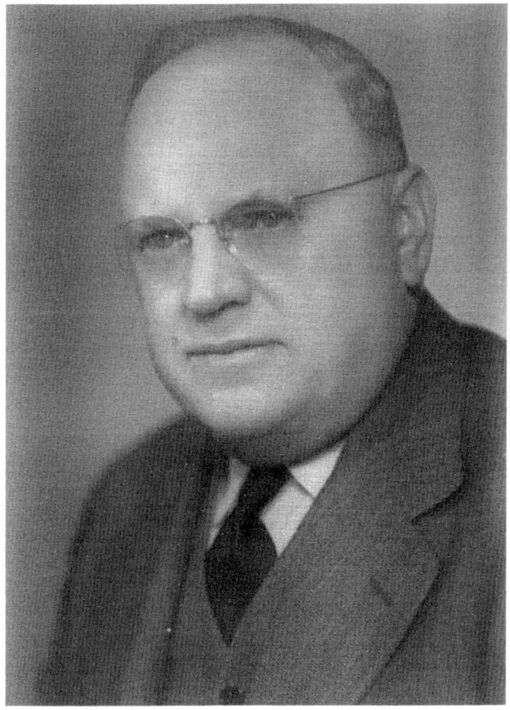

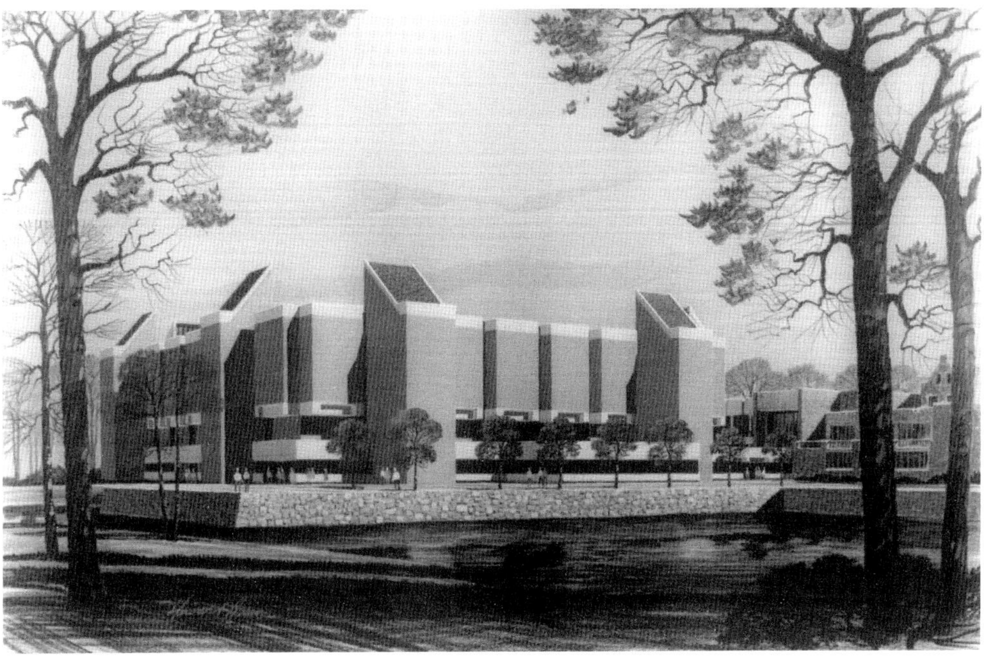

### William S. Carlson Library, Munger Munger + Associates, 1969

In his later career, Harold Munger's firm designed many important public buildings, including the William S. Carlson Library at the University of Toledo (shown here in an architects' rendering), which was under construction when Munger died in 1970. His firm was joined by other members of his family and continues today as Munger Munger + Associates.

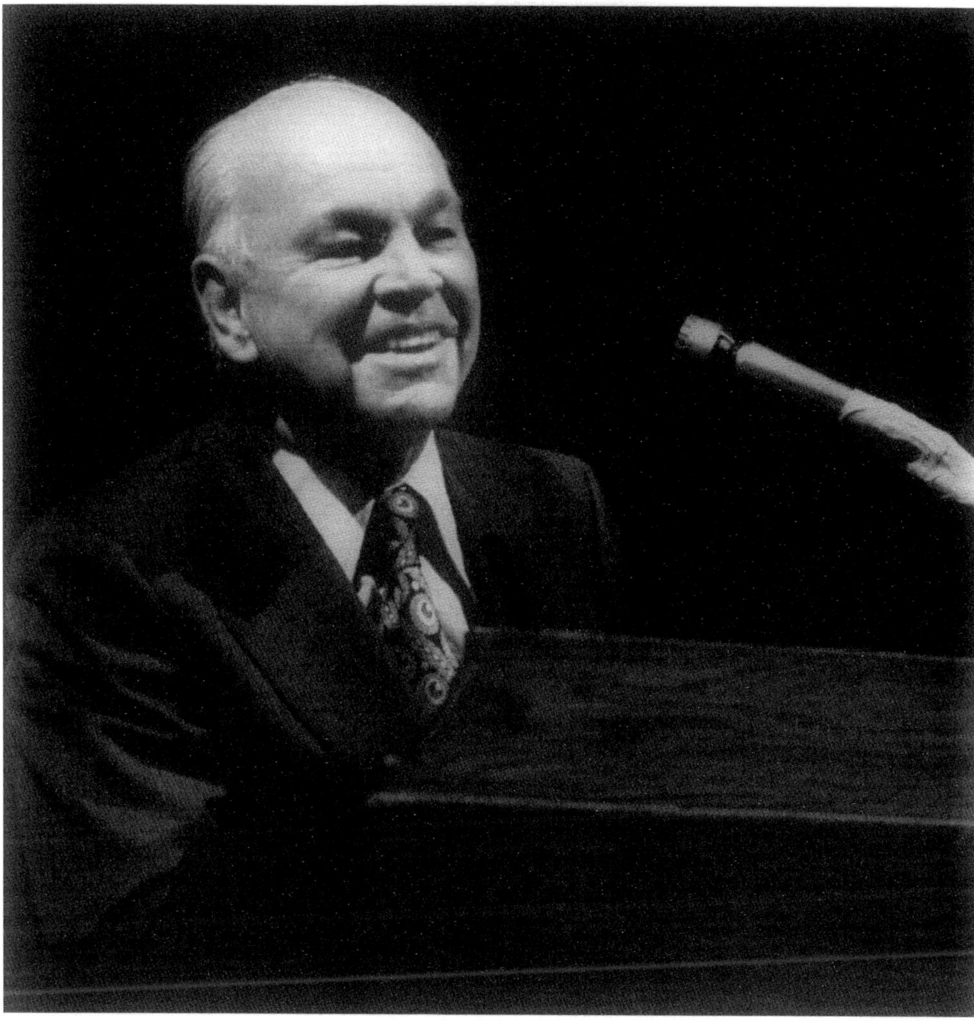

**Edward Lamb**
Born in Toledo in 1901 to a fisherman and a housekeeper, Edward Lamb attended Dartmouth College in 1920 and received a law degree from Western Reserve University in 1927. In 1934, he was asked by the protestors in the bloody Toledo Auto-Lite strike to represent them, and from that point on he became a proponent of labor unions. In the 1930s and 1940s, he represented over 75 different unions, and in 1946 he successfully argued the *Anderson v. Mt. Clemens Pottery Co.* case before the US Supreme Court. The court overturned a requirement of the pottery company that employees had to report to work early and wait, unpaid, for the shift to change.

A wise investor, Lamb became wealthy and began to acquire companies, including the Seiberling Rubber Company in 1962. In addition, he bought many media companies, particularly television stations, when they first began broadcasting.

Despite his wealth, Lamb remained a defender of the working man and a peace and civil-rights activist. In the 1950s, he was accused of being a communist. He would often travel to Cuba and meet with Fidel Castro, whom he admired. When Martin Luther King Jr. visited Toledo in 1968, Lamb hosted a reception in his honor at his home in Maumee. Lamb wrote several books in which he urged for a more equitable distribution of wealth. Lamb died in 1987, but his estate continues to assist causes through the Edward Lamb Foundation.

**The Anderson Family** (OPPOSITE PAGE)
If the trend of Toledo's economic history over the last 40 years is decline, The Andersons has bucked that trend. Not only has the company survived—it continues to diversify and thrive.

In 1927, Harold Anderson became head of the National Milling Company, a company founded by his father as a subsidiary of the National Biscuit Company. In December 1936, Anderson founded the Anderson Elevator Company in partnership with his father and wife to build a concrete grain elevator with capacity to store one million bushels of grain in Maumee, Ohio. In 1940, a second grain elevator, twice the size of the original Anderson elevator, was completed. Throughout the 1940s, the land and elevators were leased to the Cargill Corporation.

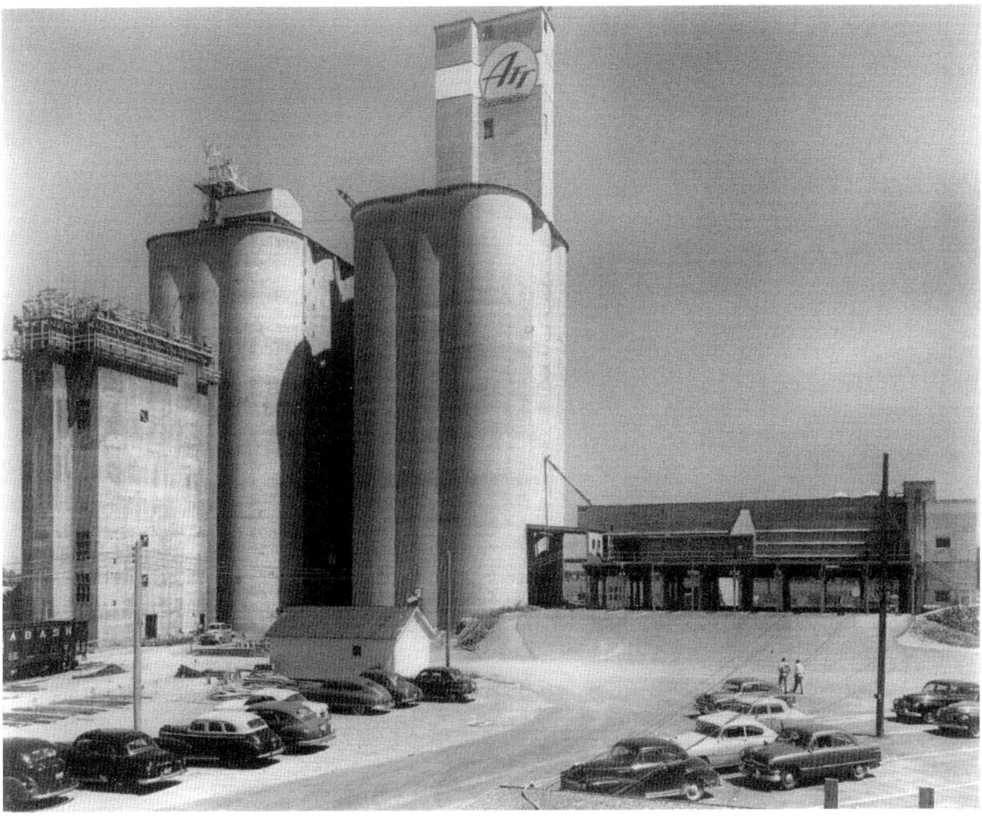

**The Andersons Truck Terminal**
In 1947, Harold Anderson, in partnership with his wife and six children, opened the Andersons Truck Terminal, consisting of a 500,000-bushel grain terminal with nine truck bays. The terminal was modern and fast.

The company was so successful that in May 1950 a new silo was built to double the capacity. It was constructed by local workers who were housed and fed in dormitories erected on the Anderson farm. They worked 24 hours a day to complete the project in seven days. In 1953, construction of another three-million-bushel grain storage elevator began. The "Big Pour," as the project became known, was even featured in *Life* magazine.

By the end of the 1950s, the Andersons owned grain elevators, grain-transfer equipment, and docks on the Maumee River, a farm, and a stone quarry. The company also opened the Andersons Warehouse Market next to the truck terminal to sell products needed by farmers at lower prices than competing stores. Harold's son Dick Anderson led the retail division.

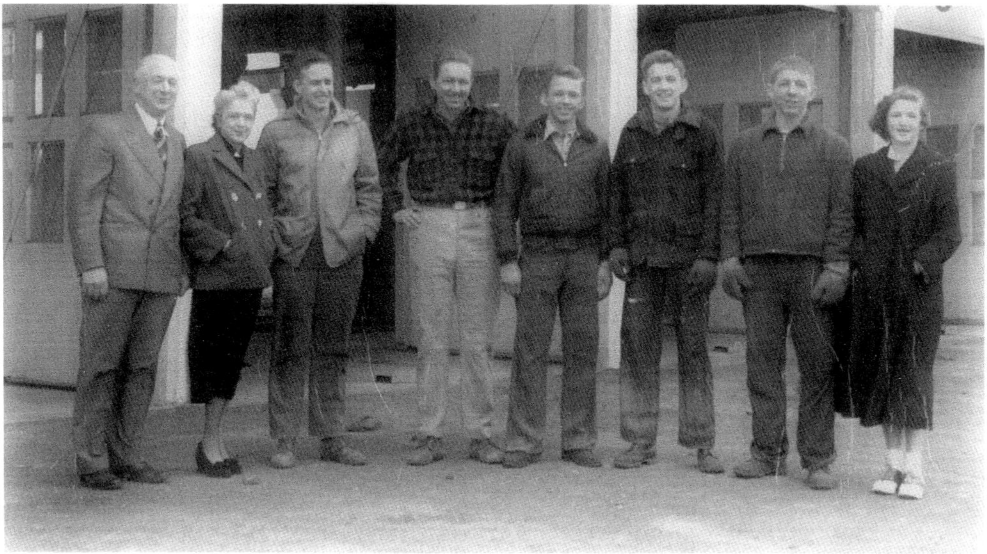

The Andersons General Store, Maumee, Ohio

In 1968, Harold Anderson stepped down, and he died unexpectedly in December. He was succeeded by his oldest son, John. The company continued its expansion through the next four decades. By 1977, The Andersons had become the nation's 25th-largest privately owned nonfinancial company. While no longer family owned, it is closely associated with them, and the Anderson family serves the community on many nonprofit boards and as leaders of charitable fund drives.

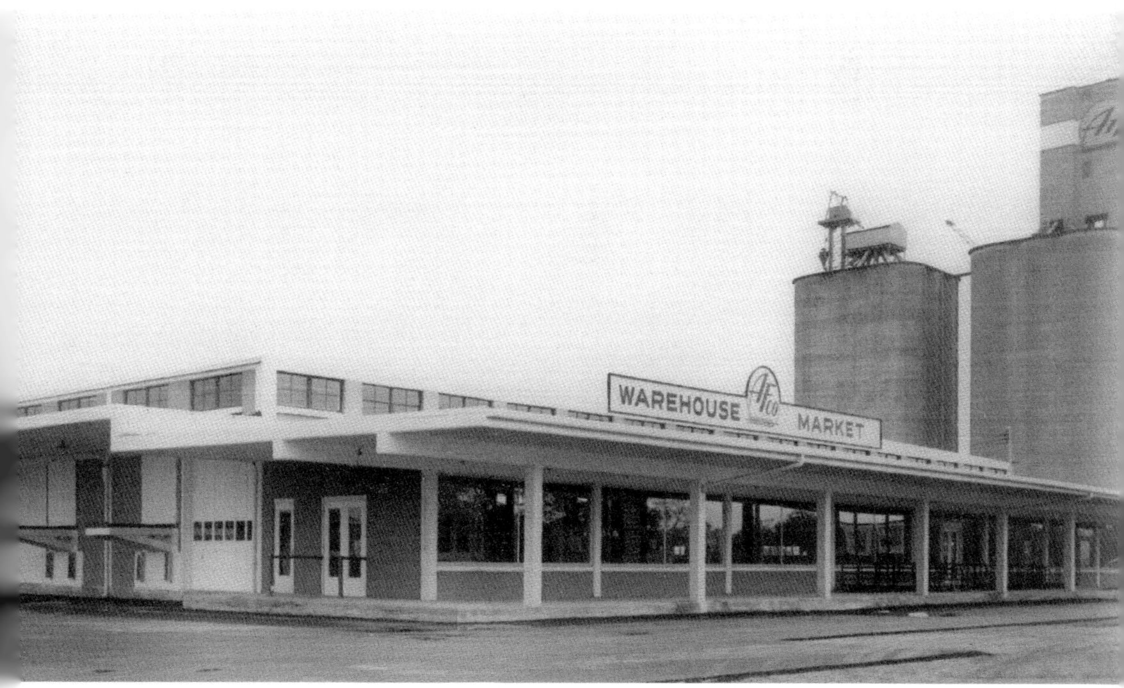

## Edwin Dodd

Edwin Dodd starting working in 1946 for the Owens-Illinois Glass Company as a trainee in the public-relations department after service as an information officer on Gen. Douglas MacArthur's staff during World War II. Carl Megowen, then O-I's president, recognized Dodd's talent for business and gave him the opportunity to travel around the country visiting O-I plants and learning all he could about the company's operations. Dodd eventually became executive director of O-I's Forest Products Division. By 1968, Dodd was named president of the Owens-Illinois, and in 1972 he became chief executive officer.

In his role as head of O-I, Dodd led the company's commitment to revitalizing downtown Toledo. In the late 1970s, O-I purchased the land along the Maumee River and began planning for the tallest building on Toledo's skyline as its new headquarters. Named One SeaGate, the building opened in 1982 and was key to the Toledo's efforts at the time to remake itself into a world-class city. Unfortunately, in 1986 Owens-Illinois was the subject of a corporate takeover, and the company's downtown workforce shrank as parts of the company were sold off. Within 20 years, the company sold its skyscraper and moved to a smaller headquarters in Perrysburg. But Dodd's risk in making O-I the cornerstone of a push to remake the downtown was a bold move that continues to leave its mark on the city. Today, One SeaGate is the headquarters of Fifth Third Bank. Dodd is pictured at left at the ground-breaking for One SeaGate in 1979.

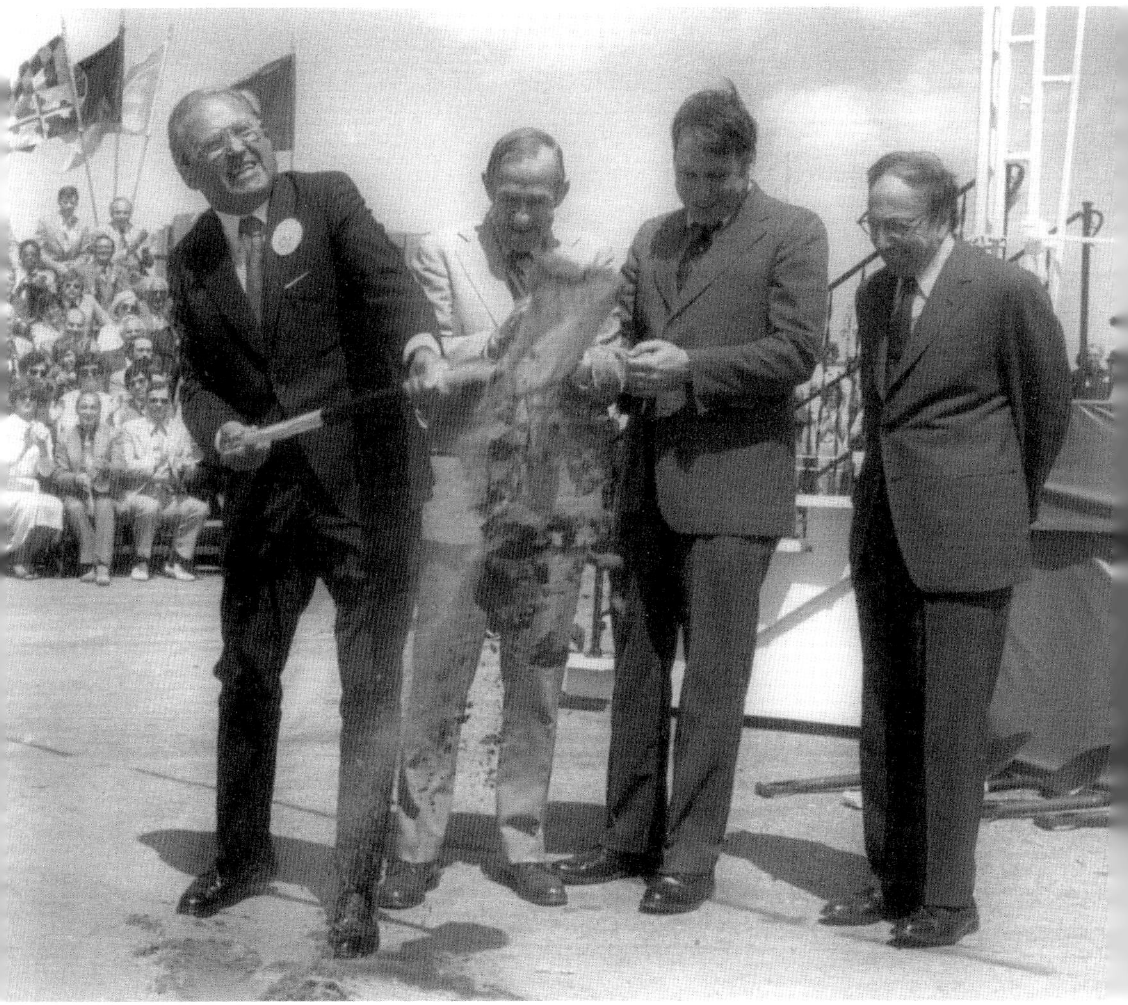

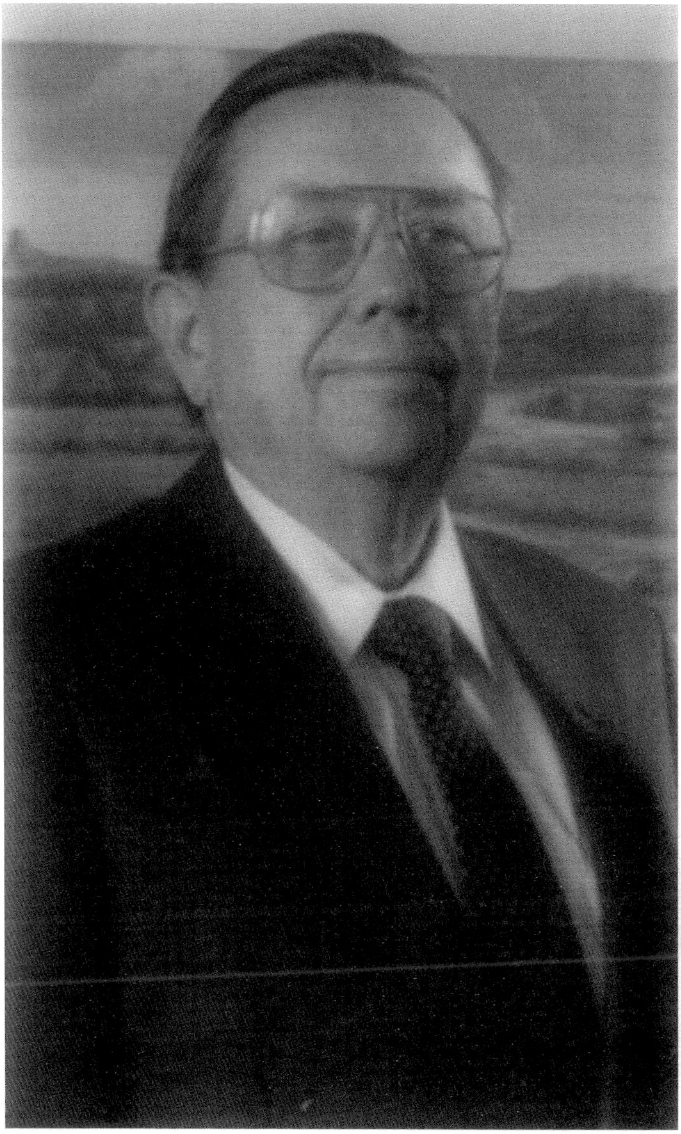

**Harold McMaster**

Harold McMaster began inventing early in life. He received his first tool set at the age of six and was building car motors by the time he was 12. After graduating from Ohio State in 1940, he went to work for Libbey-Owens-Ford, where he was responsible for numerous innovations. In 1948, he started his own company, Permaglass, making glass for appliances and electronics. In 1971, he founded Glasstech, Inc., which sold machines to produced tempered glass.

In the early 1980s, McMaster turned his attention to solar power, and in 1984 he founded Glasstech Solar. McMaster began coating glass panels with a blend of cadmium and tellurium, and in 1990, McMaster founded Solar Cells, Inc. to produce thin film semiconductors. Nine years later, he sold the company, and the name changed to First Solar. It is now one of the world's largest producers of thin film cells.

In addition to his legacy of technological innovation, Harold and his wife, Helen, created a foundation in 1988 that has supported many cultural and educational organizations. Harold McMaster died in 2003, and at the time of his death he held over 100 patents.

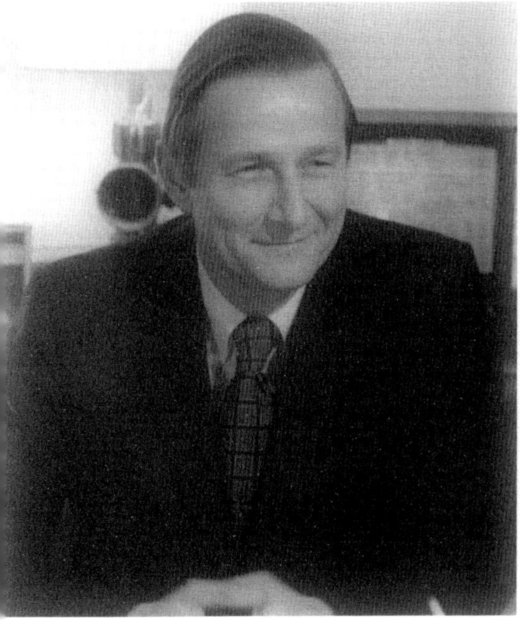

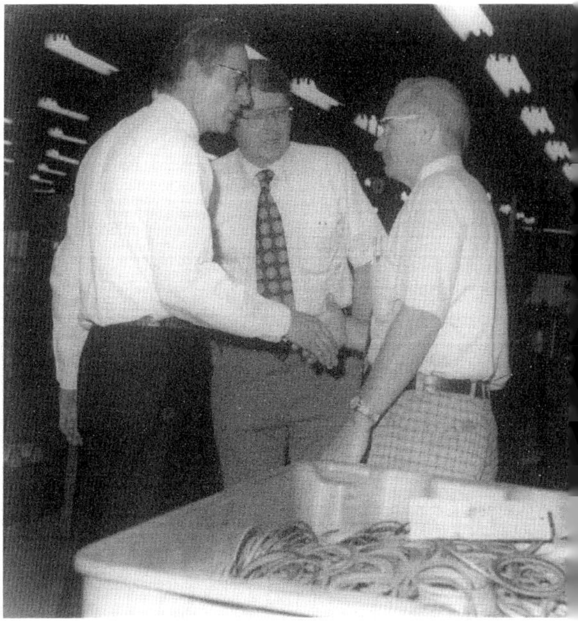

**Ren McPherson**
Ren McPherson was an internationally known businessman who believed the most important people in any corporation were the front-line workers. His philosophy helped the Dana Corporation become the 130th-largest industrial company in the United States, with sales of $2.7 billion a year.

Ren (short for Rene) joined the Dana Corporation as a sales engineer in 1952 and in 1961 became president of a subsidiary company, Hayes-Dana. The company was in danger of closing, so McPherson worked to improve efficiency and streamline paperwork, saving the company. In 1968, he returned to Toledo and became the youngest president in Dana's history. He became chairman of the company in 1972.

McPherson pioneered a new management style that focused on listening to employees. He would hold "talk back to the boss" sessions in which he encouraged those at the bottom to challenge those at the top. He gave power to the production workers and cut red tape by reducing hundreds of pages of policy to a single page. He believed that managers should treat workers as adults, so he removed time clocks. His management style was written about in the book *In Search of Excellence*.

He retired from Dana at the age of 55 to become dean of Stanford University's graduate school of business. After a serious car accident, he resigned from the position after a few struggling years. He died of pancreatic cancer in 1996.

# CHAPTER THREE

# Government and Law

Toledo's influence on government and the law has included producing a governor, a Supreme Court chief justice, leaders of the Progressive era, and the longest-serving woman in the US House of Representatives.

Two of Toledo's most important national political leaders were its Progressive-era mayors, Samuel "Golden Rule" Jones and Brand Whitlock. Jones began his career as a businessman in the city in 1893, and his company had only one rule, the Golden Rule: "Do onto others as you would have them do onto you." He paid his workers a decent wage, trusted them to keep their own time, built a recreational park for their families, and sponsored educational and cultural programing for their intellectual development. In 1899, he vowed to do for the city what he had done for his workers, and his election as mayor moved Toledo into the national spotlight as leading the Progressive movement. After he died in office in 1904, he was succeeded by Brand Whitlock, who continued Progressive reforms. Among the achievements of Jones and Whitlock were the establishment of a city park system, zoological gardens, nonpartisan elections, and reduced streetcar fares.

Other political leaders from Toledo also drew national attention. Supreme Court chief justice Morrison Waite wrote the opinion that established the right of the federal government to regulate business. Ambassador to the Soviet Union Foy Kohler represented the United States to its Cold War adversary during the delicate days after the assassination of Pres. John F. Kennedy.

Most recently, Toledo has been represented nationally in Congress by Marcy Kaptur, whose voice on behalf of the working class has again brought national attention to the city.

### Morrison R. Waite

As of this writing, Morrison R. Waite is the only person from Toledo to serve on the US Supreme Court, appointed chief justice of the court in 1874 by Pres. Ulysses S. Grant. Waite was born in Lyne, Connecticut, in 1816. He graduated from Yale in 1837 and passed the bar in 1839. Active in politics in the Whig party, he was nominated to run for Congress, elected mayor of Maumee, and served in the Ohio Legislature. In 1850, he moved to Toledo and began practicing law.

As a chief justice of the Supreme Court, he is perhaps best known for his opinion in the landmark case *Munn v. Illinois* in 1877. This case established the right of government to regulate business. But in other cases, he supported states' rights during Reconstruction. He died in 1888.

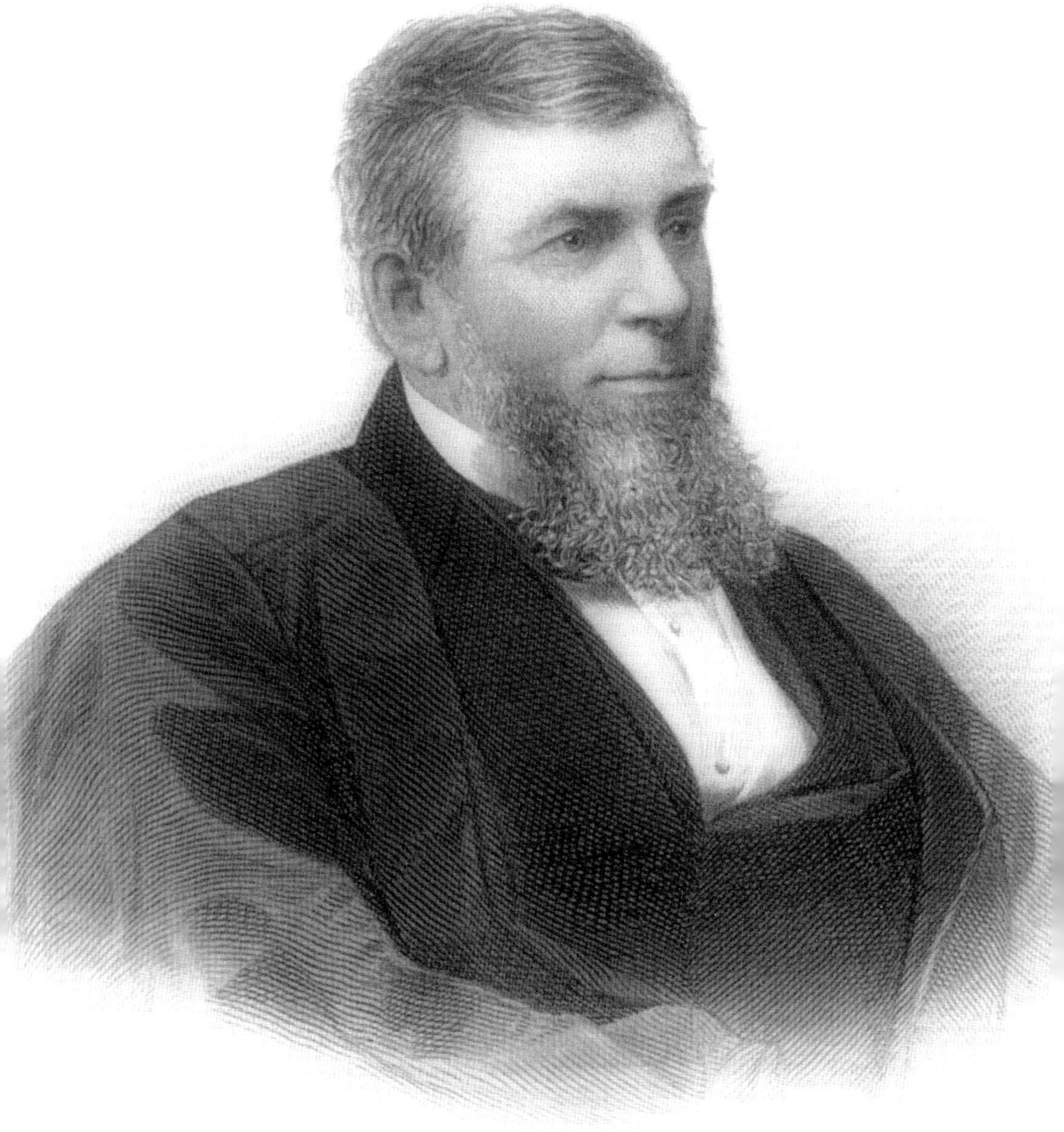

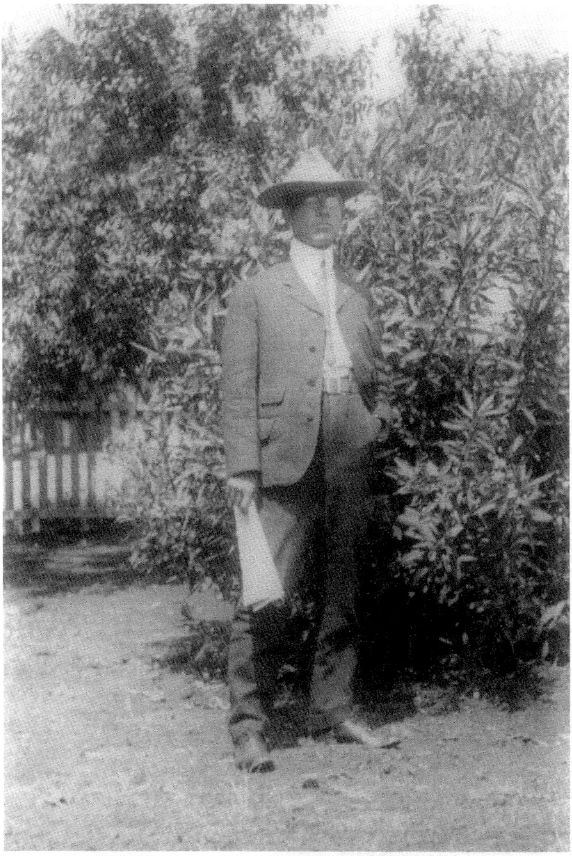

Gustavus Ohlinger

Gustavus Ohlinger was a well-known Toledo lawyer. He was born in Foochow, China, in 1877, where his parents were missionaries. Ohlinger received his law degree from the University of Michigan but returned to China, practicing law in Shanghai from 1902 to 1905. His firm represented the Russian government at the end of the Russo-Japanese War, helping to negotiate a settlement with Japan. He is pictured on a trip to Cape Town, South Africa, in 1902.

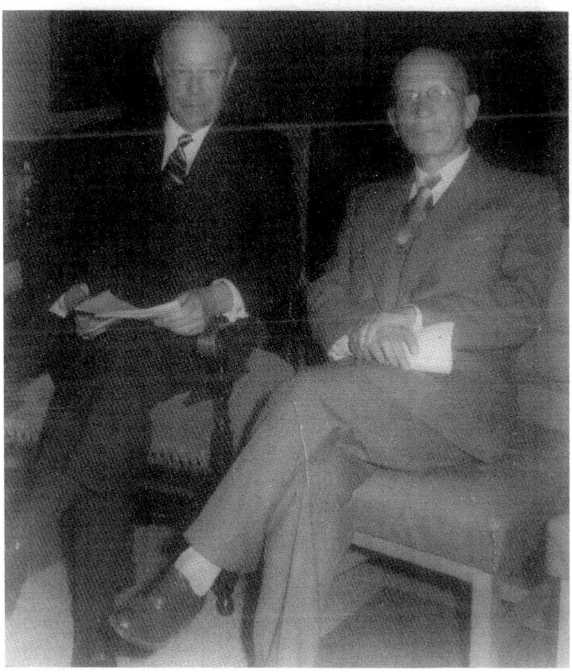

Ohlinger with Sen. Robert Taft

In 1906, Ohlinger established a law practice in Toledo, specializing in federal law. He authored *Ohlinger's Federal Practice*, which became a standard text. He served in World War I in Army intelligence and during World War II organized the Toledo Squadron of the Civil Air Patrol. Ohlinger also testified before Congress in support of Prohibition, and his testimony helped to gain passage of the 18th Amendment. He was a personal friend of Theodore Roosevelt and active in many organizations devoted to understanding world affairs, including the Toledo United Nations Association. Ohlinger died in Toledo in 1972.

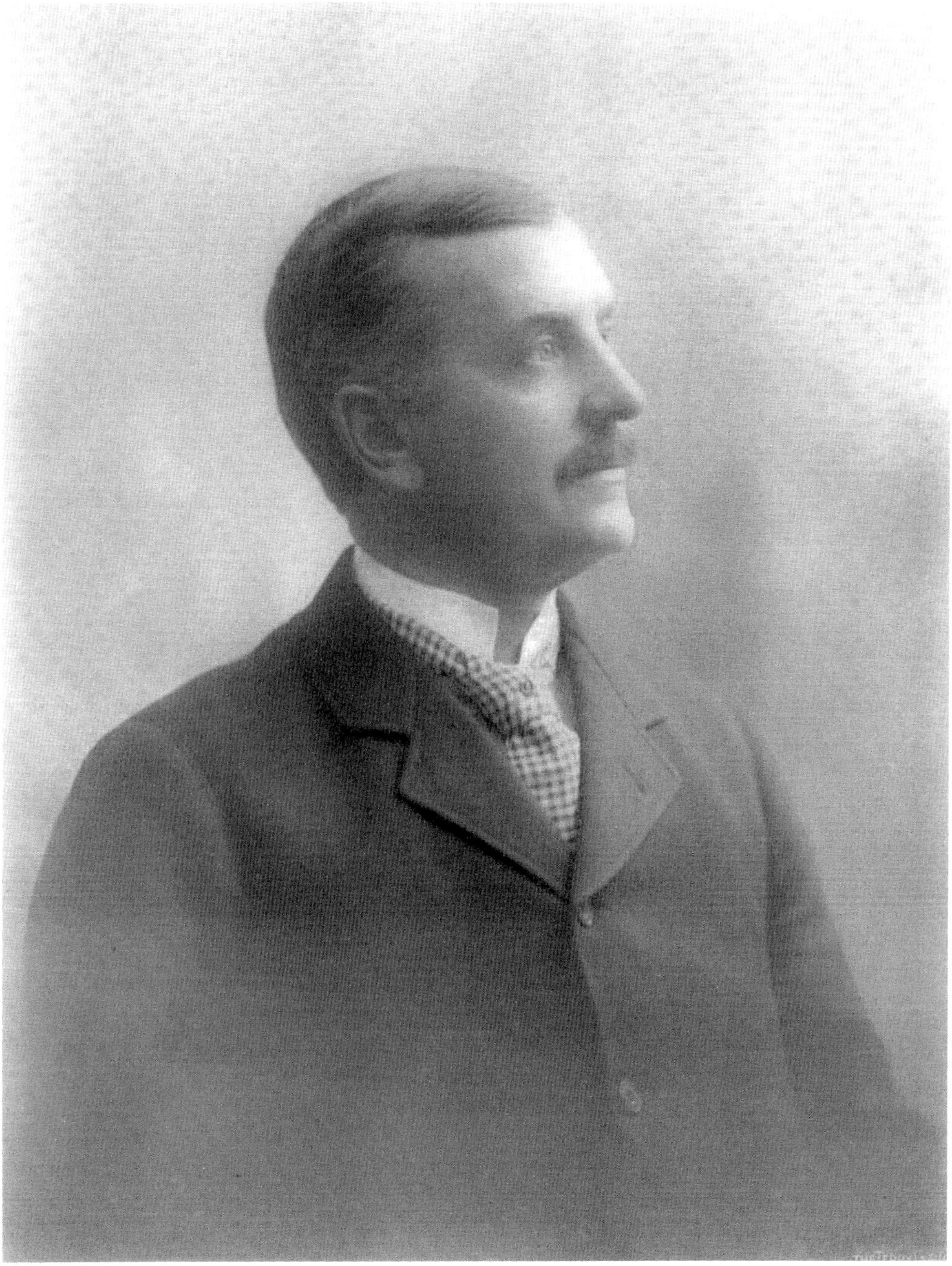

### Samuel "Golden Rule" Jones

Samuel Milton Jones was born in Wales in 1846. He came to the United States at the age of three and lived his early life in New York. He had little formal education and found work in the oil fields of Pennsylvania at the age of 18. After the death of his wife, he moved to Ohio and established the Ohio Oil Company, which was later purchased by Standard Oil. His knowledge of the oil business led him to invent the sucker rod, used in deep-well drilling. This invention made his fortune, and he founded the Acme Sucker Rod Company in Toledo to produce it.

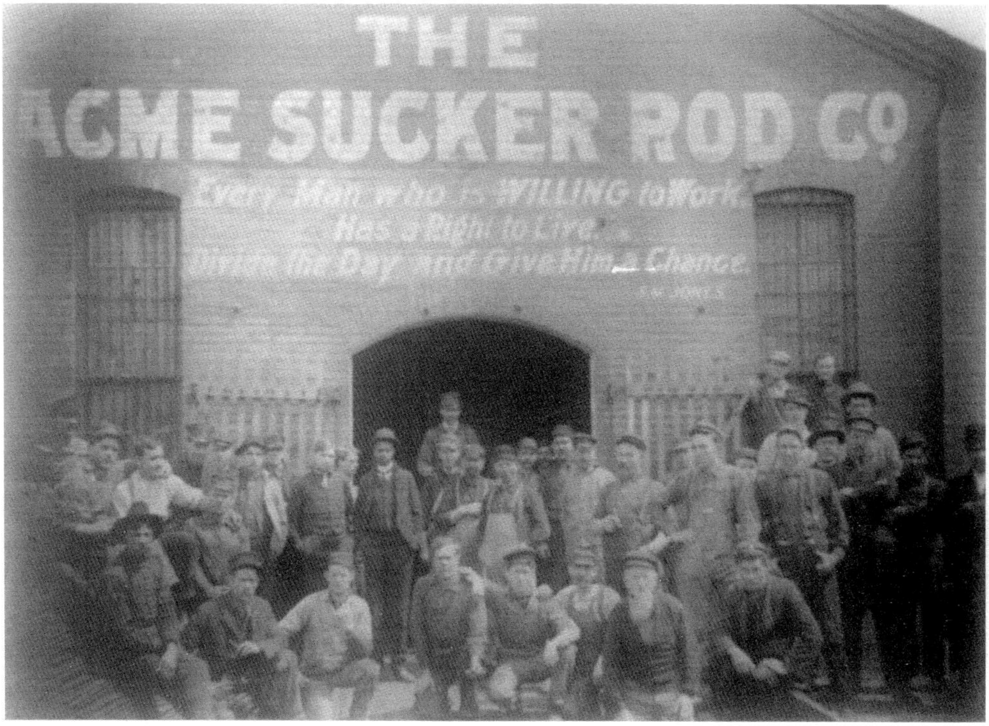


Workers at the Acme Sucker Rod Company

As an employer, Jones was known for treating his employees well. He instituted an eight-hour workday and paid vacations. He established a park for the children of his workers, sponsored lectures and cultural programs, and even bought musical instruments for a company band. He had only one rule for his business—the Golden Rule. In the middle of the economic depression known as the Panic of 1893, his generosity earned him great love and respect by the people of Toledo. (Courtesy of the Toledo-Lucas County Public Library.)

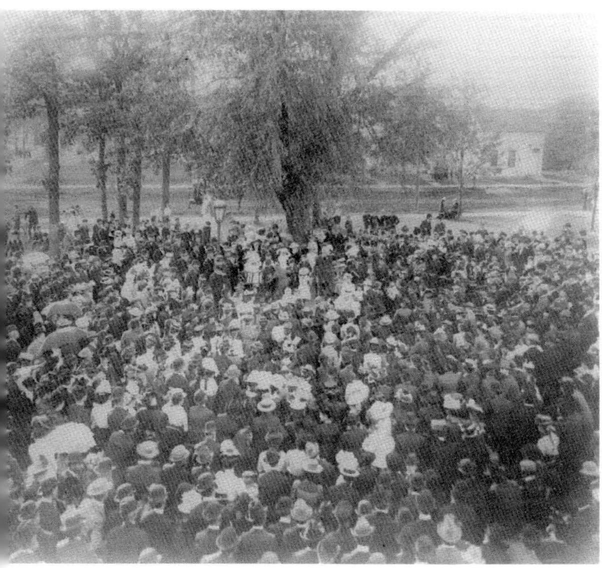

Jones Campaigning to Become Toledo's Mayor, 1897

In 1897, Jones ran for mayor of Toledo as a Republican and soon became known for the Progressive-era reforms he enacted. These included establishing city parks, fighting corruption, improving the industrial areas of the city, and instituting municipal ownership of utilities. His reforms were not popular with the Republican Party, so Jones ran for reelection as an independent and won by a landslide. He was elected mayor four more times and served until 1904, when he died in office. He is remembered today as one of the country's most important Progressive-era mayors.

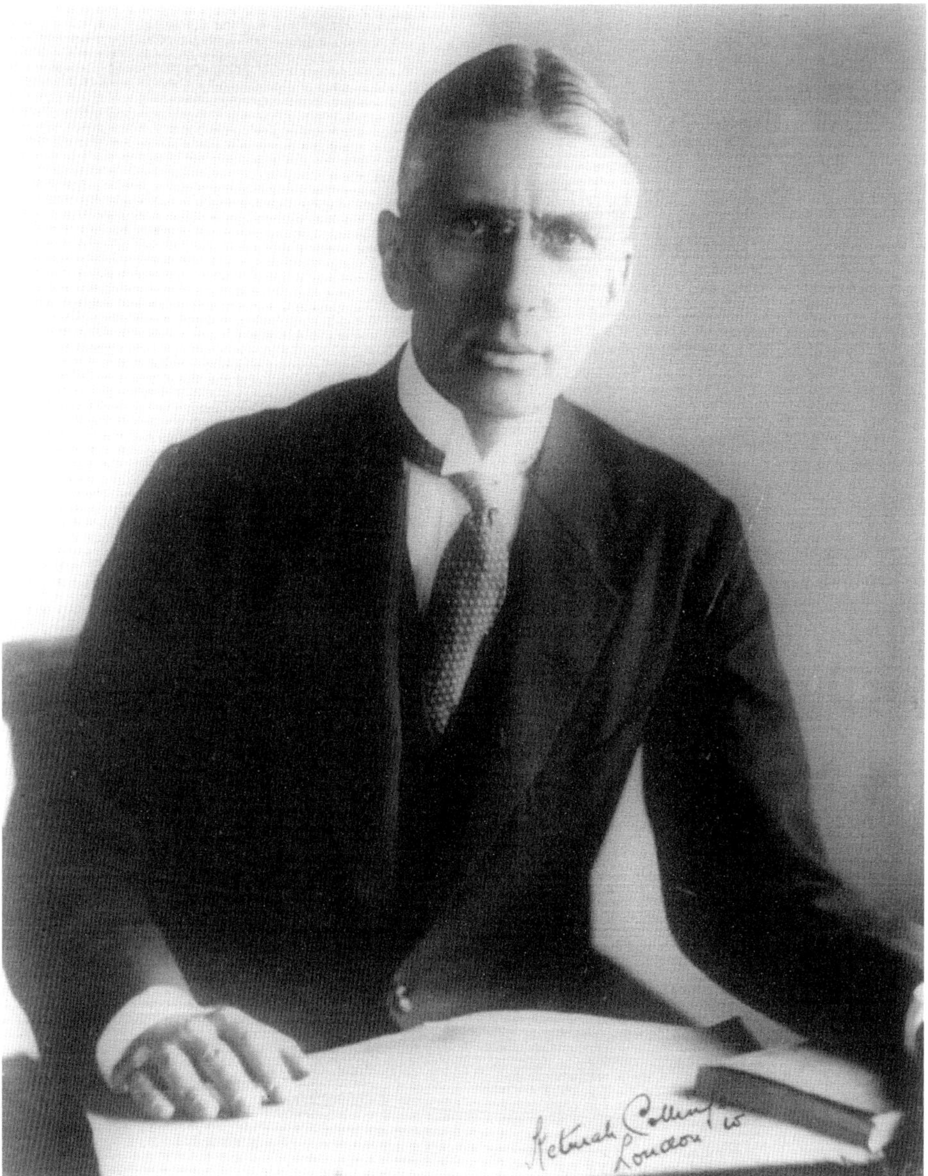

Brand Whitlock

Brand Whitlock began his career as a reporter. He moved to Toledo from his hometown of Urbana, Ohio, to work for the *Toledo Blade* and in 1891 went to Chicago to work for the *Chicago Herald*. There, he became active in Progressive-era politics working for Illinois governor John Altgeld. While living in Springfield, Whitlock also studied law, and he was admitted to the bar in 1894.

In 1896, Altgeld's political career ended when he pardoned the Haymarket Square rioters using documents that Whitlock had drafted. Whitlock returned to Toledo after Altgeld's reelection defeat, and he became a lawyer and supporter of the city's Progressive mayor, Samuel "Golden Rule" Jones. After Jones's death, Whitlock ran for Toledo mayor as an independent and was elected in 1906, serving four terms in the position. Whitlock was not just a politician, however. While mayor of Toledo, he also wrote several novels.

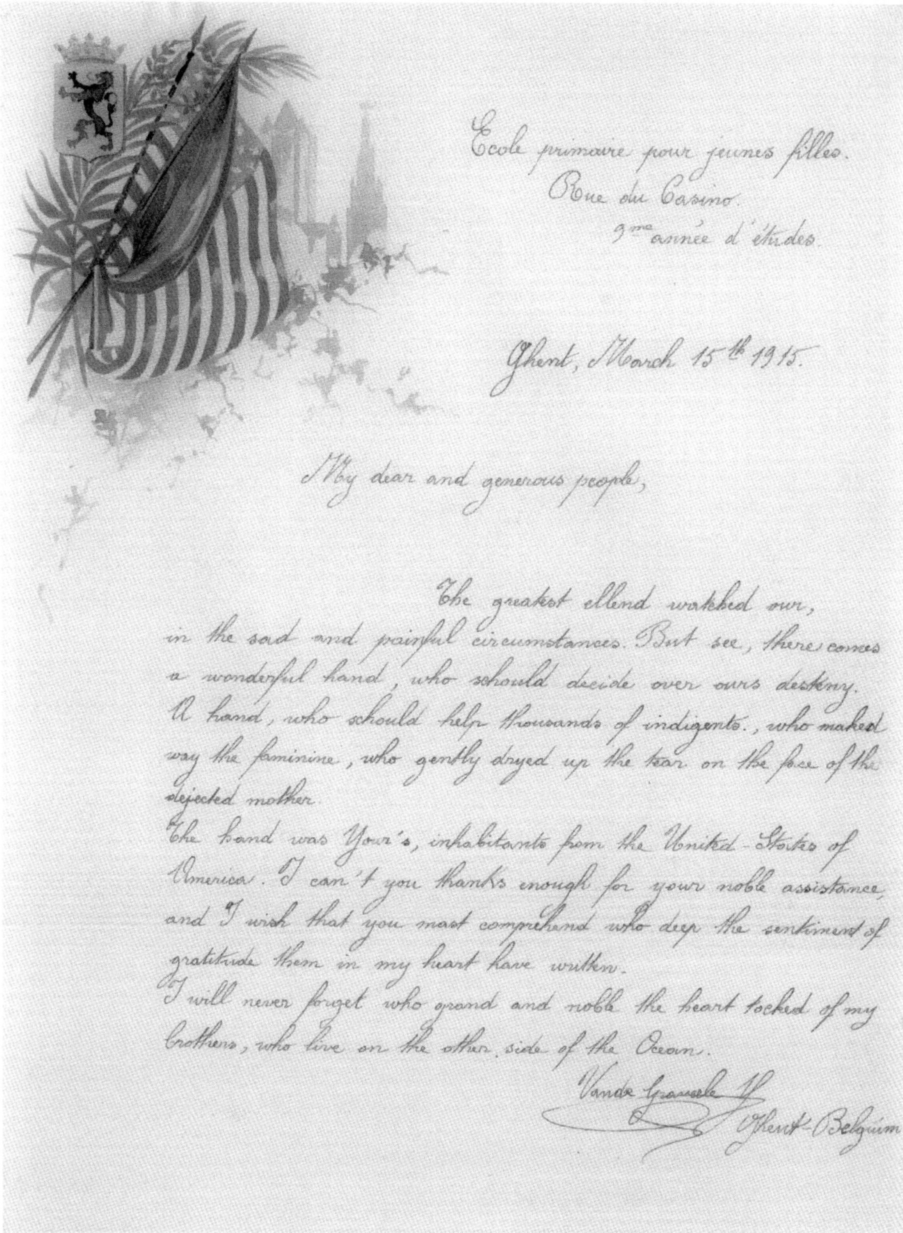

École primaire pour jeunes filles.
Rue du Casino.
9me année d'études.

Ghent, March 15th 1915.

My dear and generous people,

The greatest ellend watched our, in the sad and painful circumstances. But see, there comes a wonderful hand, who schould decide over ours destiny. A hand, who schould help thousands of indigents, who maked way the faminine, who gently dryed up the tear on the face of the dejected mother.
The hand was Your's, inhabitants from the United-States of America. I can't you thanks enough for your noble assistance, and I wish that you most comprehend who deep the sentiment of gratitude them in my heart have written.
I will never forget who grand and noble the heart toched of my brothers, who live on the other side of the Ocean.

Vande Graveele Y.
Ghent-Belgium

**Letter from a Citizen of Belgium, 1915**
In 1914, Whitlock was appointed minister to Belgium by Pres. Woodrow Wilson and began perhaps his most important phase of his life. When World War I broke out, Germany occupied Belgium, and the people of the country were faced with extreme hardship. Whitlock stayed in Brussels to oversee the distribution of food sent by the Committee for Relief of Belgium, helping to save thousands from starvation. It was only after America declared war on Germany that Whitlock left the country. When the war ended, Whitlock returned to Belgium and resumed his position as minister. He also continued to write, including an autobiography. In all, Whitlock authored 18 books. He died in Cannes, France, in 1934.

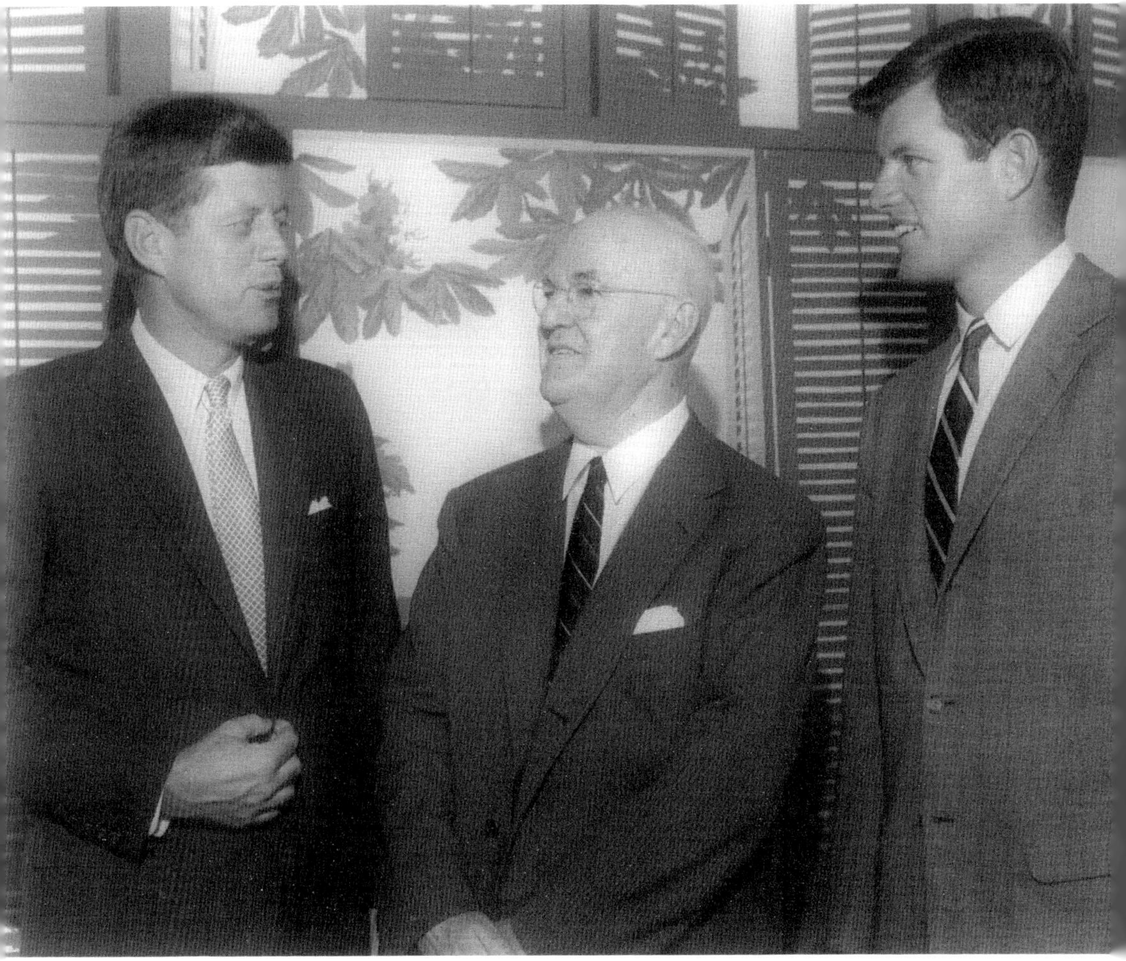

## John P. Kelly

In a city that has traditionally had strong roots in the Democratic Party, John P. Kelly was a Democrat's Democrat. Born in Toledo in 1896, he started working in the public sector as a deputy sheriff in Lucas County in 1919. He would go on to serve as a deputy county engineer, as Lucas County Commissioner, as a member of Toledo City Council, and as a clerk and a member of the Lucas County Board of Elections.

His political involvement began in 1932, when he became a Democratic ward chairman, a position he held for nearly 50 years. From 1945 to 1966, he was the chairman of the Lucas County Democratic Party's executive committee. He was also active in state and national politics, including serving as a presidential elector in 1948 and 1964, as an advisor to the national Democratic Party, and as vice chairman of the Ohio Democratic Party. In his many roles, he had the opportunity to work closely with many national political leaders, including John F. and Robert F. Kennedy, with whom he is pictured here in 1960. Kelly died in 1989.

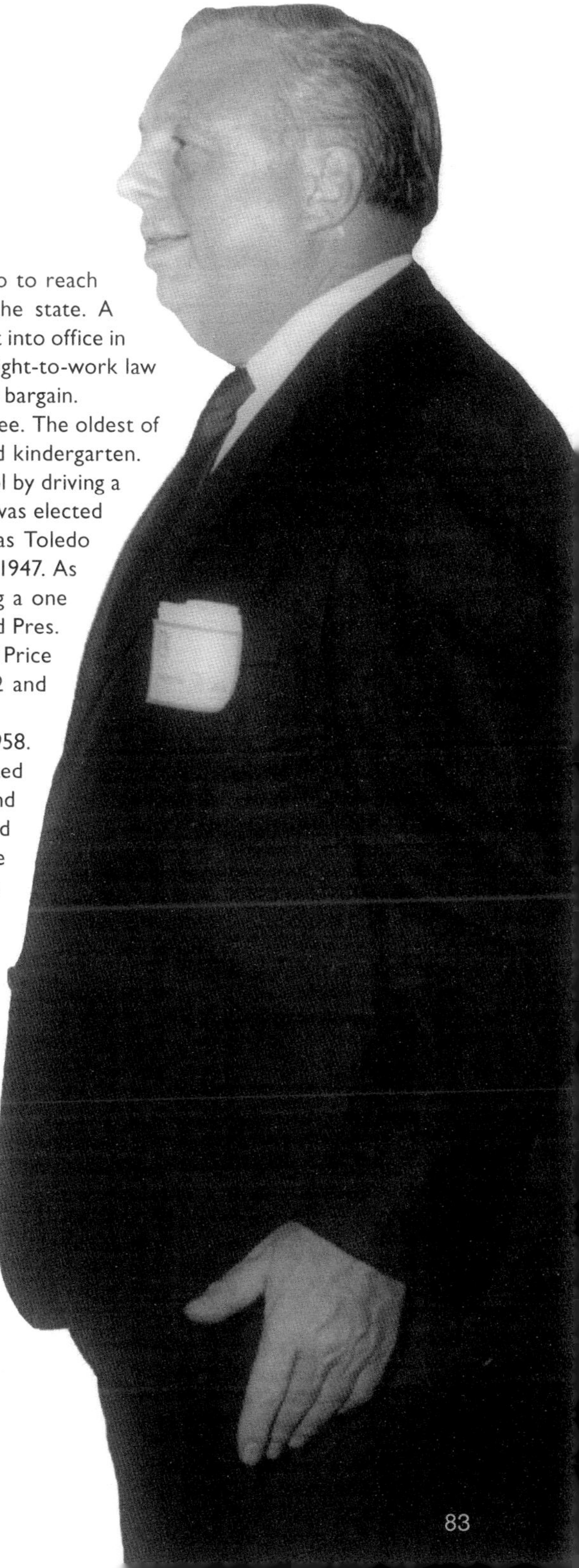

Michael V. DiSalle

Michael V. DiSalle was the only person from Toledo to reach Ohio's pinnacle of political power—governor of the state. A Democrat and a friend of labor, in 1958 he was swept into office in a race where the biggest issue on the ballot was a right-to-work law that threatened the ability of workers to collectively bargain.

DiSalle's family moved to Toledo when he was three. The oldest of seven children, he spoke only Italian until he started kindergarten. He worked his way through Georgetown Law School by driving a delivery truck. He began practicing law in 1932 and was elected to the state legislature in 1936, served two terms as Toledo vice mayor beginning in 1944, and became mayor in 1947. As mayor, he stabilized the city's finances by instituting a one percent personal and business income tax, which led Pres. Harry S. Truman to appoint him head of the Office of Price Stabilization in 1950. He ran for the Senate in 1952 and governor in 1956, losing both races.

But the support of labor pushed him ahead in 1958. With the help of a Democratic legislature, he enacted the largest tax increase in the state's history to fund reform programs. But he also strongly opposed the death penalty, which cost him support. Still, he considered running for the presidency in 1960, but after a series of secret meetings, threw his support to John F. Kennedy, helping to ensure Kennedy's victory. In 1962, DiSalle lost his bid for reelection as governor to Republican James A. Rhodes, and he retired from politics to run several businesses and write a book against the death penalty. DiSalle died suddenly in 1981.

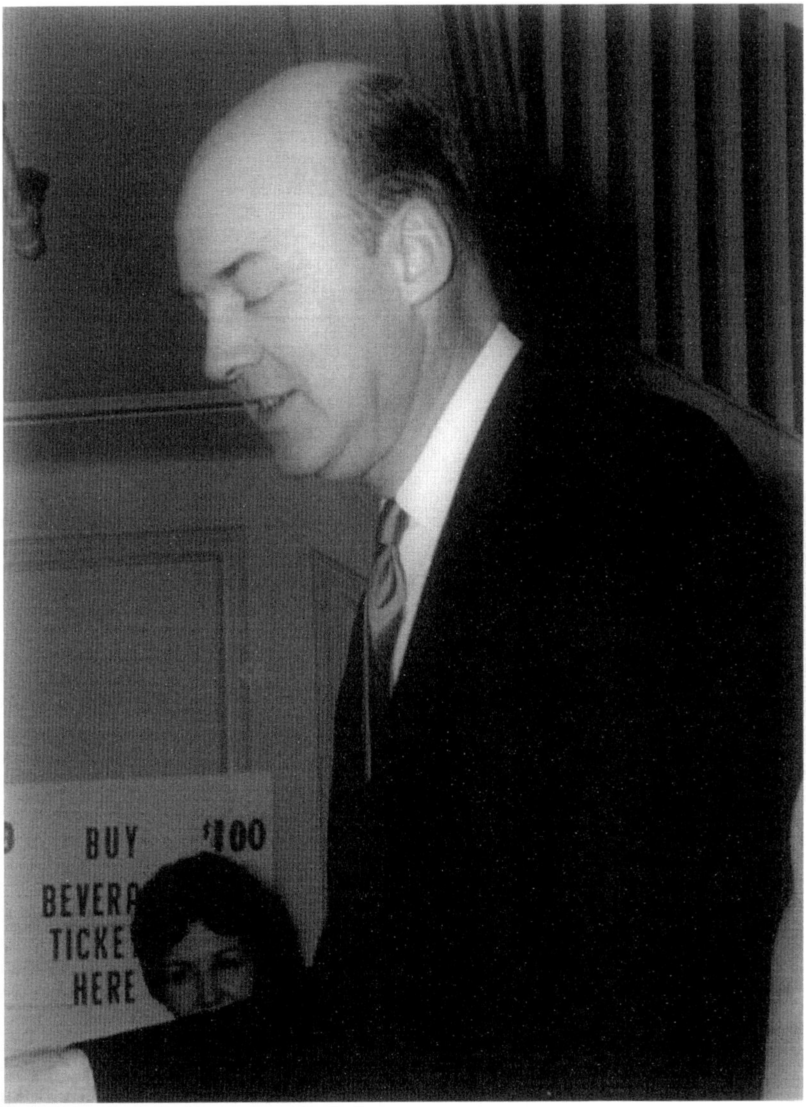


**John W. Potter**

John Potter not only served as Toledo's mayor but also as a state and federal judge.

Potter's family moved to Toledo from England before he was born, in 1918. Potter received a bachelor's degree in political science from the University of Toledo and a law degree from the University of Michigan. After service in World War II, he returned to Toledo and began a career in law.

But he was also drawn to politics. He began as a precinct committeeman in West Toledo, which led to his election to city council. In 1961, he was elected mayor and reelected in 1963. It was during his tenure as mayor that Toledo saw its first efforts in urban renewal with the development of Riverview, which included a new world headquarters for Owens-Corning Fiberglas called the Fiberglas Tower. He was also instrumental in the development and expansion of Toledo Express Airport.

After serving as mayor, Potter was elected to the Sixth Ohio District Court of Appeals in 1969 and reelected in 1974. After four years as presiding judge of courts from 1971 to 1975, he was appointed by Pres. Ronald Reagan to the US District Court in 1982, serving full-time for 10 years before acquiring senior status as a federal judge. He died in 2013.

### Thomas Ludlow Ashley

Thomas Ludlow Ashley had politics in his blood. His great-grandfather was James Ashley, who represented Toledo in Congress from 1859 to 1869 and is considered the author of the 13th Amendment to the Constitution, which outlawed slavery. Thomas Ludlow Ashley, known as "Lud," was born in Toledo in 1923. He attended Yale, where he became friends with George H.W. Bush, and received his law degree from Ohio State University. He was elected to Congress in 1955 and served 13 terms until 1981.

In Congress, Ashley was a great champion for public housing and assistance for the poor. He also helped to get federal money to improve the Port of Toledo and fund downtown redevelopment in late 1970s. But in the Reagan landslide of 1980, Ashley lost his seat to Republican Ed Weber.

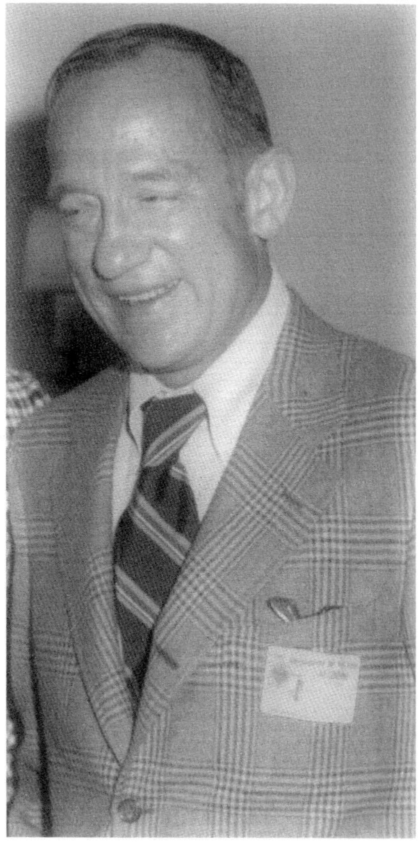

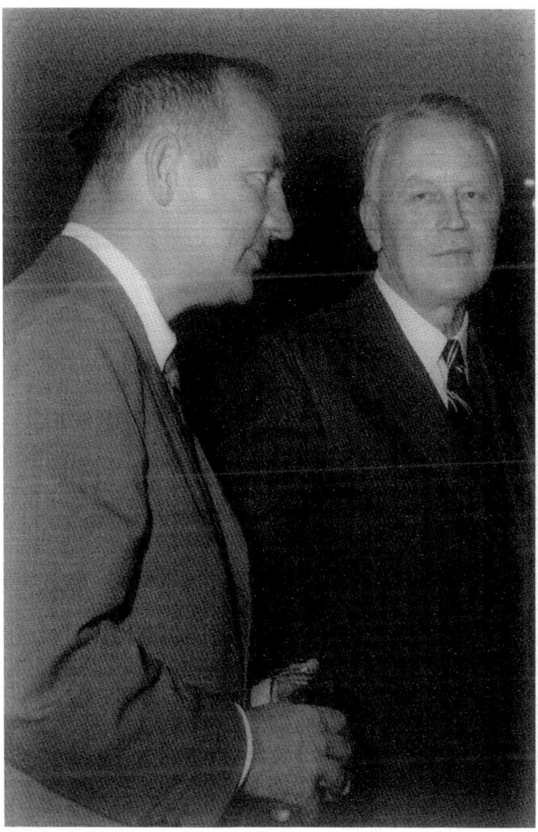

### Thomas Ludlow Ashley with University of Toledo President William S. Carlson, c. 1968

Ashley died in 2010. Two years later, the federal courthouse in Toledo was named the James M. and Thomas W. Ludlow Ashley United States Courthouse.

## Foy D. Kohler

As the US ambassador to the Soviet Union in 1963, Foy D. Kohler (center) was in Moscow at the height of the Cuban Missile Crisis when the United States and the USSR threatened each other with nuclear annihilation. Fortunately, Pres. John F. Kennedy and Soviet premier Nikita Khrushchev were able to end the standoff peacefully for the sake of the world's survival.

Born in 1918, Kohler attended the University of Toledo from 1924 to 1927. His early diplomatic posts were in Canada, Romania, Yugoslavia, Greece, and Egypt.

In 1959, he was appointed deputy assistant secretary of state for European affairs and coordinated Vice Pres. Richard Nixon's visit to the Soviet Union. He witnessed the famous "kitchen cabinet" debate between Nixon and Khrushchev over which country was more advanced.

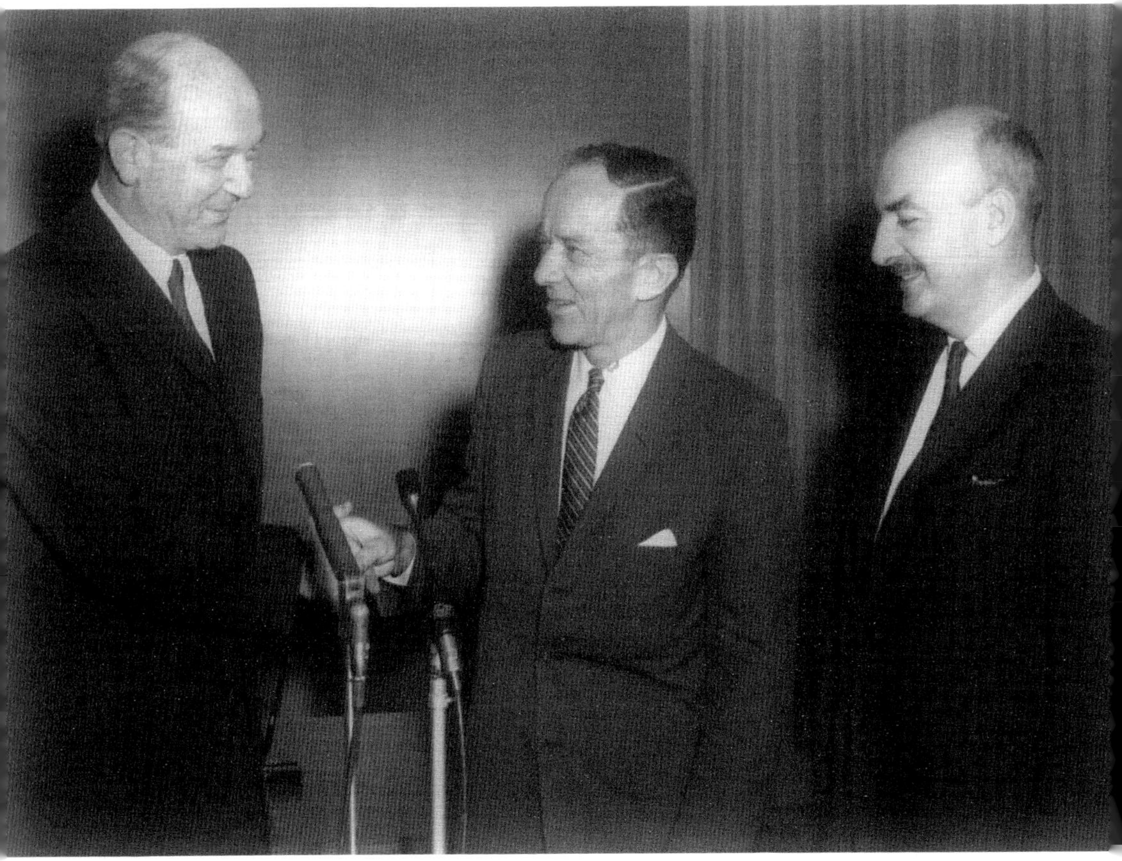

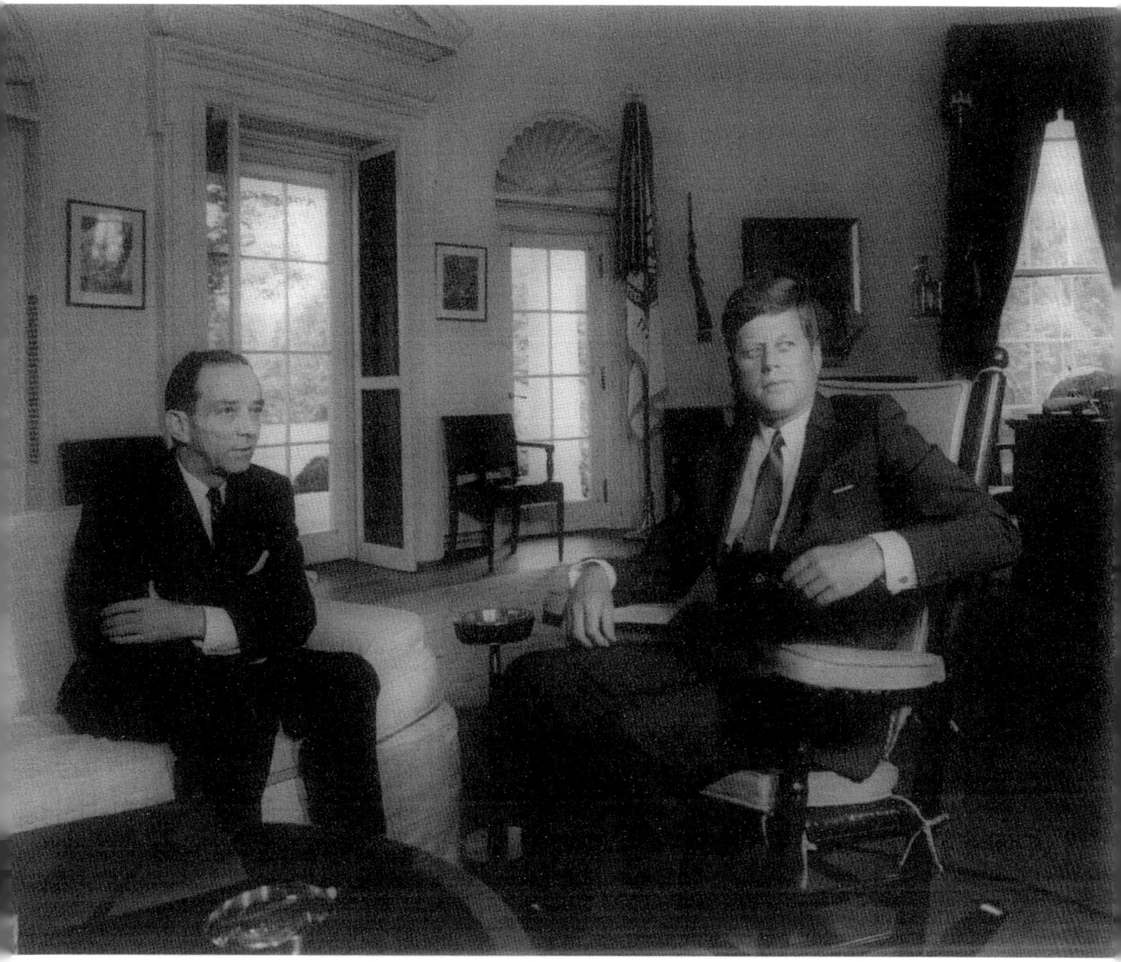

**Ambassador Foy Kohler and Pres. John F. Kennedy in the Oval Office, 1962**
In 1962, Kohler was appointed ambassador to Russia by Kennedy. After Kennedy's assassination, Kohler held a memorial service at the American Embassy in Moscow, receiving the Soviet leaders. Kohler remained as ambassador until 1966.

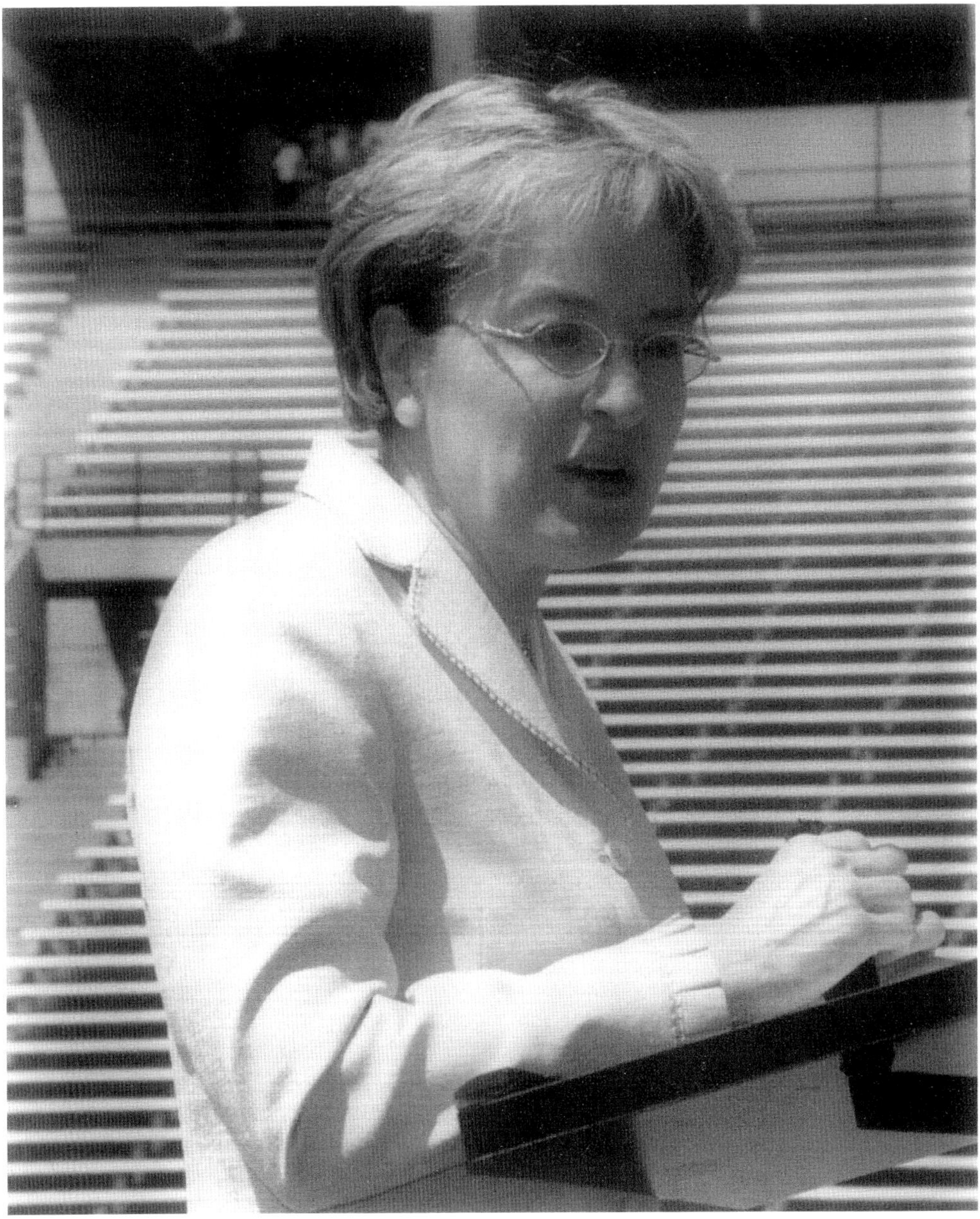

Marcy Kaptur

Marcy Kaptur rose from humble roots in Toledo's Polish American community to the halls of Congress, and as of this writing, she is the longest-serving female member of the House of Representatives.

Kaptur was born in 1946 and grew up in the Kuhschwantz neighborhood, where her parents ran a small grocery store. Active in the Democratic Party, she started volunteering in elections at the age of 13. She received degrees in history and urban planning from the University of Wisconsin and served as a regional planner before joining the Carter administration as an urban advisor. Kaptur had begun the doctoral program in urban planning at the Massachusetts Institute of Technology when she was asked by party leaders to return to Toledo and run for Congress in 1982 against incumbent Ed Weber. She won that election by 19 points and has won 16 elections since.

**Marcy Kaptur Receiving Honorary Degree from the University of Toledo, 1993**
Kaptur is known in Congress as a supporter of the working class and unions and as an opponent of the North American Free Trade Agreement (NAFTA). She has also championed the causes of veterans and helped to establish the National World War II Veterans Memorial in Washington, DC.

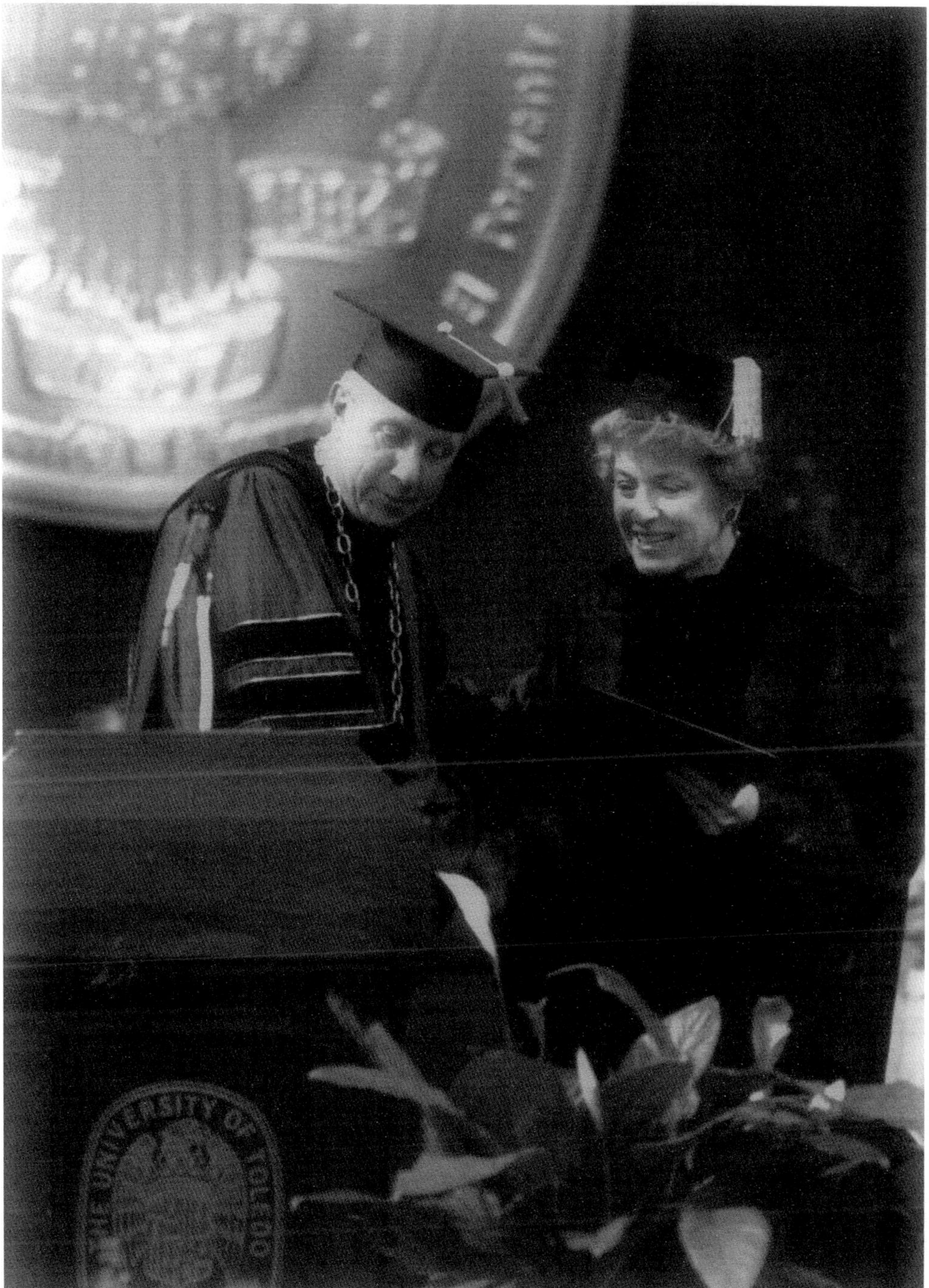

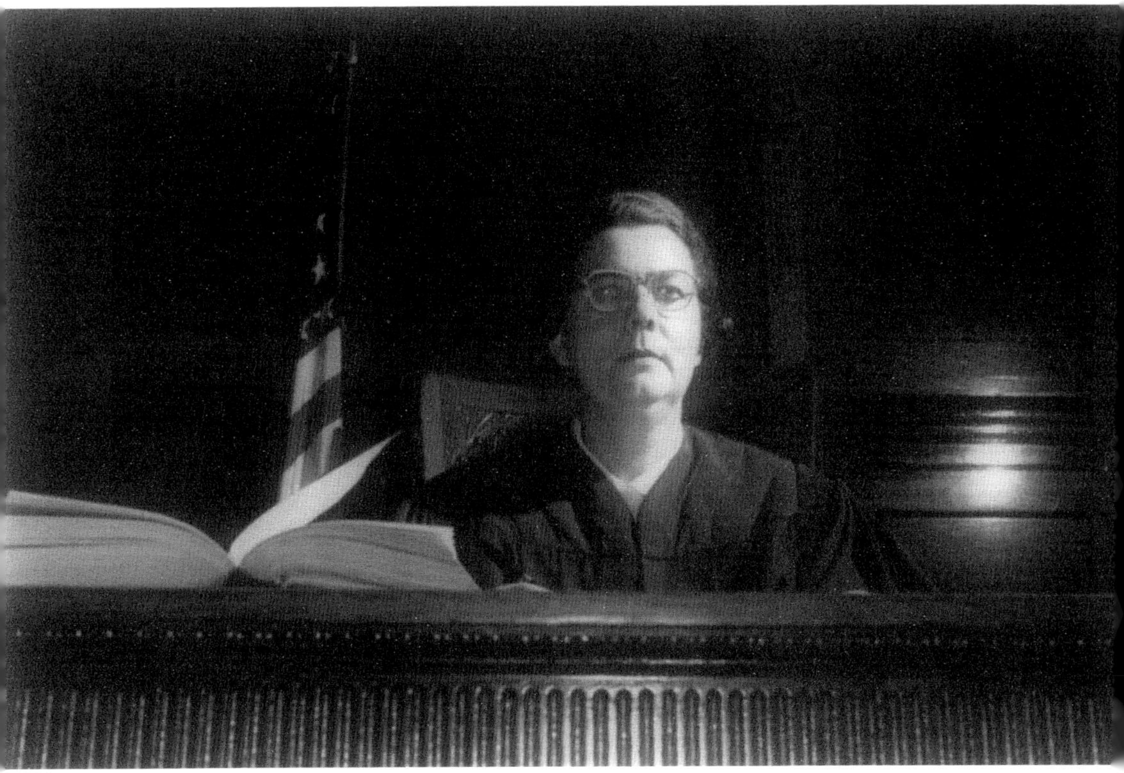

### Geraldine Macelwane

Geraldine Macelwane became a judge at a time when there were few women lawyers. She was born in Detroit in 1909, but her family moved to Toledo in 1924. After graduating from high school in 1926, she immediately started working as a clerk for the railroads. But when she lost that job due to the Depression, she began to attend law school at night and was admitted to the Ohio Bar in 1932 even before receiving her law degree. She received the degree from the University of Toledo in 1938.

Macelwane practiced law until 1937, when she became a prosecutor for Lucas County. There, she specialized in child-neglect cases. She married architect John P. Macelwane in 1938, and the couple had two children.

In 1952, she was elected the first woman judge to the Toledo Municipal Court, and in 1956, she was appointed by Ohio governor Frank Lausche as the first woman judge of the Lucas County Common Pleas Court. Macelwane was elected to the position for four additional terms. One of her specialties in law was the development of standardized instructions to jurors. She died in 1974. (Courtesy of the Toledo-Lucas County Public Library.)

# CHAPTER FOUR

# The Arts, Entertainers, and Sports Figures

While thousands of miles away from the sports, entertainment, and art hubs of New York and Los Angeles, Toledo has still impacted these fields in numerous and profound ways. Many of those who called Toledo home moved on to New York or Los Angeles in order to be successful—and were. Who can forget Danny Thomas's television show *Make Room for Daddy*, Teresa Brewer's song "Music! Music! Music!," or Jamie Farr's character Corporal Klinger? Helen O'Connell, Art Tatum, Steve Mix, and Joe E. Brown were other national stars in the entertainment and sports fields from Toledo.

But Toledo also produced men and women who, while less well known, were nonetheless stars. Bill Jones, for example, may have been the first African American to play on an integrated professional basketball team. Lee Richmond was the first to pitch a perfect professional baseball game. Joe Scalzo brought the world's attention to Toledo when he organized the Amateur Wrestling World's Championships in the city in 1962. And Noah Swayne, while not a player himself, brought baseball to the city. Today, Toledo's Mud Hens are one of the most recognizable names in the minor leagues.

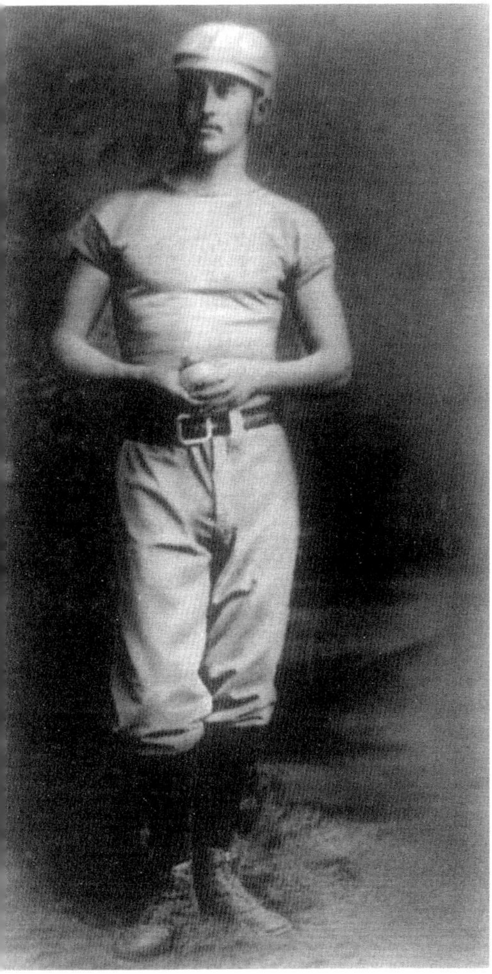

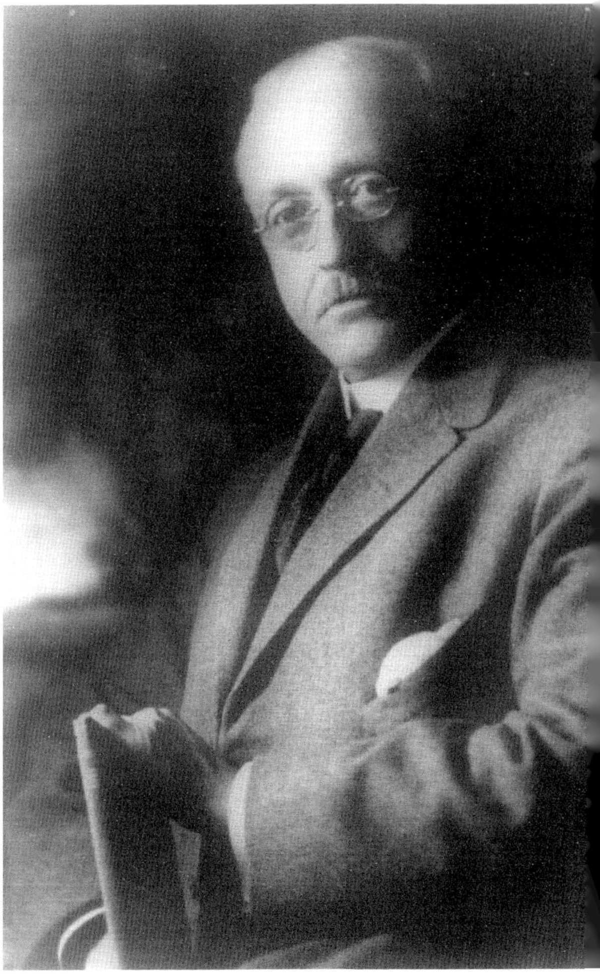

**Lee Richmond**

Lee Richmond was born in 1857 in Sheffield, Ohio, and began playing baseball in 1874. Five years later, he was described by many as the best pitcher in collegiate sports when he led Brown University to the national championship. The following year, he signed with the Worcesters, a professional team in Worcester, Massachusetts. In a game against Cleveland on June 12, 1880, he kept all of Cleveland's players from getting on base—thus pitching a perfect game—and Worcester won by a score of 1-0. It was the first perfect game pitched in professional baseball.

Richmond played professionally for six seasons before entering medical school. He practiced medicine for a few years and then moved to Toledo, where he taught high school math for 32 years and then became a professor of hygiene and physical education and dean of men at the University of Toledo. He died in Toledo in 1929.

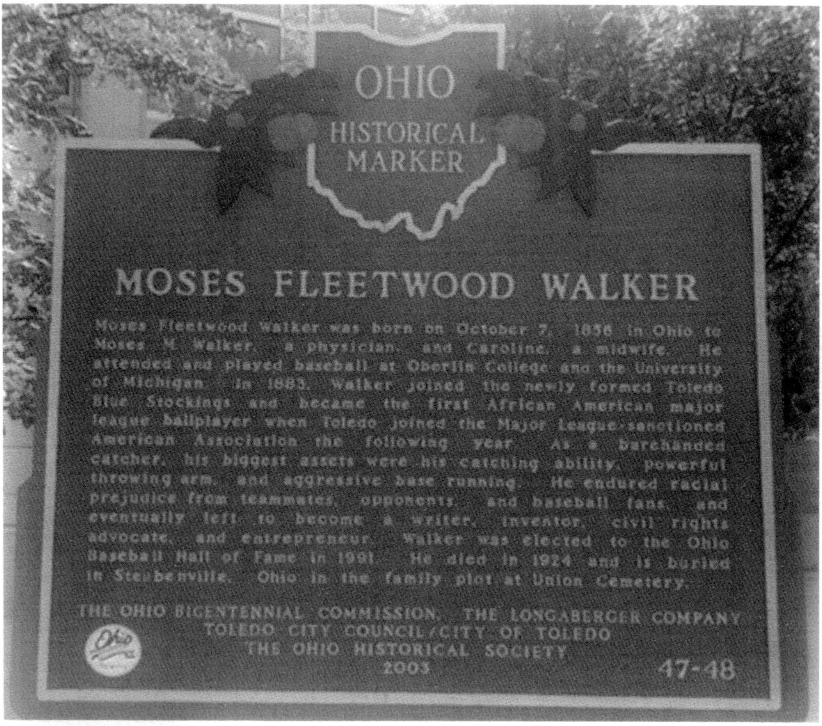


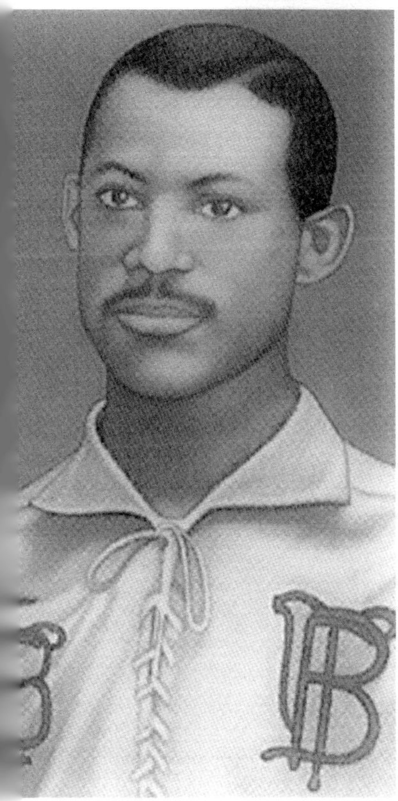

## Moses Fleetwood Walker

While most Americans probably believe Jackie Robinson was the first African American to play baseball in the major leagues, that title rightly goes to Moses Fleetwood Walker, who did it while playing in Toledo.

Born in Mount Pleasant, Ohio, before the Civil War, Walker graduated from the University of Michigan. After college, he joined the Toledo Blue Stockings, an all-white minor-league baseball team, as a catcher in 1883. At the time, segregation in sports teams was not a league policy, just the preference of many players and fans. The following year, the Blue Stockings joined the American Association of the National League, becoming a major-league franchise. On May 1, 1884, Moses Fleetwood Walker played in the opening game of the season, officially breaking the color barrier in the major leagues 63 years before Jackie Robinson.

After playing in 42 games in 1884, Walker was injured, and the following year the Toledo Blue Stockings folded. Walker could only find work with minor-league teams, and in 1889 professional baseball officially banned African American players. His life went downhill after that, and in 1891 he killed a man in self-defense. He was acquitted, but his anger led him to become a vocal opponent of racial integration. He died in 1924.

Pictured above is the historical marker honoring Moses Fleetwood Walker outside the Toledo Mud Hens Stadium in downtown Toledo.

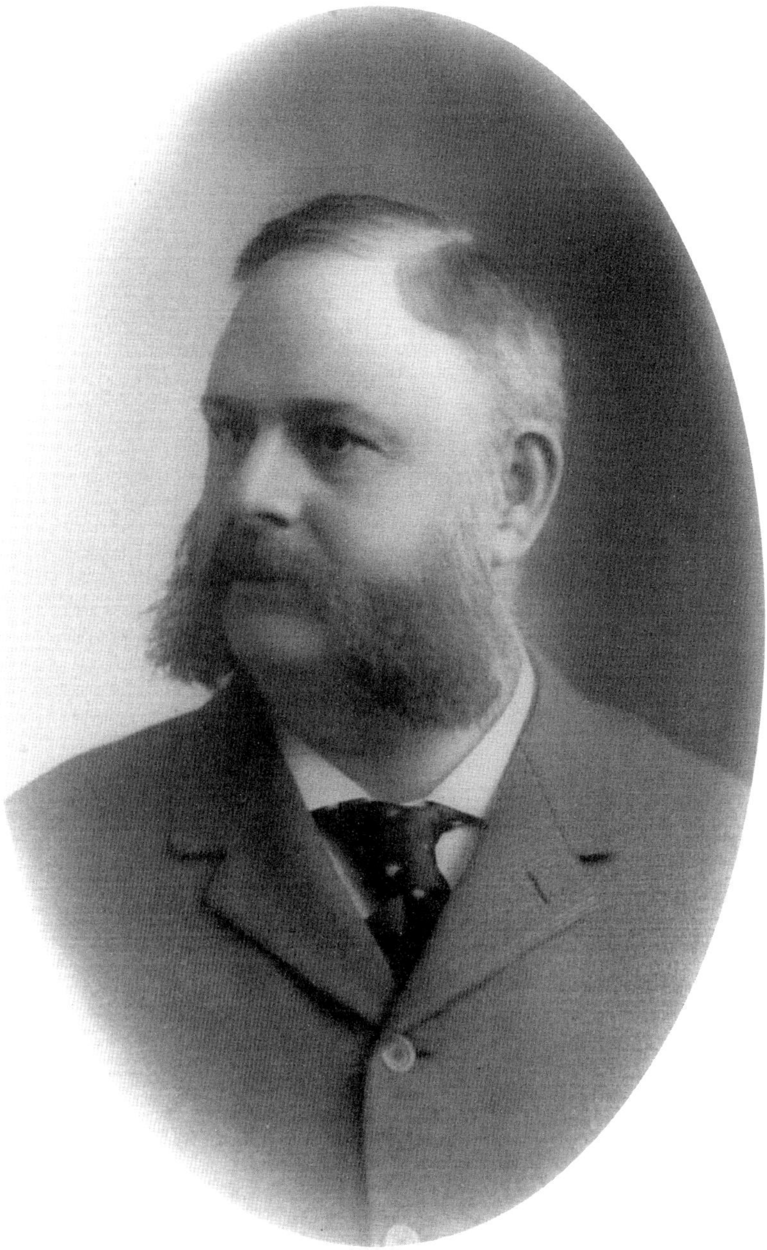

Noah Swayne

Noah Swayne was a noted lawyer and politician who was best known for bringing baseball to Toledo. Born in Maryland in 1848, Swayne was the son of an associate justice on the US Supreme Court. He graduated from Yale in 1870 and after receiving his law degree, came to Toledo to work for the firm of his brother, Swayne, Hayes & Fuller. Elected to the Ohio Legislature in the 1880s, Swayne was one of the chief advocates for the establishment of the Toledo State Hospital, which opened in 1888.

In his youth, Swayne played amateur baseball in the early years of the sport. In 1883, he was a member of the board of directors of Toledo's first professional team, the Blue Stockings, which won its first game over Bay City by a score of 5-4.

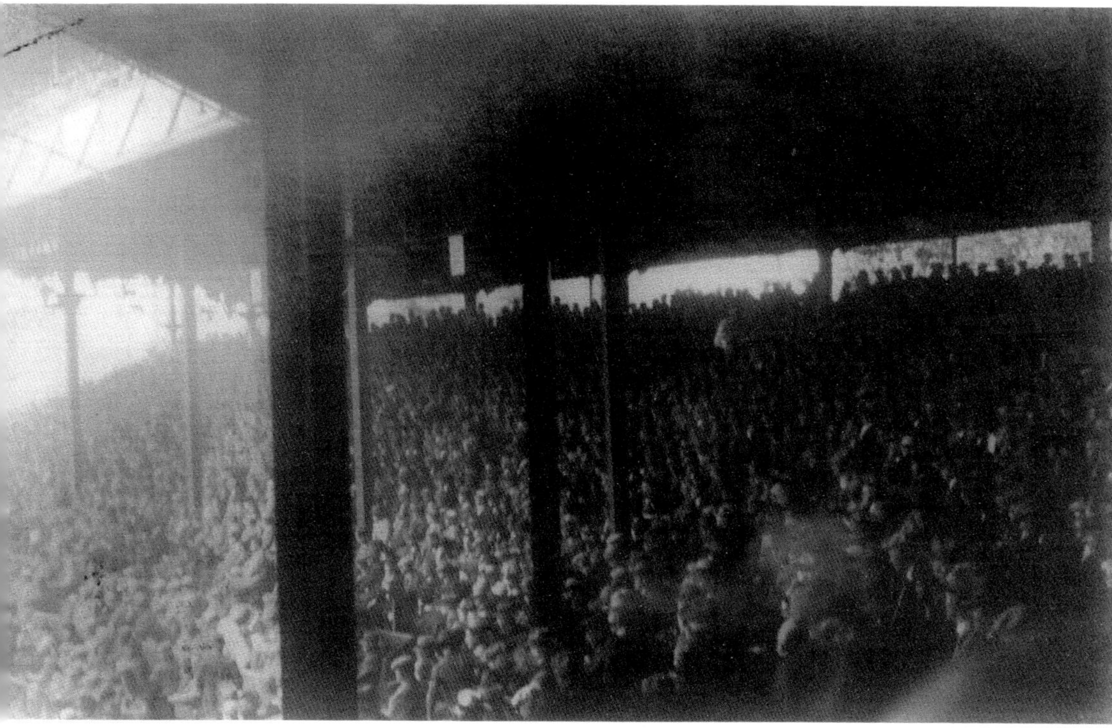

**Baseball at Swayne Field, c. 1925**
Noah Swayne gave a large tract of land at the corner of Detroit and Monroe Streets for the city's first baseball field in 1909. Named Swayne Field, it continued as Toledo's baseball field until 1955. (Both, courtesy of the Toledo-Lucas County Public Library.)

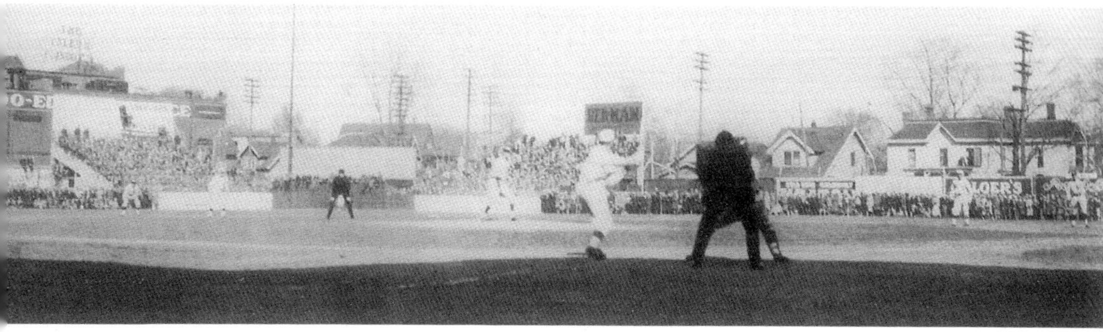

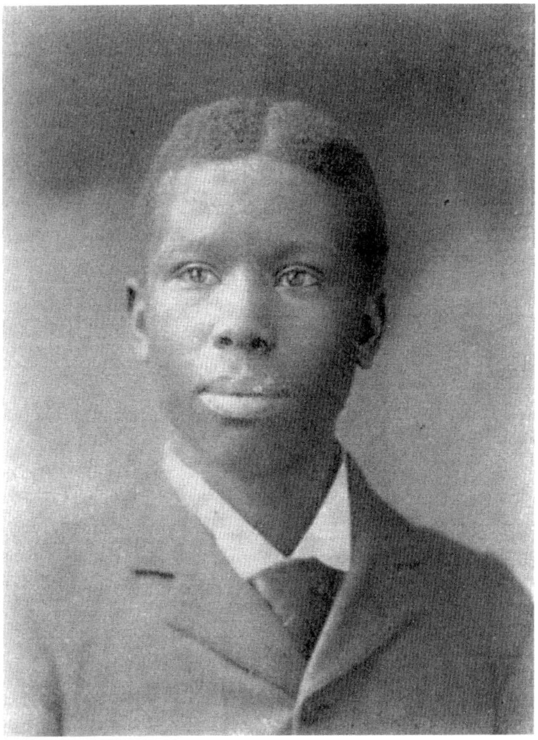

**Paul Lawrence Dunbar**

Paul Lawrence Dunbar was not born in Toledo and only lived in the city for a short time. But during this time he published perhaps his most important work, establishing his reputation as a poet thanks to the support of two prominent Toledoans. Dunbar was born in Dayton in 1872 to freed slaves. He began publishing poetry in Dayton's newspapers at the age of 14. While an excellent student, he could not afford to go to college, and instead worked as an elevator operator.

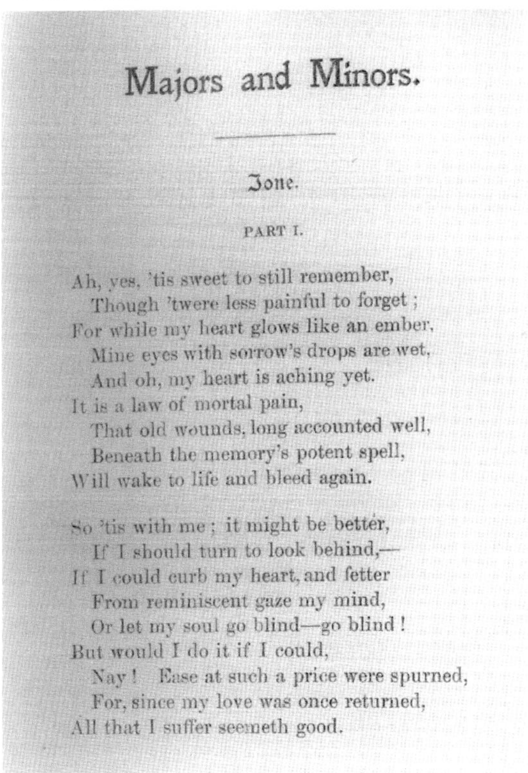

Majors and Minors.

Ione.

PART I.

Ah, yes, 'tis sweet to still remember,
Though 'twere less painful to forget;
For while my heart glows like an ember,
Mine eyes with sorrow's drops are wet,
And oh, my heart is aching yet.
It is a law of mortal pain,
That old wounds, long accounted well,
Beneath the memory's potent spell,
Will wake to life and bleed again.

So 'tis with me; it might be better,
If I should turn to look behind,—
If I could curb my heart, and fetter
From reminiscent gaze my mind,
Or let my soul go blind—go blind!
But would I do it if I could,
Nay! Ease at such a price were spurned,
For, since my love was once returned,
All that I suffer seemeth good.

***Majors and Minors* by Paul Lawrence Dunbar, 1896**

In 1893, Dunbar self-published his first book of poetry, *Oak and Ivy*, which came to the attention of Henry A. Tobey, a Toledo psychiatrist who was superintendent of the Toledo State Hospital, and attorney Charles A. Thatcher. In 1896, Tobey and Thatcher underwrote the publication of Dunbar's second book of poetry, *Majors and Minors*. While primarily written in a classical style, several poems in the book included "Negro dialect." The work was favorably reviewed, and Dunbar's reputation as a poet grew.

Dunbar went on to write several novels and many lyrics to musical works. In 1898 he married Alice Ruth Moore, who became an established author in her own right. Dunbar contracted tuberculosis in 1900 and suffered from alcoholism and depression. In 1904, he returned to his native Dayton, where he died two years later.

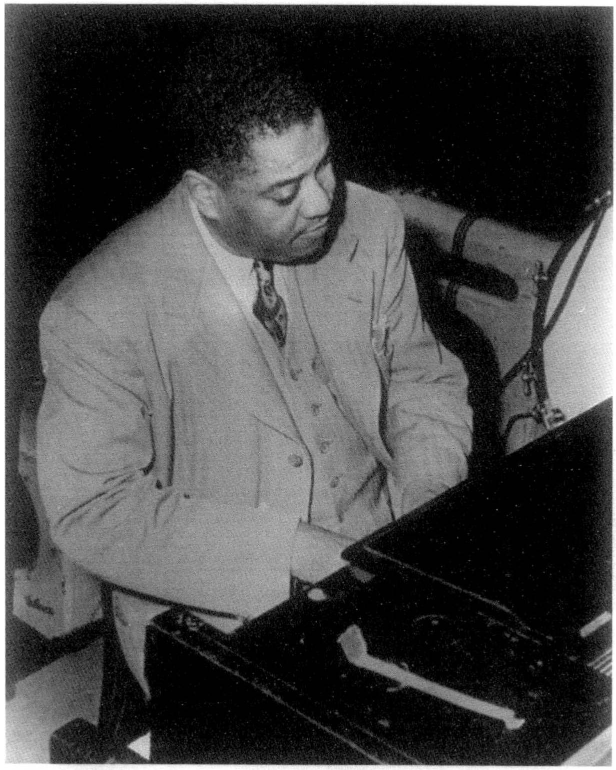

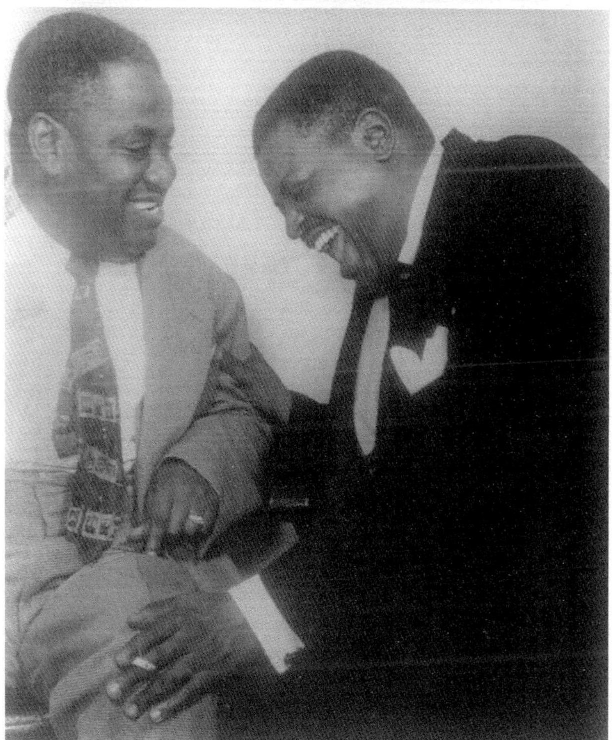

Art Tatum

Though blind nearly from birth, Art Tatum became one of the greatest jazz pianists of all time. He was born in South Toledo in 1910. His father was a guitarist, and his mother played the piano. He began playing piano at the age of 8, and at the age of 17 Tatum was featured on WSPD radio playing musical interludes that became so popular he was given his own show. He also played with local bands at clubs such as Chateau La France and Chicken Charlie's.

Tatum moved to New York in 1931, where he quickly established a reputation for his talent on the keyboard. His style featured quick tempos and improvisation, and it was said that he never played a song the same way twice. He recorded his first solo album in 1933. When he died in 1956 at the age of 47, many entertainers performed tributes at his funeral, including Ella Fitzgerald and Sarah Vaughn. While he had moved away from Toledo many years before, he never forgot his hometown, and in 1941 he honored the city by recording "Toledo Blues." Here, Tatum (left) is pictured with Oscar Peterson. (Both, courtesy of the Toledo-Lucas County Public Library.)

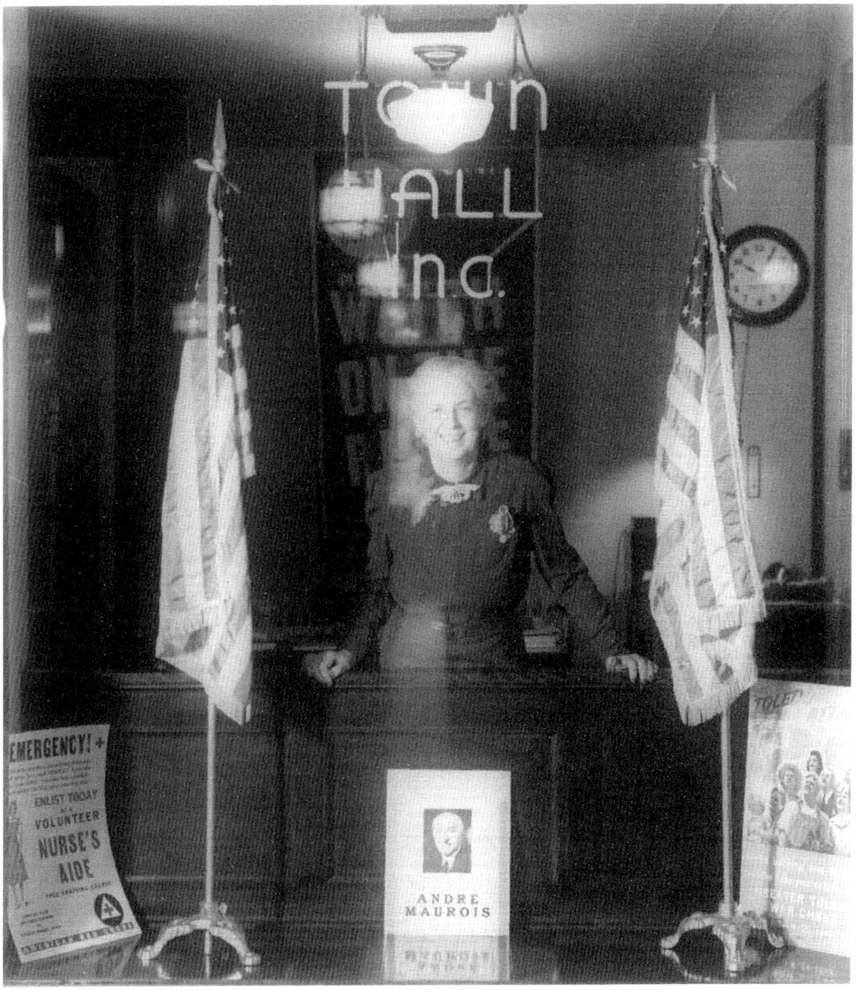


**Flora Ward Hineline**

Flora Ward Hineline brought culture to Toledo through her town hall lecture series from 1929 to the mid-1950s. The series brought people such as Orson Welles, Helen Hayes, Gertrude Stein, Winston Churchill, Marion Anderson, Ethel Barrymore, and Eleanor Roosevelt to Toledo for lectures and theatrical performances.

Flora Ward was born in Pittsfield, Ohio, in 1879 and began teaching in public schools in 1898. In 1902, she married Herbert Bey Hineline but made it clear she intended to continue to work outside the home. She gave birth to a son, and the family moved to Toledo in 1908. When she was told she could not be a teacher because she was married, she became a journalist, writing a column for the *Toledo Blade* and the *Toledo Sunday Times* on society happenings and music. After her husband's and son's deaths less than a year apart, she decided to change course again, establishing the town hall series, modeled after the town hall forum in New York City.

A one-woman operation, Hineline handled all of the arrangements and publicity. In 1945, the Schubert Brothers of New York transformed a theater at Orange and St. Clair Streets in downtown Toledo into the Town Hall Theatre. But she soon broke with the Schuberts.

Hineline received many accolades for her work, but it drained her finances. She ended the series in 1956. She was able to move into the Sunset House in Ottawa Hills thanks to an anonymous donor, and she died there in 1962.

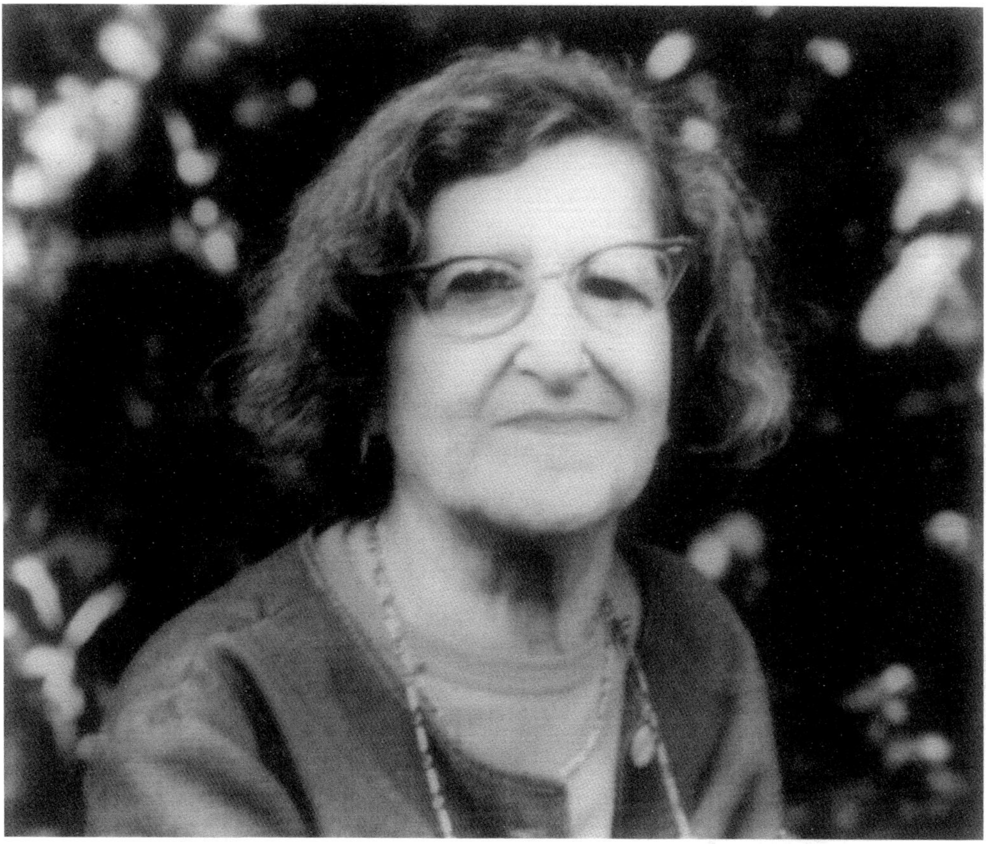

**Jean Gould**

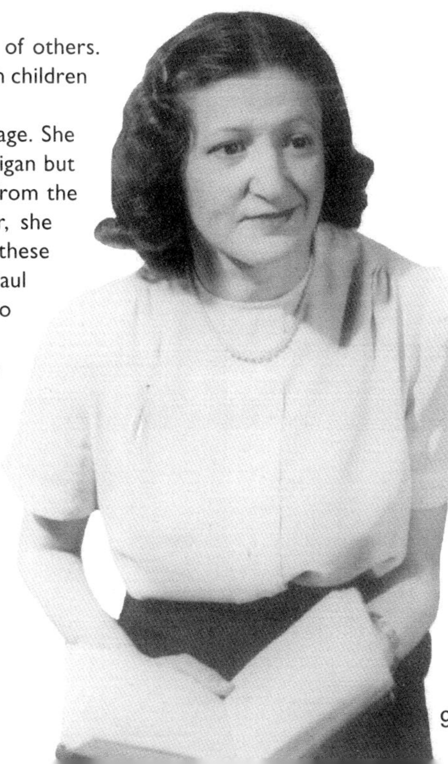

Jean Gould was a writer who wrote about the lives of others. Throughout her career she wrote biographies for both children and adult readers.

Born in 1909, Gould moved to Toledo at a young age. She began her collegiate studies at the University of Michigan but graduated with degrees in literature and journalism from the University of Toledo in 1937. As a freelance writer, she began writing books for children in 1941. Some of these works were about the lives of literary figures like Paul Lawrence Dunbar, and this turned her interest to writing biographies.

Jean Gould's books, published by Dodd, Mead, were about author Herman Melville; Franklin Roosevelt and his fight with polio; artist Winslow Homer; poets Robert Frost, Edna St. Vincent Millay, and Amy Lowell; and two volumes about modern American women poets. She also published shorter works in many popular magazines, including the *New Republic*, the *New York Times*, the *New York Review of Books*, and *Saturday Review*. She lived most of her life in New York's Greenwich Village but died in Toledo in 1993.

## Mildred Benson

Mildred Benson had a secret that was as compelling as the mysteries solved by character Nancy Drew in the books that featured the teenage sleuth. Mildred Benson wrote 23 of the first 30 Nancy Drew books, beginning in 1930, but under the name Carolyn Keene. Few people were aware of Benson's contributions to the iconic book series, which inspired many young girls to be adventurous and sold more than 80 million copies overall.

Benson was born in 1905 in Ladora, Iowa, and received a bachelor's and master's degree from the University of Iowa. After working for a newspaper, she went to New York to inquire about writing fiction works for the Stratemeyer Syndicate. In 1930, she was offered the chance to write the first Nancy Drew book, titled *The Secret of the Old Clock*. Almost an immediate success, Benson started turning the books out quickly, once writing 13 in one year. Other writers also wrote books in the series under the name Carolyn Keene, but Benson was the first.

Nancy Drew was such a popular character because she was different from young female characters in most popular fiction of the time. She was fearless, adventuresome, and independent—attributes that many young girls found appealing. Nancy Drew (and her creator, Mildred Benson) no doubt influenced the life choices of many young women of the day.

In 1944, Benson moved to Toledo, where she worked for the *Toledo Times* and later the *Toledo Blade* newspapers. She covered politics and crime, among other beats, for the papers. She was not generally recognized and honored as the author of the early Nancy Drew novels until the 1990s.

Benson died in Toledo in May 2002 at the age of 96. She was still working as a writer for the *Blade* when she died. (Courtesy of the *Toledo Blade*, © 1949.)

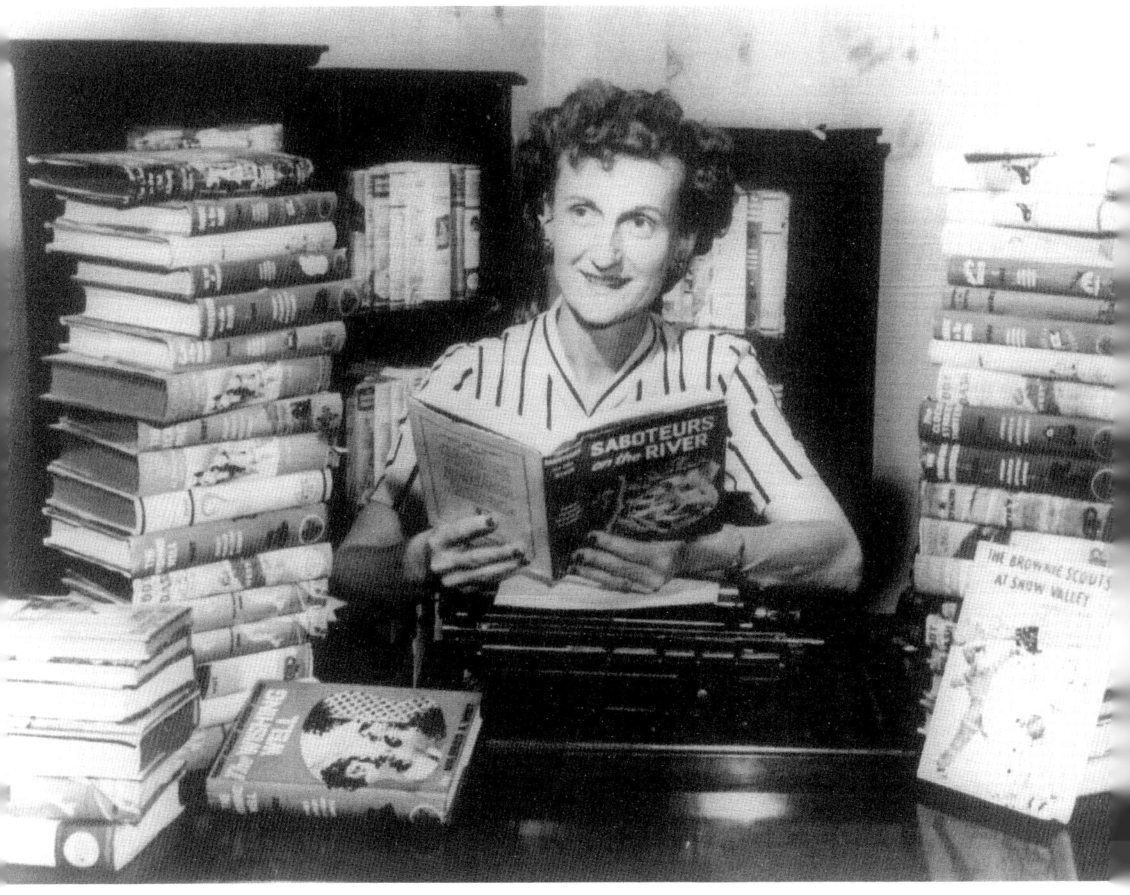

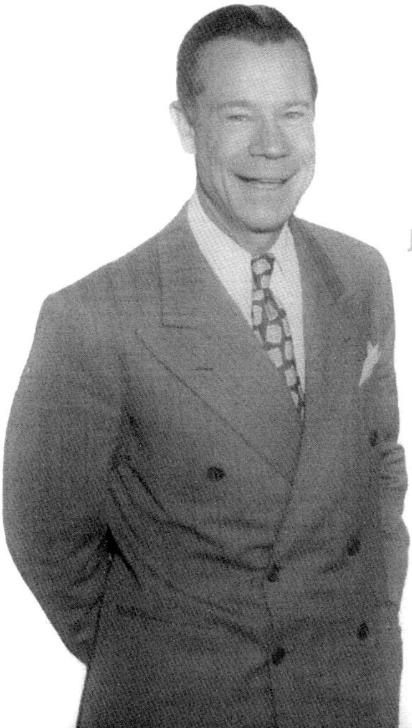

Joe E. Brown

Joe E. Brown's wide smile and seemingly elastic face made him one of the most popular comedians in the country in the 1930s. He was born in Holgate, Ohio, in 1891 but lived most of his early life in Toledo. At the age of nine he joined the circus and even became a professional baseball player. Much of his early entertainment career was spent in vaudeville. In 1929, Brown appeared in Warner Bros. first all-color talking musical *On with the Show*. He soon became a headliner, appearing in one hit after another throughout the 1930s. (Courtesy of the Toledo-Lucas County Public Library.)

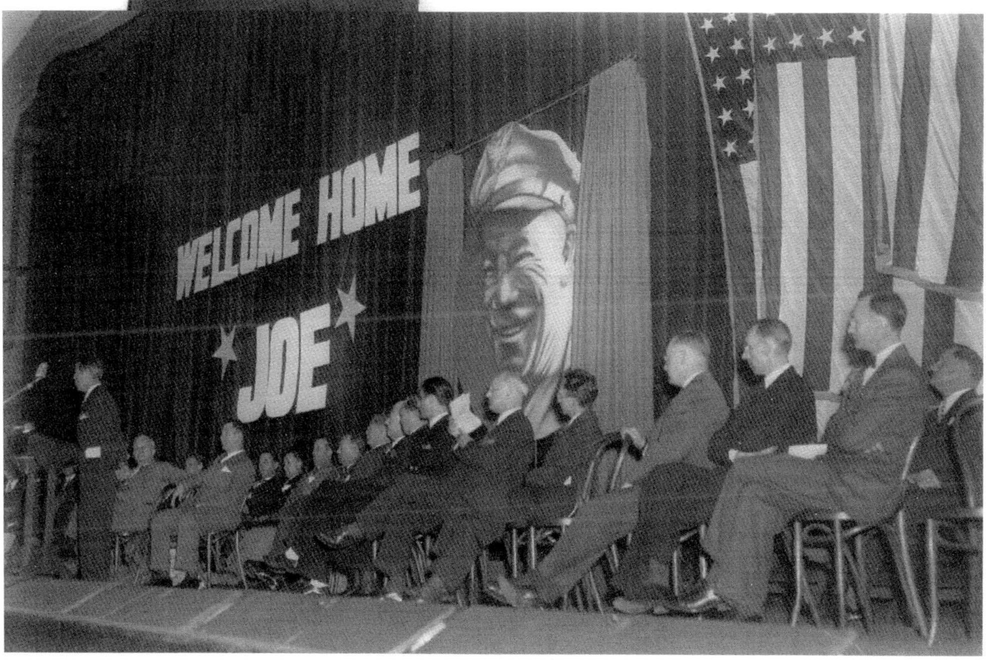


Joe E. Brown Day in Toledo, December 7, 1945

During World War II, Brown spent a lot of his time entertaining the troops with the USO. In recognition of this, the City of Toledo honored him with Joe E. Brown Day on the fourth anniversary of the bombing of Pearl Harbor. In the 1950s, he appeared in the play *Harvey* and won a Tony award. He had cameo roles in some of the most popular movies of the 1950s and early 1960s, including *Around the World in 80 Days* and *It's a Mad, Mad, Mad, Mad World*. He died in Los Angeles in 1973. Toledo named Joe E. Brown Park on the city's east side in his honor. (Courtesy of the Toledo-Lucas County Public Library.)

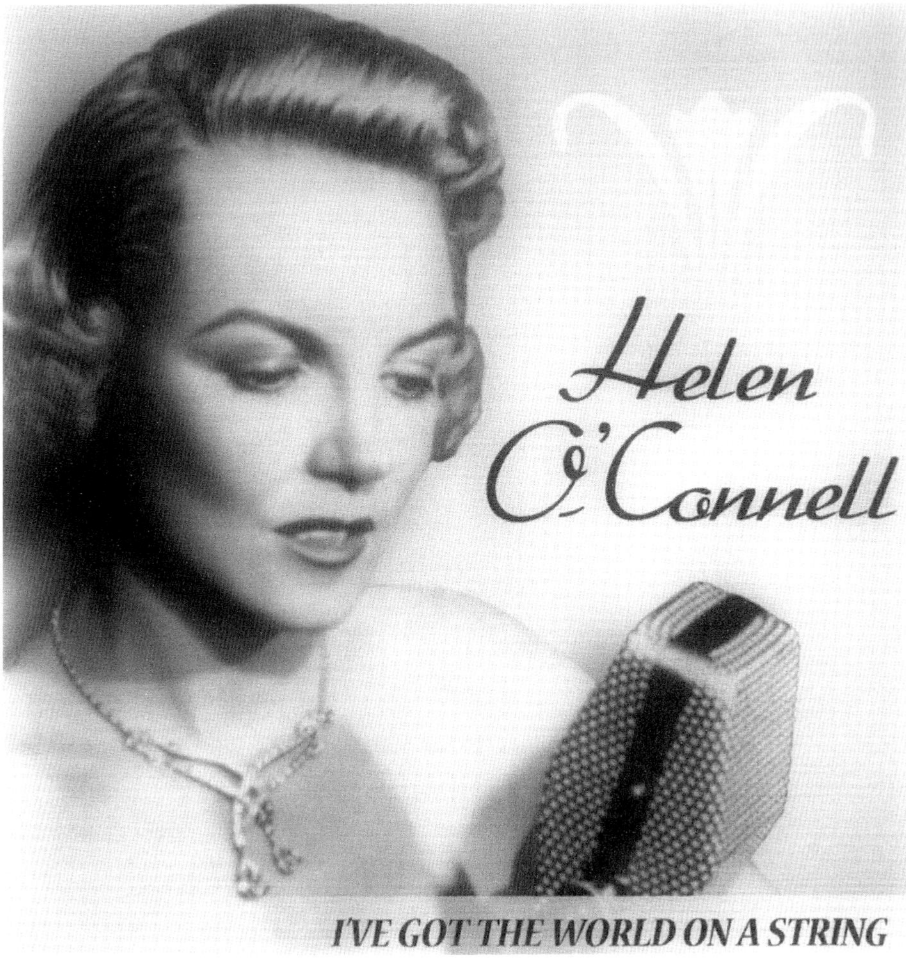


Helen O'Connell

Helen O'Connell became a big-band singer out of necessity. She was born in Lima, Ohio, in 1920, but her family moved to Toledo when she was six. As a child, she sang duets with her sister Alice on the local radio station WSPD. She had to drop out of high school her freshman year after her father died unexpectedly. One night, Helen subbed for her sister at a local club, and she became an immediate hit. She decided to try becoming a professional singer.

Her national singing career began at the age of 16 when Jimmy Dorsey's manager discovered her singing in Cleveland. She traveled with the band for four years. "I left town with just two dresses, one just barely good enough to wear in front of a band," she later recalled. Her first record hit was "Green Eyes," which she recorded with Bob Eberly in 1939. Other hits would include "Tangerine," "I Remember You," and "When the Sun Comes Out."

Despite her popularity among the GIs during World War II, O'Connell quit her singing career in 1943 to raise a family. She had four daughters with two husbands before returning to singing in the 1950s. She worked with the Artie Shaw, Woody Herman, and Glenn Miller orchestras. She also hosted the CBS television show *TV's Top Tunes* in 1953 and was a regular on *The Russ Morgan Show* in 1956. From 1956 to 1958, she worked with Dave Garroway on NBC's *Today Show* and in 1957 had her own show on NBC.

She continued performing later in life a part of an act called "Four Girls Four" with Rosemary Clooney, Margaret Whiting, and Rose Marie in the late 1970s. She also toured with big bands until the last month of her life. She died in California in 1993.

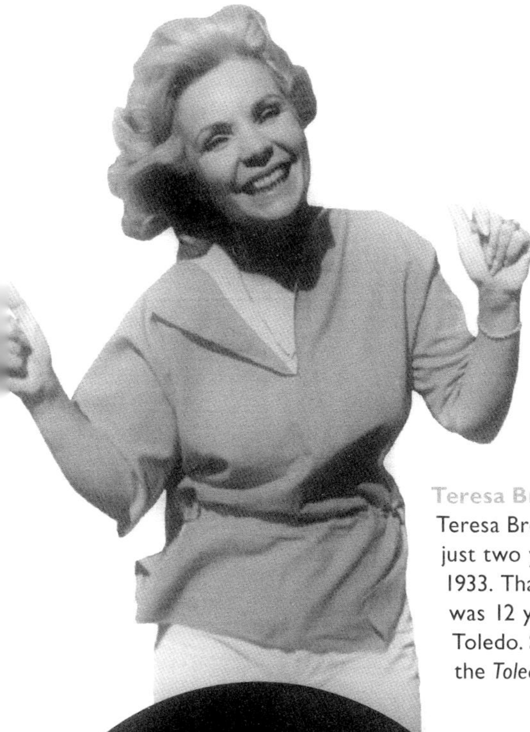

**Teresa Brewer**

Teresa Brewer's career started at a very young age. She was just two years old when she performed on WSPD radio in 1933. That led to a stint with a touring radio show until she was 12 years old, when she returned to her hometown of Toledo. She is pictured here in Toledo in 1981. (Courtesy of the *Toledo Blade*, ©1981.)

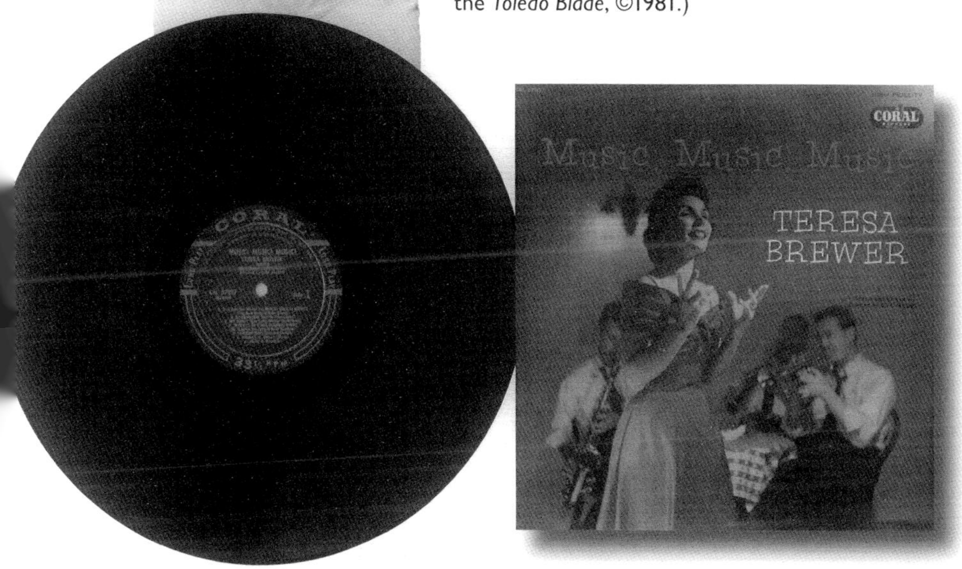


**"Music! Music! Music!" Released by Coral Records, 1955**

In the late 1940s, Brewer signed a recording contract. Her first single had the song "Music! Music! Music!" (sometimes known as "Put Another Nickel in the Nickelodeon"), which became a million seller. Her career took off from there, and she had numerous hits in the 1950s, including "Till I Waltz Again with You," "Mutual Admiration Society," and "Have You Ever Been Lonely." After marrying Bob Thiele, her songs became jazzier. After Thiele's death in 1996, Brewer did not record again. She has a star on the Hollywood Walk of Fame and was inducted into the Hit Parade Hall of Fame. She died in 2007.

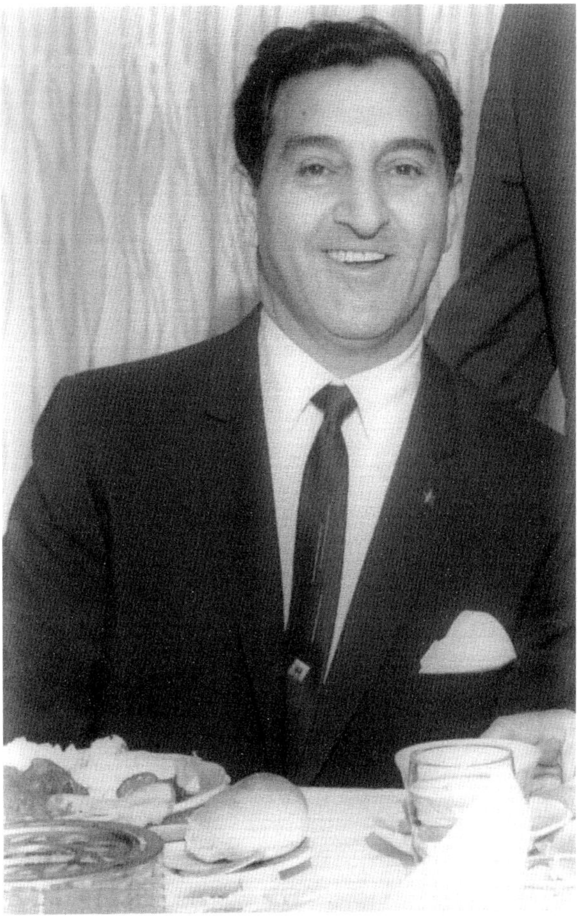

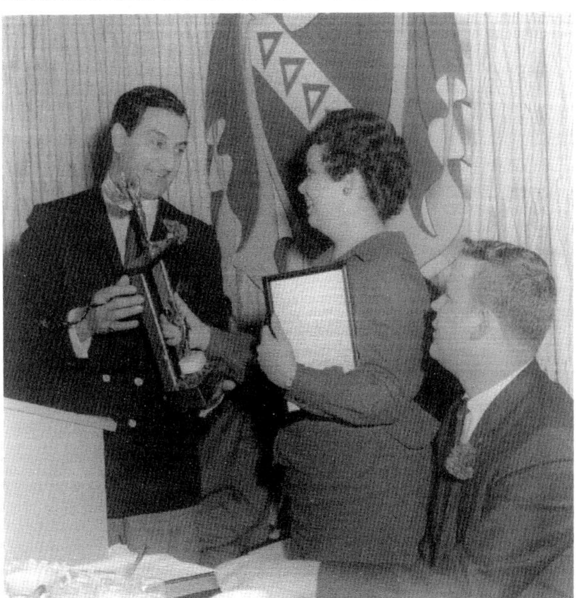

### Danny Thomas

Danny Thomas was an actor, comedian, and television star. But his charitable work as the founder of the St. Jude Children's Research Hospital in Memphis, Tennessee, has been his lasting legacy.

Thomas was born Amos Jacobs in 1912 in Deerfield, Michigan. One of 10 children, his Lebanese family moved to Toledo. He dropped out of Woodward High School to break into show business. He adopted the stage name of Danny Thomas based on the names of two of his brothers, and he got his first big break in Chicago in 1940 as a comic at the Northside Club. He moved to Hollywood, where he made movies with MGM and Warner Bros. In 1953, he took his most endearing and enduring role as nightclub singer Danny Williams in *Make Room for Daddy*, which costarred Marjorie Lord. The show aired until 1964. Many of the show's characters were loosely based on people Thomas knew in Toledo, including Uncle Tonoose, who was modeled after his real uncle.

In 1962, he founded the children's hospital with a research agenda to find the cure for childhood cancer. He died in Los Angeles in 1991 at the age of 77.

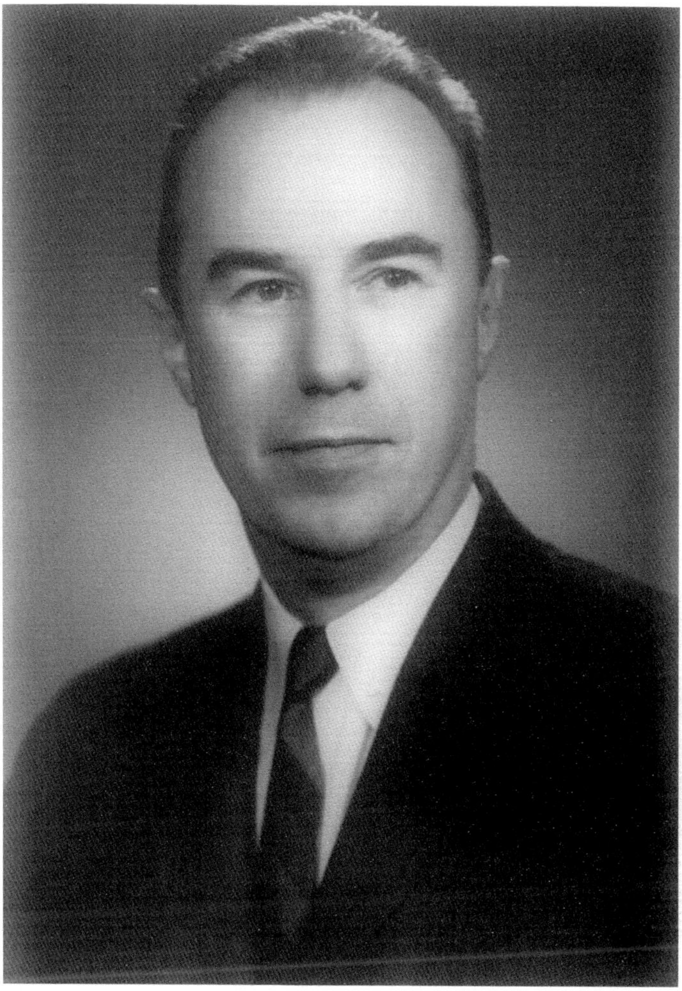

Otto Wittmann Jr.

Otto Wittmann Jr. was committed to preserving works of art.

He began his career as a curator after graduating from Harvard in 1933. His first job was with the Rockhill Nelson Gallery of Art in Kansas City (now known as the Nelson-Atkins Museum of Art). From 1938 to 1941, he was an instructor of art history at Skidmore College and curator of the Hyde Collection in upstate New York.

But Wittmann's work to preserve art extended to his service in Europe during World War II. He was tapped to join the Art Looting Investigation Unit in the Office of Strategic Services. In this position, he traveled through Europe as one of the "Monument Men," investigating the theft of artwork from Jews. He also learned much about European art and made many connections that would serve him in his next career.

Wittmann was named associate director of the Toledo Museum of Art in 1946 and became director in 1959. He transformed it into a world-class museum, tripling the collection and using his keen eye to purchase many important works. He was also active professionally, serving twice as president of the American Association of Art Museum Directors and as an advisor to the National Endowment for the Arts and National Endowment for the Humanities. After his retirement from the Toledo Museum of Art, he moved to California, where he served on the boards of the Los Angeles County Museum of Art and the J. Paul Getty Museum. He died in California in 2001.

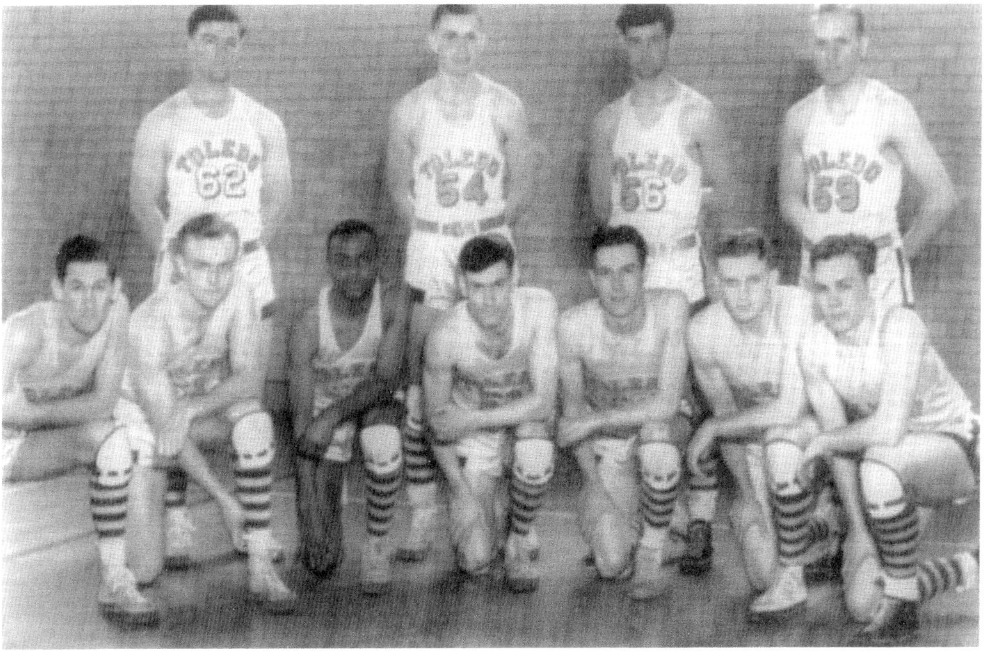

Bill Jones and Members of the University of Toledo Basketball Team, 1938

Bill Jones may have been the "Jackie Robinson" of basketball—one of the first African Americans to play on a white professional team.

He was born in Toledo in 1914. At Woodward High School, he helped to win back-to-back city-league basketball championships in 1929 and 1930. He played for the University of Toledo from 1936 to 1938, and the Toledo team became wildly popular.

After graduation, Jones played for the Toledo White Huts, a semiprofessional team. Against all odds, the team went to the World's Professional Basketball Tournament in Chicago in 1941, where they made it to the semifinals. On the success of the White Huts, Toledo landed a National Basketball League franchise, the Jim White Chevys. The team signed four African American players, with Bill Jones being the first.

Steve Mix at the University of Toledo, 1967

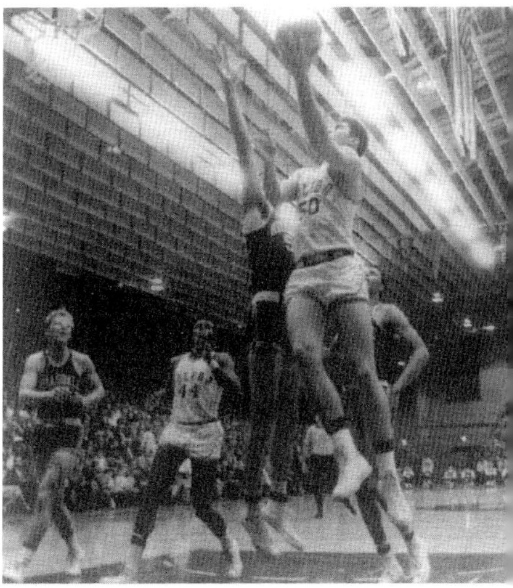

Steve Mix was born in Toledo in 1947. At six-foot-seven, he quickly became a basketball stand-out at Rodgers High School, where he was named to the All Ohio team three years in a row. Mix attended the University of Toledo, where he became the university's all-time leading scorer with 1,676 points and a rebounding average of 11.9 per game.

Mix was a fifth-round NBA pick, selected by the Detroit Pistons, with whom he played from 1969 to 1971. After a brief stint with the Denver Rockets, he played for the Philadelphia 76ers from 1973 to 1982. He was named to the NBA All-Star team in 1974 and 1975. In 787 professional games, he scored 8,357 points. After retiring, he worked as a sports commentator, and from 2012 to 2014 he was head women's basketball coach for Trine University.

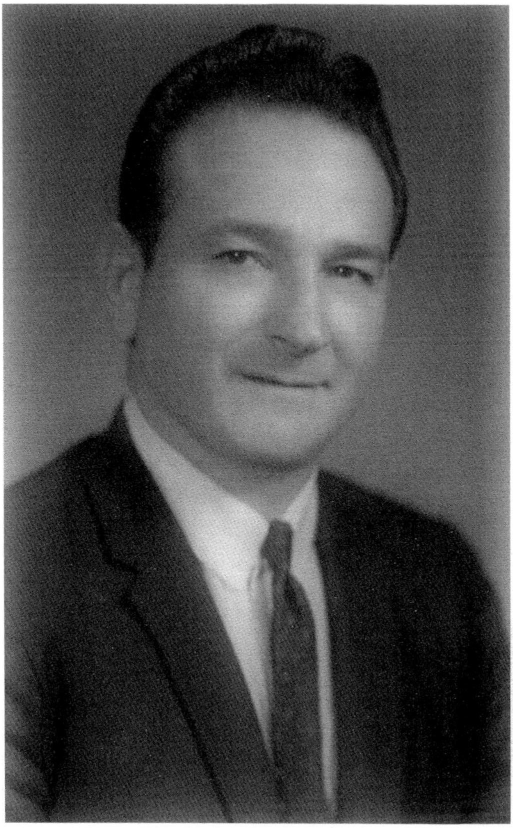

### Joseph R. Scalzo

Joseph Scalzo was an intercollegiate wrestling champion in the 1930s. He moved to Toledo in 1944 to work for Sun Oil and took classes in the evening at the University of Toledo College of Law, graduating in 1948. While at UT, he formed a wrestling team, which he coached for 17 years, and also coached two teams at the YMCA. Scalzo was an official at the 1952 Olympic Games in Helsinki and the 1960 games in Rome. In 1956, he was the coach of the US Olympic Greco-Roman wrestling team in Melbourne, Australia. He held positions with the International Amateur Wrestling Federation, including vice president in 1980, and was also a member of the International Olympic Committee and the US Olympic Committee.

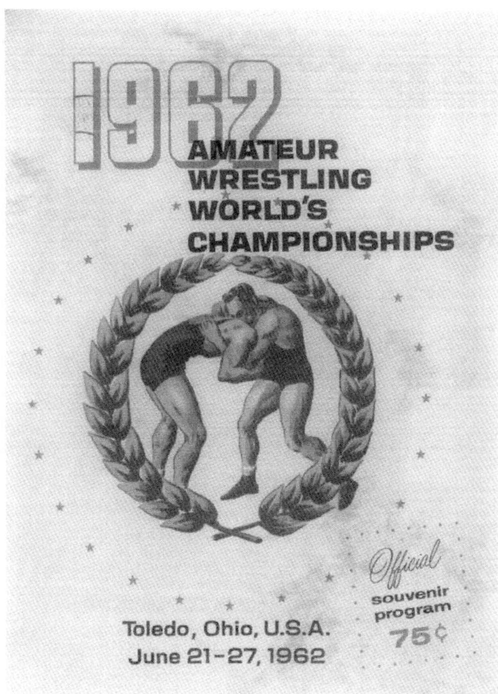


### Program, Amateur Wrestling World's Championships, 1962

Joe Scalzo brought the Amateur Wrestling World's Championships to Toledo in 1962 and 1966 and focused an international spotlight to the city. Scalzo died of a heart attack in 1986 while doing what he loved—watching the World Freestyle Greco-Roman Wrestling Championships.

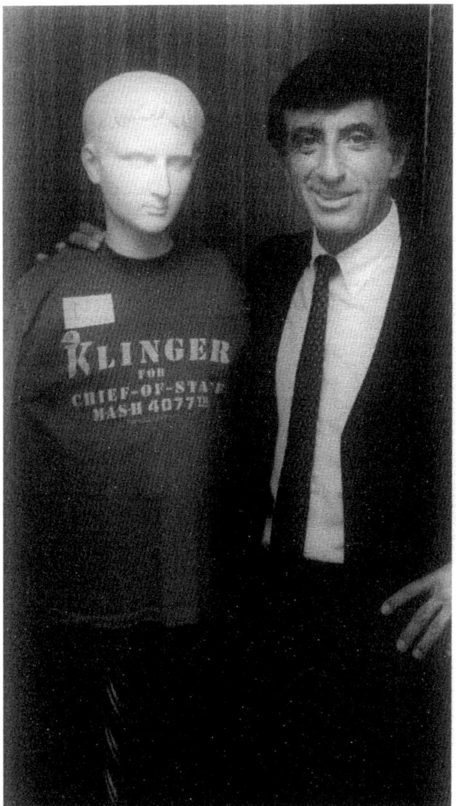


### Jamie Farr

Jameel Farah was the son of a Lebanese grocer and born in Toledo in 1934. Shortly after graduating from high school, he moved to California to become an actor, changing his name to Jamie Farr. He found some small parts in movies such as *The Blackboard Jungle* in 1954 and *No Time for Sergeants* in 1956, and in the 1960s he landed some continuing roles on television, including *The Red Skelton Show*, *The Danny Kaye Show*, and *F-Troop*.

His big break came in 1972 when he was tapped to play Corporal Klinger on the new series *M*A*S*H*, a dark comedy about the Korean War. His character tried to get out of the war by passing himself off as mentally deranged, dressing as a woman. The role became popular with viewers, and Farr became a regular by the third season. As Klinger, Farr often talked about his love for his hometown of Toledo. He would incorporate people and places from Toledo into the script, including Tony Packo's, the Hungarian hot dog restaurant.

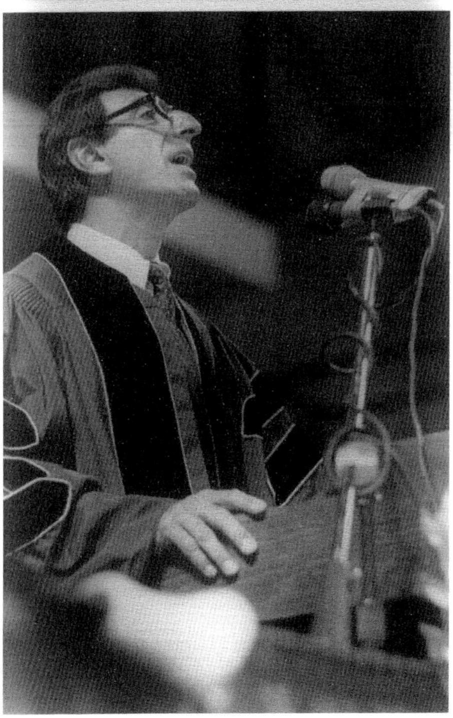

### Jamie Farr Receiving Honorary Degree from the University of Toledo, 1983

*M*A*S*H* ended in 1983, still one of the most popular shows on television. Farr continued in the sequel *After M*A*S*H* in 1983–1984. He was awarded an honorary degree from the University of Toledo in 1983 and for many years was the host of the Jamie Farr Classic, an LPGA tournament held in Toledo.

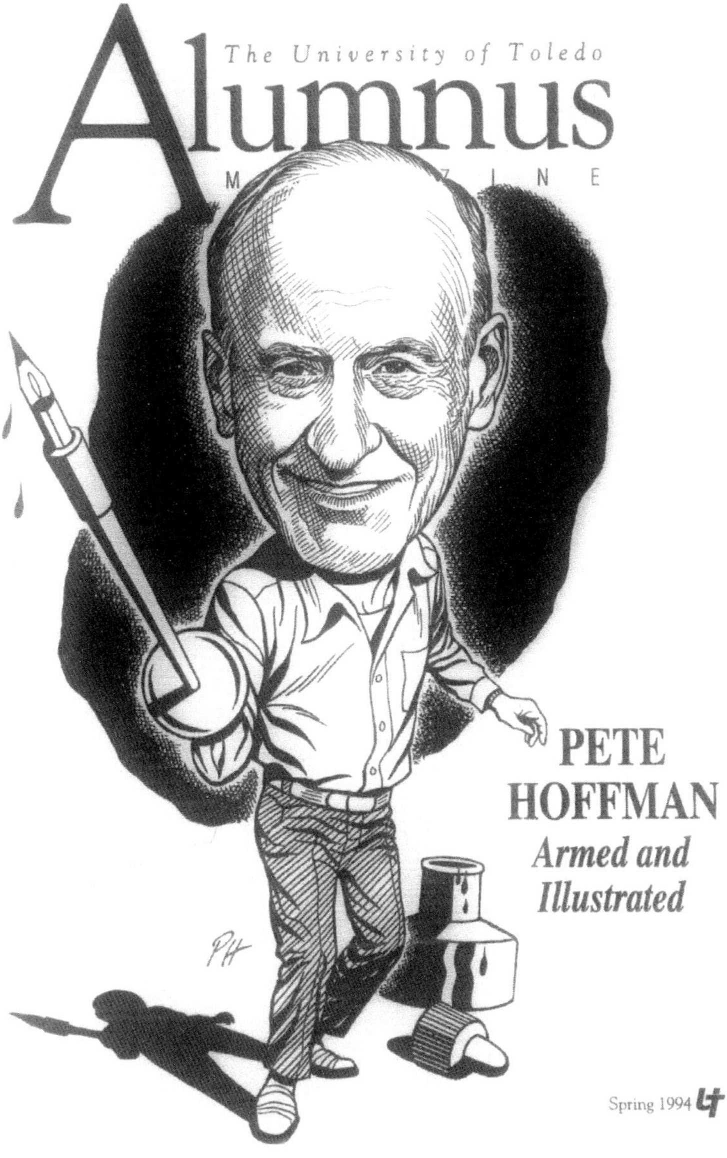


### Pete Hoffman

Peter Hoffman was a self-taught artist who became a nationally syndicated cartoonist. He was born in Toledo in 1919 and published his first drawing in the local newspaper at the age of four. While a student at the University of Toledo, Hoffman drew for the campus newspaper and yearbook, and after graduation he got a job drawing advertisements for Tiedtke's department store. During World War II, he was popular for the caricatures he drew of the men in his unit.

After the war, he got a job with Allen Saunders drawing Saunders's comic strip *Steve Roper.* He left that job in 1954 and developed a comic strip for General Features Syndicate about investigative journalism reporter Jeff Cobb. He researched and wrote the daily strip until 1978. It was published in over 100 newspapers in North America and overseas, with its largest fan base in Sweden. Hoffman retired but would do freelance work, including the illustrations for UT's homecoming Golden Alumni Society publications. He died in 2013.

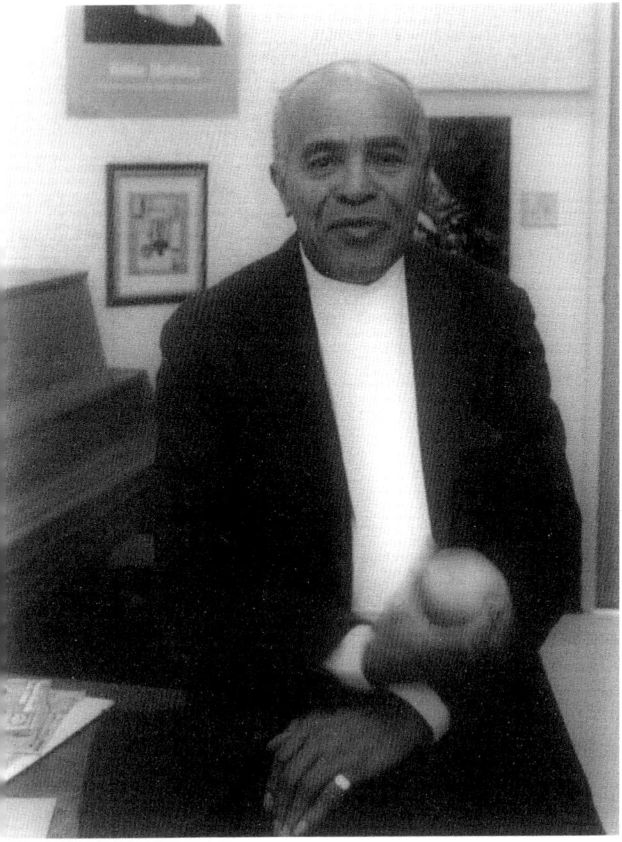

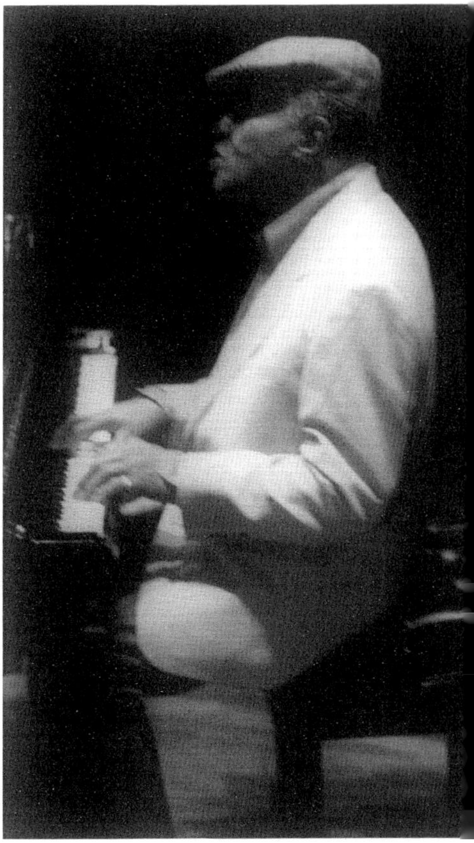

**Jon Hendricks**

While a child, Jon Hendricks studied singing with his neighbor, jazz great Art Tatum. Hendricks's big break came in 1950 when he was still a college student. He often worked nights as a drummer and singer at various Toledo clubs, but one night he got the chance to perform with Charlie "Bird" Parker in Toledo's Civic Auditorium. Parker was so impressed he encouraged Hendricks to come to New York. Hendricks did so two years later and found Parker playing at the Apollo Bar. Parker introduced him to other jazz greats of the time such as Dizzy Gillespie.

In 1955, Jon Hendricks began recording vocalese versions of Count Basie songs with Dave Lambert. British singer Annie Ross joined the group, and they would replicate the parts traditionally played by instruments with their voices. The group found much success as Lambert, Hendricks, and Ross. Their style would influence many other jazz singers, including Bobby McFerrin and the Manhattan Transfer. In the 1970s, he recorded with the Manhattan Transfer and won a Grammy Award for a duet with McFerrin. In 1992, he received the National Endowment for the Arts American Jazz Masters Fellowship, the highest honor for a jazz singer. He was also honored at a 75th-birthday tribute at Lincoln Center and programs on National Public Radio. In 1999, he returned to his alma mater of the University of Toledo to receive an honorary degree and teach the history of jazz as a distinguished professor.

# CHAPTER FIVE

# Unsung Heroes

In the history of every city, there are those whose contributions to its development are known by few and appreciated by even fewer. These unsung heroes are people who may have played roles behind the scenes that received little attention. Or they might be those whose sacrifices were important for a brief period of time but are long since forgotten. Or they might be people who, because of their place in society, were little noticed. Or they might be well-known individuals—but not for their service to others. All have stories that should not be forgotten.

The unsung heroes in Toledo's past include businessmen like John Gunckel, Charles Feilbach, and Jefferson Robinson—men with established careers, but whose real passion was in helping others. They include people like Edward Bowsher, the beloved superintendent of Toledo Public Schools who held that position for 20 years. Such a track record is all but unheard of today. They include those who sacrificed their lives in war such as Carl Joseph and Robert Craig. And lastly, they include the likes of Alva Bunker, who was born without hands and legs but inspired an international effort to assist children with disabilities that continues today.

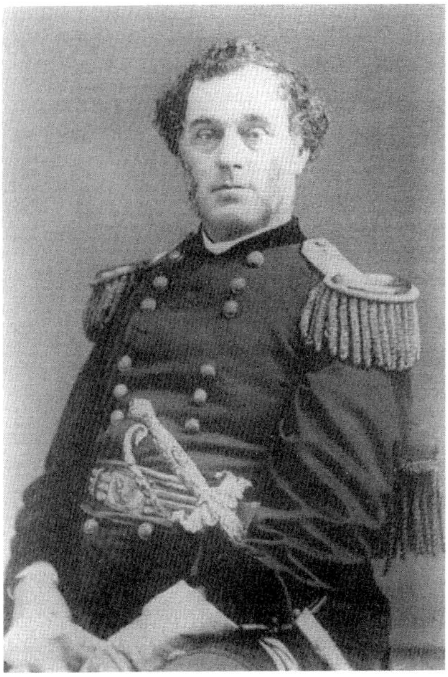

## James Steedman

James Steedman was born in Pennsylvania and orphaned as a young child. As the eldest of three children, he took a job as a printer's apprentice at the age of 15. He joined the Texas independence movement, and he later moved to northwest Ohio to become a contractor on the Erie and Wabash Canal project. In 1849, he joined the California Gold Rush.

He served as editor of the *Toledo Times* between 1857 and 1861 and supported Stephen Douglas (a personal friend) for president over Abraham Lincoln. Steedman ran for Congress against James Ashley in 1861 but lost.

When the Civil War broke out, Steedman helped to organize the 14th Ohio Regiment. In 1863, he became commander of the 1st Division of Reserve Corps. On September 20 of that year, the division held their positions in the battle of Chickamauga, helping to bring about a Union victory. He was called the hero of the battle and was promoted to major general.

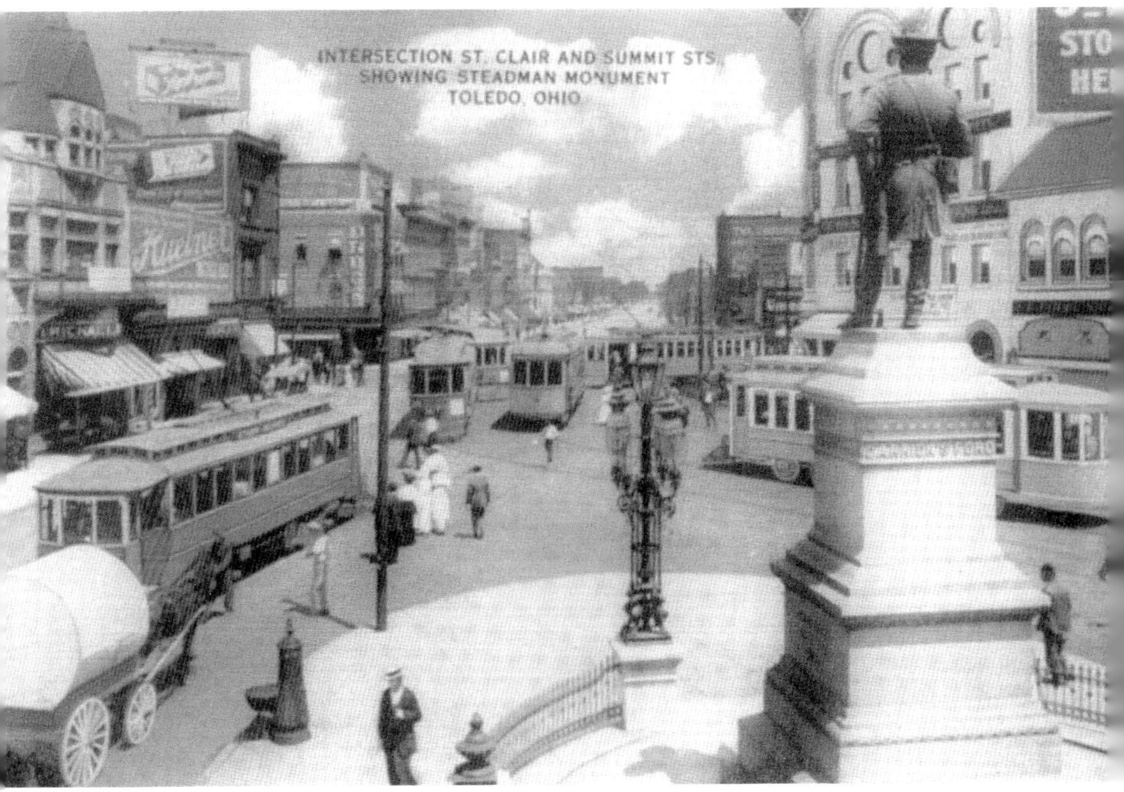


## James Steedman Statue in Downtown Toledo

Steedman returned to Toledo in 1869 and was active in politics. His last position was as Toledo chief of police. He died in 1883, and a statue of him was erected at the intersection of Summit and St. Clair Streets in 1887. It was later moved farther north on Summit Street, where it is displayed today.

### Jefferson D. Robinson

Jefferson Robinson accompanied Edward Drummond Libbey in 1888 from Cambridge, Massachusetts, when Libbey brought the New England Glass Company to Toledo. He would eventually become president and chairman of the board of directors for Libbey Glass.

His most noteworthy contribution to Toledo, however, was his philanthropic work. He was a charter member of the Toledo Museum of Art, a major supporter of Toledo Hospital, and the first chairman of the Community Chest. But the agency that meant the most to him was the Newsboys Association. When he died in 1929, his estate established a trust to support the Newsboys (which later became the Boys' Club of Toledo) and provide care to indigent children at Toledo Hospital. In recognition of his service on the Toledo Board of Education, in November 1929 the new junior high school building was named the J.D. Robinson School.

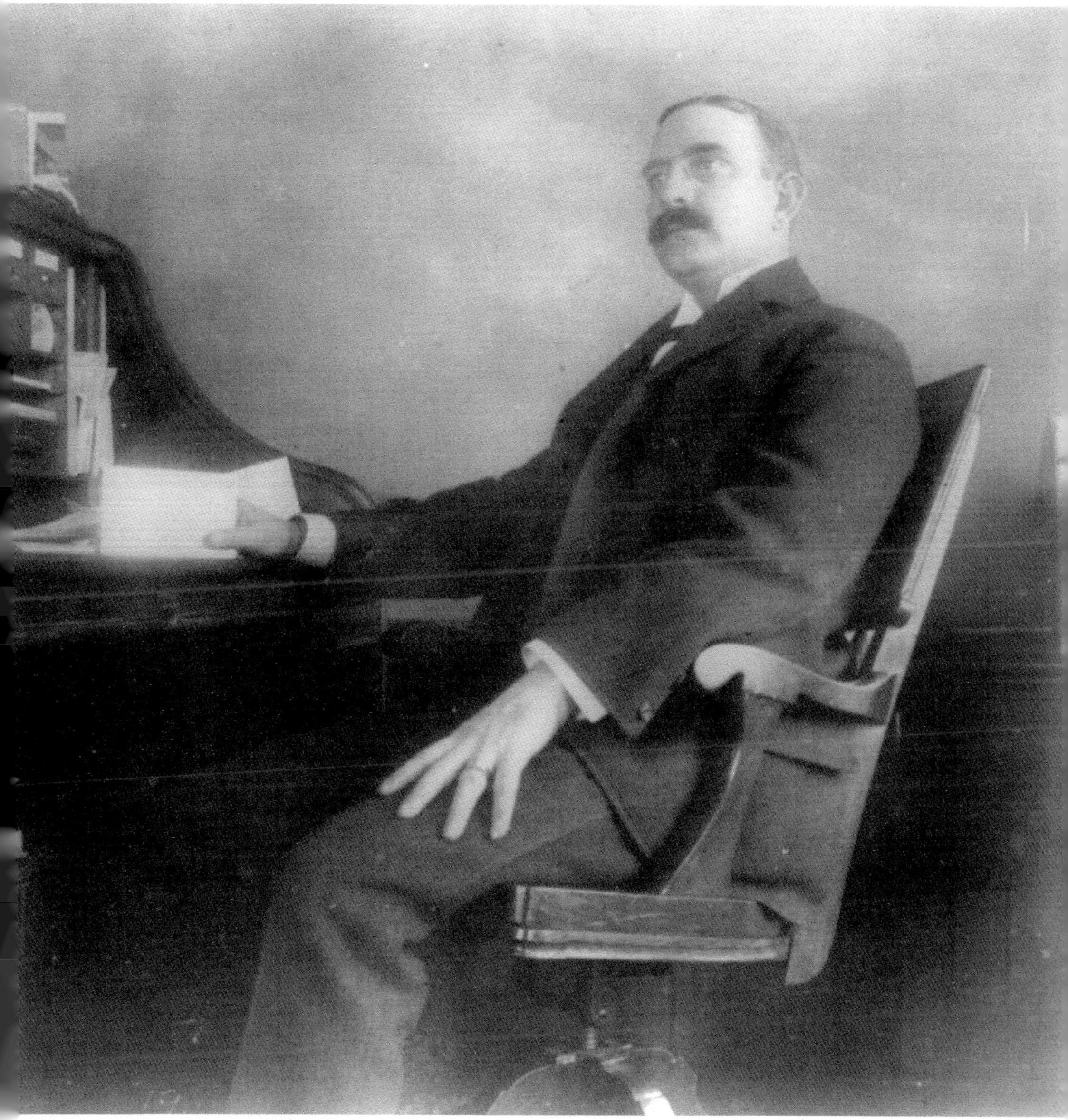

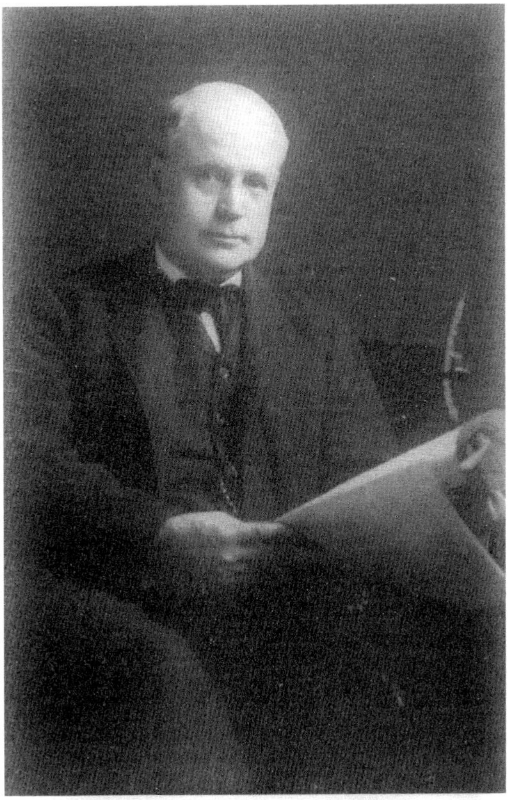

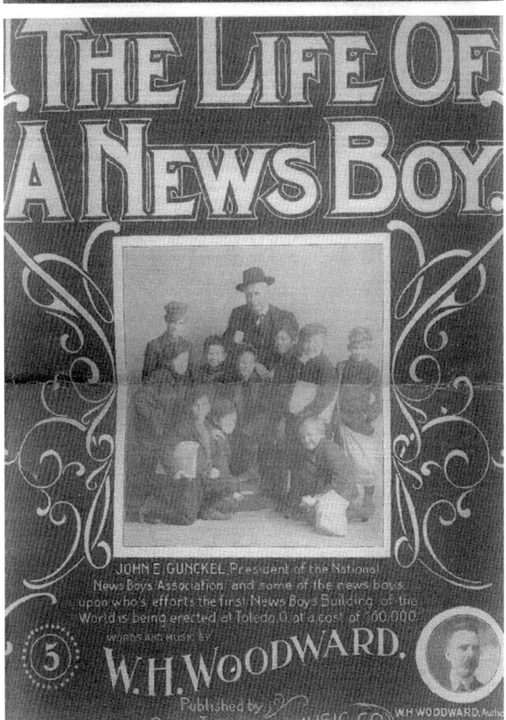


### John Gunckel

John Gunckel moved to Toledo in 1875 to become a ticket agent for the Lake Shore and Michigan Southern Railway. His office in the downtown Boody House hotel gave him a window into the lives of young boys, often orphans, who sold newspapers for a penny on the streets. Gunckel would invite the newsies into his office to get warm in the winter, and he sought to help them in a more meaningful and lasting way.

On December 25, 1892, he invited them to a Christmas dinner at the Marine Building on Water Street. After the party, he helped the newsboys create an association founded on the ideas of responsibility, self-governance, and the chance for a better life. The Toledo Newsboys Association was governed by elected officers. Members had to agree not to lie, steal, gamble, smoke, or drink.

In 1908, Gunckel led a campaign to raise $100,000 to build the Newsboys Building. Similar organizations were created in many cities modeled after the Toledo organization, and in 1915, Gunckel led the effort to create a National Newsboys Association. When Gunckel died in 1917, a massive pyramid of 30,000 stones contributed by schoolchildren marked his grave in Woodlawn Cemetery.

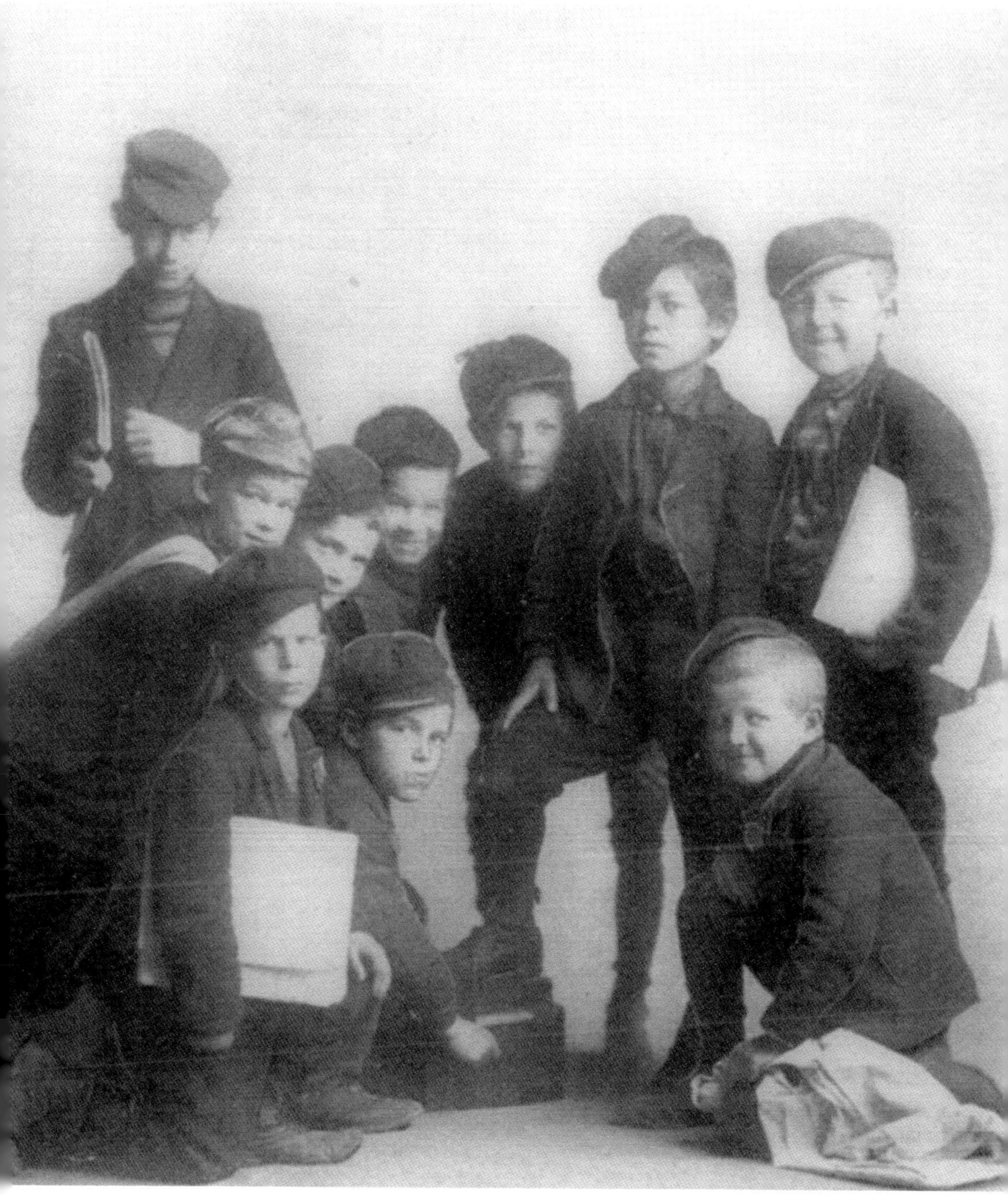

Members of the Toledo Newsboys Association

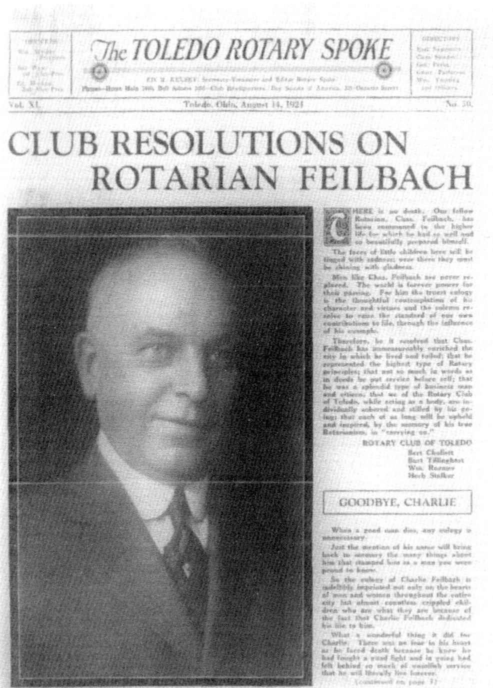

The TOLEDO ROTARY SPOKE

Vol. XI. Toledo, Ohio, August 14, 1924 No. 30.

CLUB RESOLUTIONS ON ROTARIAN FEILBACH

THERE is no death. Our fellow Rotarian, Chas. Feilbach, has been summoned to the higher life for which he had so well and so beautifully prepared himself.

The faces of little children here will be tinged with sadness; over there they must be shining with gladness.

Men like Chas. Feilbach are never replaced. The world is forever poorer for their passing. For him the truest eulogy is the thoughtful contemplation of his character and virtues and the solemn resolve to raise the standard of our own contributions to life, through the influence of his example.

Therefore, be it resolved that Chas. Feilbach has immeasurably enriched the city in which he lived and toiled; that he represented the highest type of Rotary principles; that not so much in words as in deeds he put service before self; that he was a splendid type of business man and citizen; that we of the Rotary Club of Toledo, while acting as a body, are individually sobered and stilled by his going; that each of us long will be upheld and inspired, by the memory of his true Rotarianism, in "carrying on."

ROTARY CLUB OF TOLEDO
Bert Chollett
Burt Tillinghast
Wm. Roemer
Herb Stalker

GOODBYE, CHARLIE

When a good man dies, any eulogy is unnecessary.

Just the mention of his name will bring back to memory the many things about him that stamped him as a man you were proud to know.

So the eulogy of Charlie Feilbach is indelibly imprinted not only on the hearts of men and women throughout the entire city but almost countless crippled children who are what they are because of the fact that Charlie Feilbach dedicated his life to him.

What a wonderful thing it did for Charlie. There was no fear in his heart as he faced death because he knew he had fought a good fight and in going had left behind so much of unselfish service that he will literally live forever.

(continued on page 3)

## Charles Feilbach

Charles Feilbach's obituary in 1924 stated, "Perhaps few business men of Toledo have been more generally beloved than Mr. Feilbach, whose attention has been particularly directed to the crippled children in the last seven years." The president of Feilbach Co., a wholesale grocer, he led the Toledo Rotary when the club took up the cause of assisting disabled children.

He went on to be president of the Toledo Society for Crippled Children, vice president of the Ohio Society for Crippled Children, and a director of the International Society for Crippled Children, organizations he not only helped to lead but also played a role in founding.

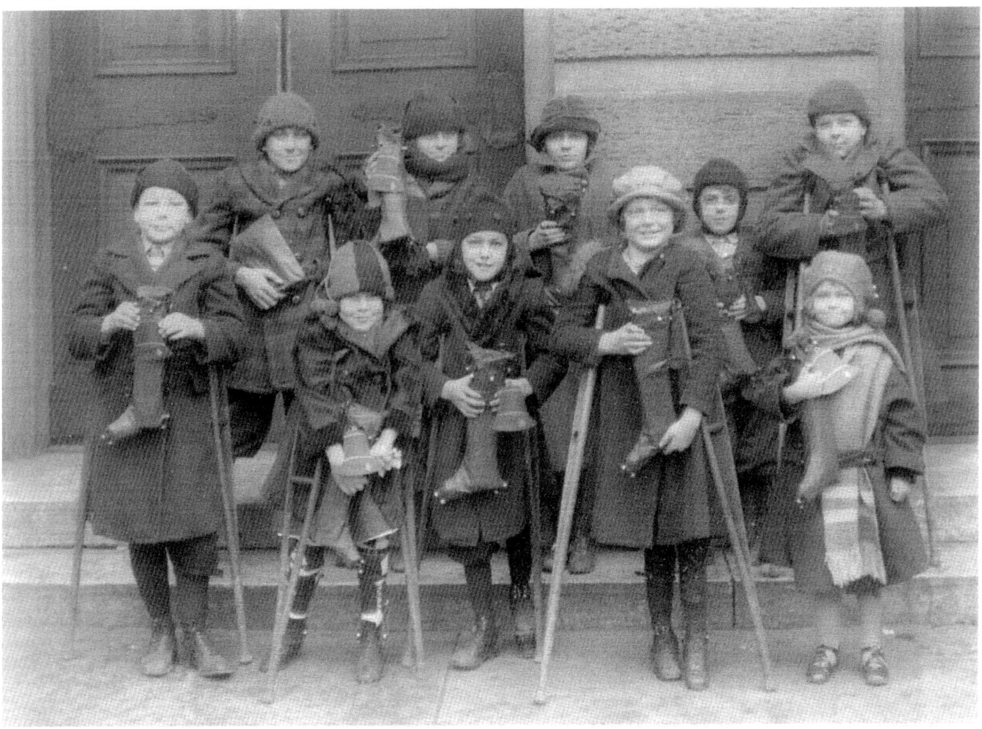

## Feilbach School Students

Children at the Feilbach School for Crippled Children received Christmas gifts in 1931.

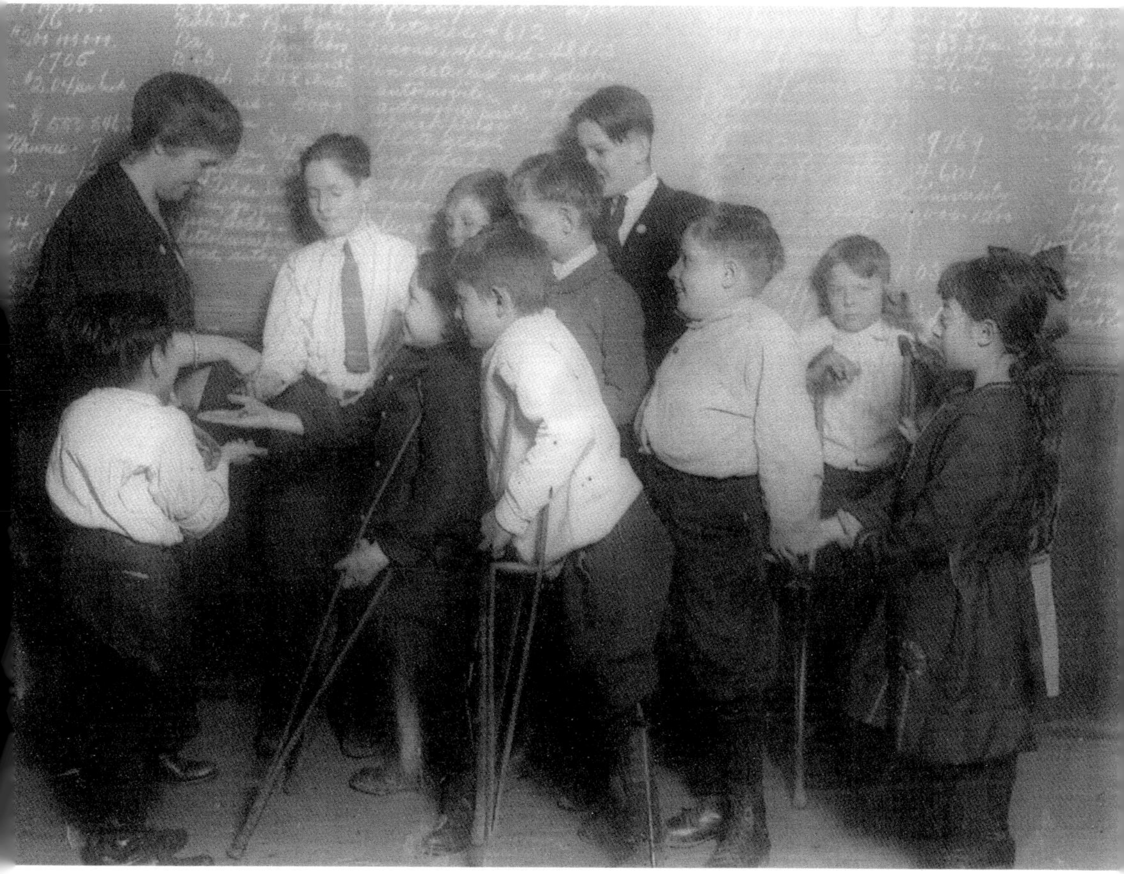

**Students at the Feilbach School for Crippled Children, c. 1920**
Charles Feilbach was a member of the Toledo Board of Education from 1919 until his death. In this capacity, he urged the district to create a school for disabled children. Created in 1919, the school was later named in Feilbach's honor after his death in 1924.

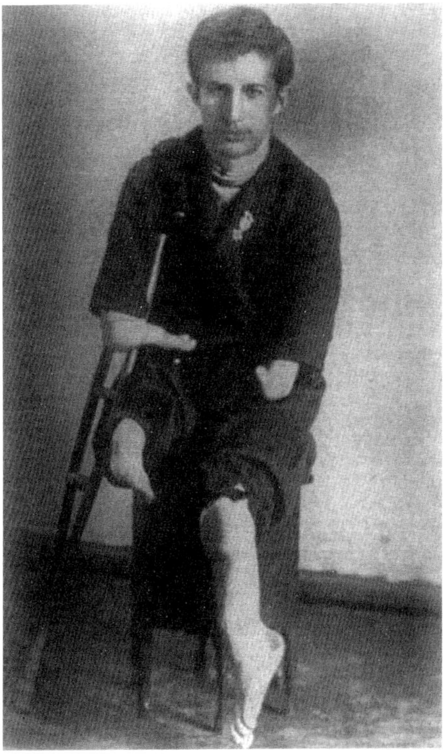

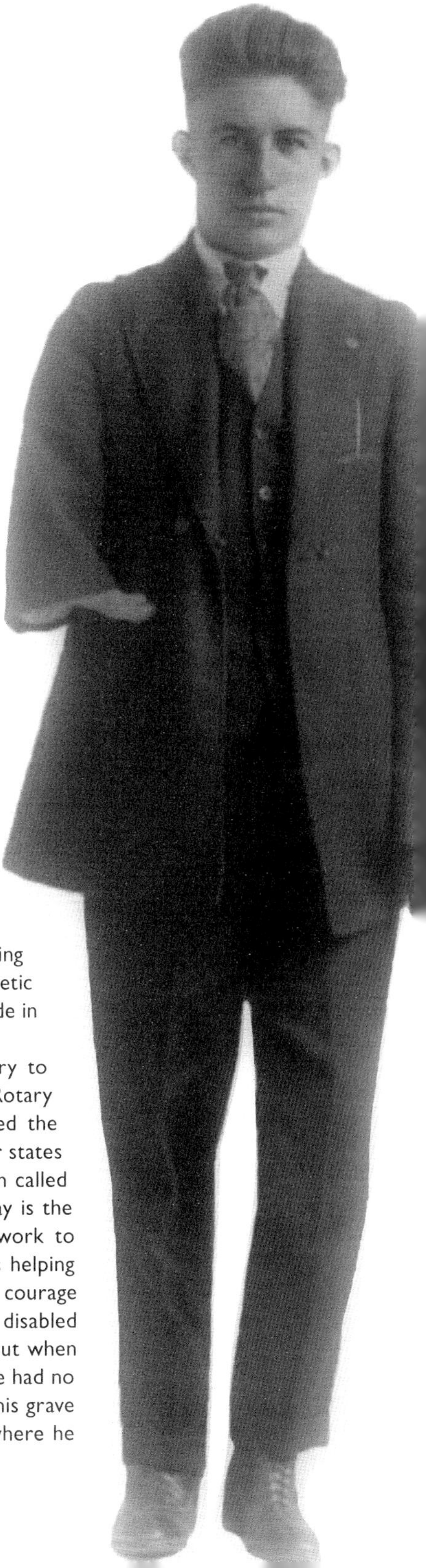

## Alva Bunker

In 1900, Alva Bunker was born in north Toledo to a working-class family. His arms ended at the elbows, and he had only one misshaped foot attached near the knee. Because of his severe disabilities, his family kept him at home, and he could barely speak. Most people believed he was developmentally disabled.

In 1917, the Toledo Rotary decided to assist Bunker by sending him to Detroit for surgery, where he was fitted with prosthetic legs. He attended classes and graduated from the eighth grade in eight months. He also learned to stand and walk.

Alva Bunker's transformation inspired the Toledo Rotary to work on behalf of disabled children. With other Ohio Rotary clubs, they advocated for a new law in 1921 that required the state to provide care and education for such children. Other states followed with similar laws. They created a new organization called the International Society for Crippled Children, which today is the National Easter Seal Society. Rotarians everywhere also work to raise millions of dollars to eradicate polio worldwide, thus helping to insure that fewer children will be disabled. Because of the courage of Alva Bunker and the work of Rotary International, today disabled children can go to school and receive necessary services. But when Bunker died in 1979, all of this had been forgotten. His grave had no headstone. In 2012, the Toledo Rotary placed a marker on his grave and dedicated a monument to his name in the cemetery where he is buried.

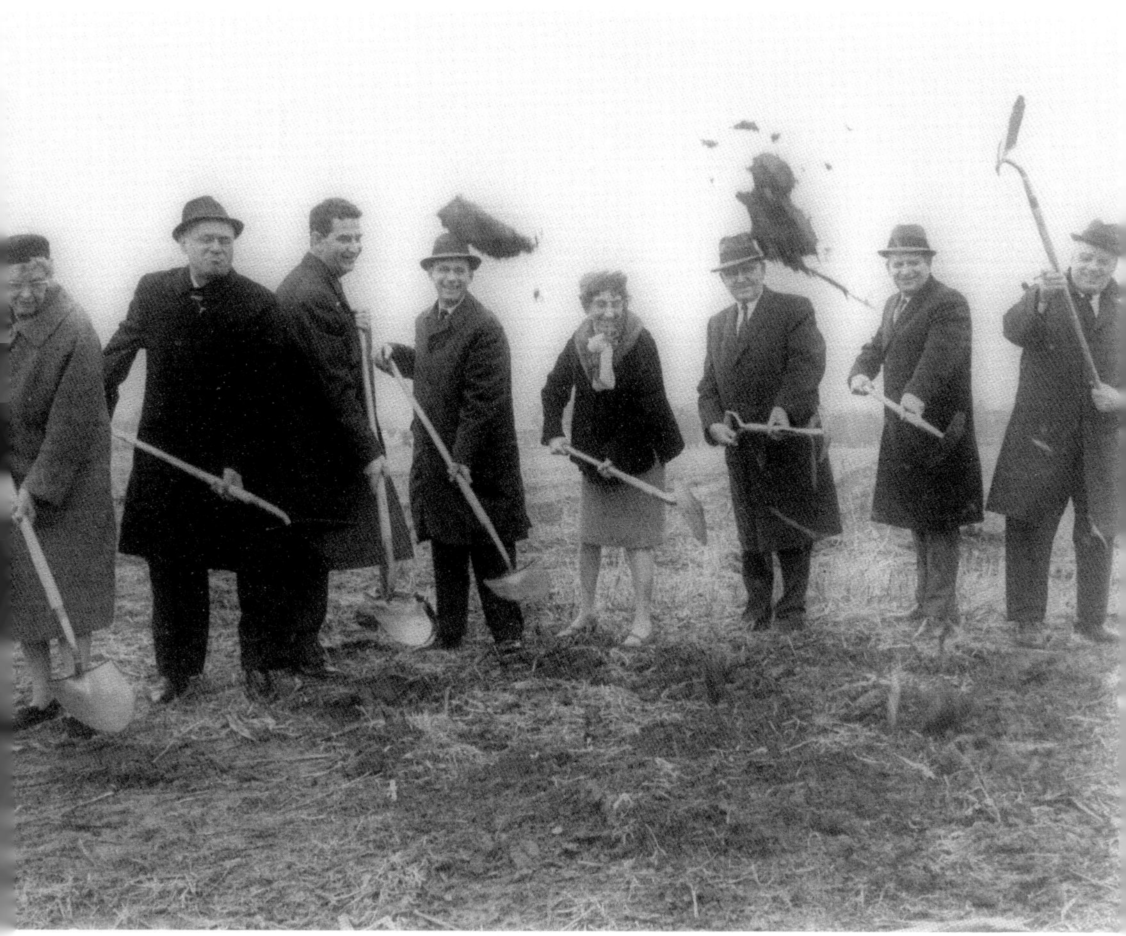

**Josina Lott at the Ground-breaking for Larc Lane School, 1960**

Josina Lott (center) started a school in her apartment in Toledo in 1938 based on one simple premise—that every child should have the chance to go to school, no matter their mental limitations. She started the school for the developmentally disabled with one student and soon had a class of 15. Her work got the attention of a small group of people, some of them parents of developmentally disabled children, who helped her create the Lott Day School in 1945. It was not until 1950 that the State of Ohio enacted legislation requiring counties to provide education to such children.

Lott was concerned not only about developmentally disabled children but also what would happen to these children when they became adults. She started a sheltered workshop to train them in vocational skills, one of the first such workshops in the country. In 1957, county voters agreed to support Lott's school and workshop with tax money. With the support of parents, a new school called Larc Lane (whose name came from the Lucas County Association for Retarded Children) opened in 1961. Josina Lott died in 1972, but Lott Industries continues today to provide work and training for developmentally disabled adults.

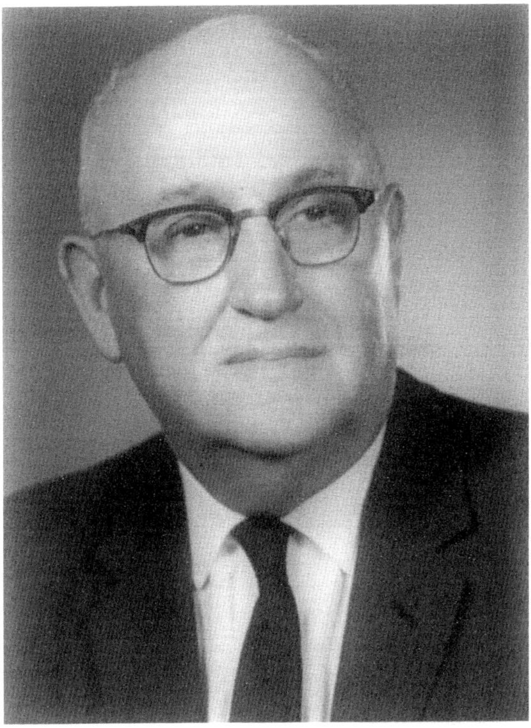

**Edward L. Bowsher**

Edward Bowsher served as superintendent of the Toledo Public Schools for 20 years, a remarkably long tenure for such a political position. Bowsher was born in Cridersville, Ohio, in 1891, and graduated from Defiance College in 1913. He began teaching in a one-room school, where he also was expected to sweep the floors and stoke the fire. He served as superintendent of schools in Wauseon, Waverly, and Ashland. In 1935, he became state director of education, a position he held for two years until he became superintendent of Toledo Public Schools.

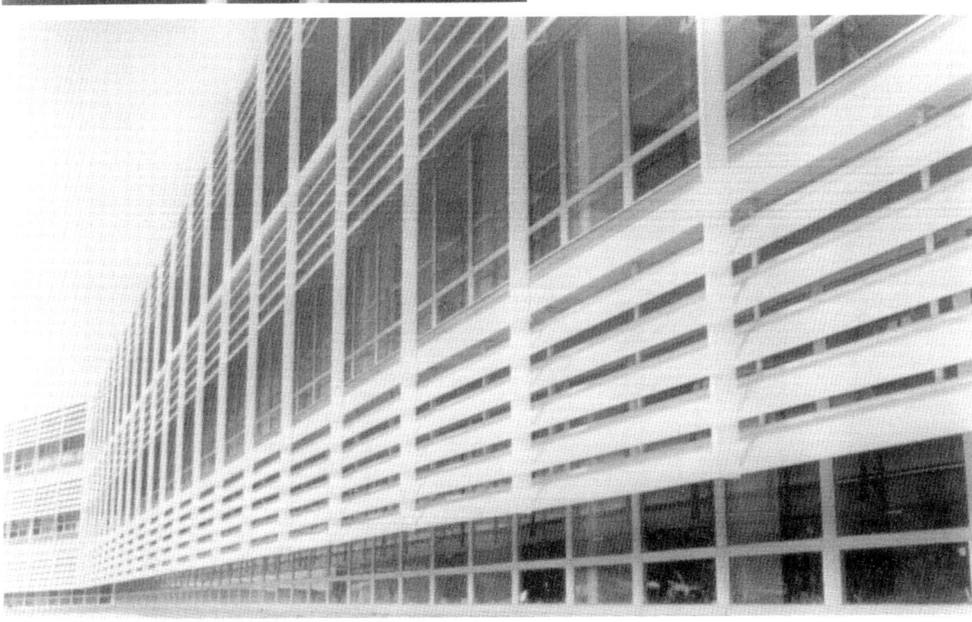

**Bowsher High School, 1962**

He came to Toledo during the Great Depression and had to convince Toledoans that investment in schools would improve the city. He advocated for adult and recreational programs, unions, music and arts education, and allowing married women to be teachers, a concept not endorsed at the time. When he retired in 1957, he was loved by students and parents. In 1962, the high school under construction on the south side was named E.L. Bowsher High School.

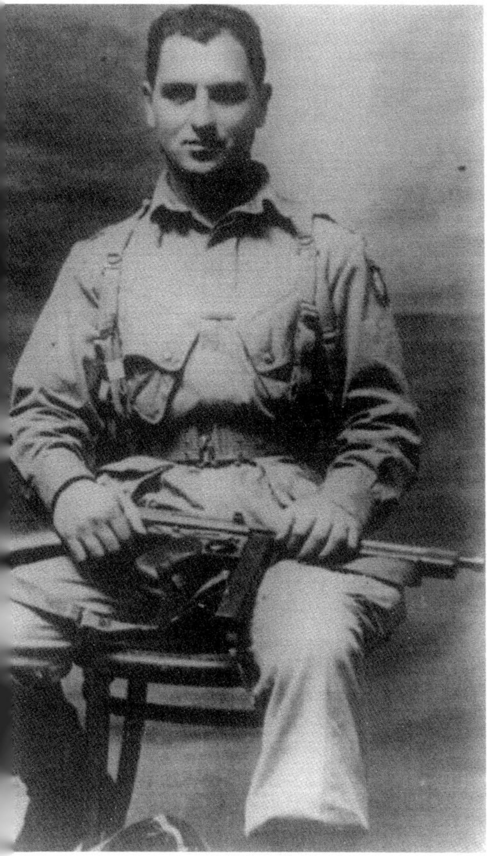

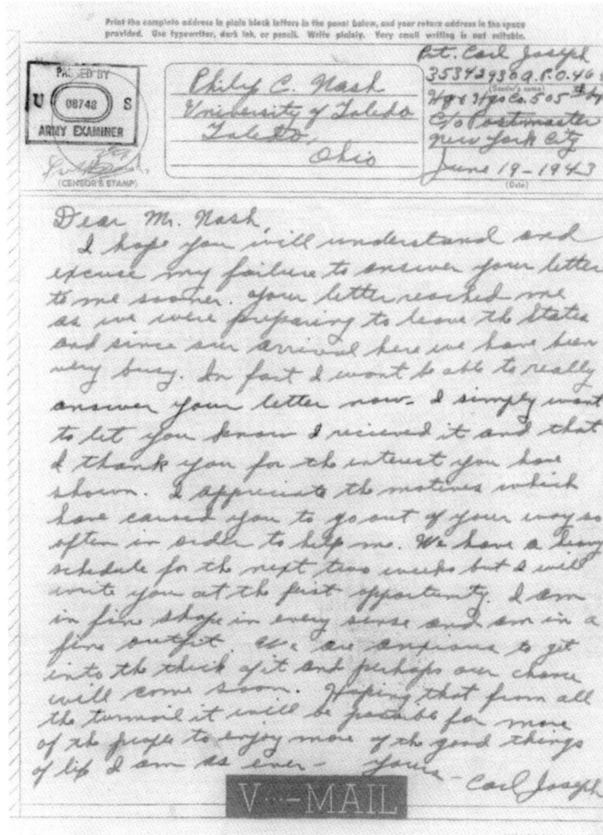

Print the complete address in plain block letters in the panel below, and your return address in the space provided. Use typewriter, dark ink, or pencil. Write plainly. Very small writing is not suitable.

PASSED BY
U 08748 S
ARMY EXAMINER
(CENSOR'S STAMP)

Philip C. Nash
University of Toledo
Toledo,
Ohio

Pvt. Carl Joseph
35342938 A.P.O. 469
(Sender's name)
Hq & Hq Co. 505 Pcht Inf
c/o Postmaster
New York City
June 19 - 1943
(Date)

Dear Mr. Nash,
I hope you will understand and excuse my failure to answer your letter to me sooner. Your letter reached me as we were preparing to leave the States and since our arrival here we have been very busy. In fact I won't be able to really answer your letter now. I simply want to let you know I recieved it and that I thank you for the interest you have shown. I appreciate the motives which have caused you to go out of your way so often in order to help me. We have a heavy schedule for the next two weeks but I will write you at the first opportunity. I am in fine shape in every sense and am in a fine outfit. We are anxious to get into the thick of it and perhaps our chance will come soon. Hoping that from all the turmoil it will be possible for more of the people to enjoy more of the good things of life I am as ever - Yours - Carl Joseph

V-MAIL

**Carl Joseph**

Carl Joseph was a troubled youth. While a student at Waite High School, he was labeled disruptive. In 1934, he was arrested during the Toledo Auto-Lite Strike. Four years later, while president of the International Longshoremen's Association Local 1353, he was charged with participating in communist activities. When he applied to the University of Toledo in 1941, dean Raymond Carter tried to keep him out because of his radicalism.

But other members of the community came to Joseph's defense. UT president Philip Nash not only admitted Carl Joseph but also took him under his wing. The two developed a close friendship built on the ideas of peace and equality.

In 1943, Joseph enlisted in the Army as a paratrooper. While overseas, he corresponded with Nash and sent books for the university's library. In February 1944, Joseph told Nash, "I've thought a lot about what I can do as my share and it boils down to just this: To do my job as a soldier so well that the fellow in my right and the fellow on my left will have a better chance of coming through alive."

On D-Day, June 6, 1944, Joseph jumped with the 504th Regiment of the 82nd Airborne Division and was shot by a sniper. The man who many questioned his allegiance to his country died defending it.

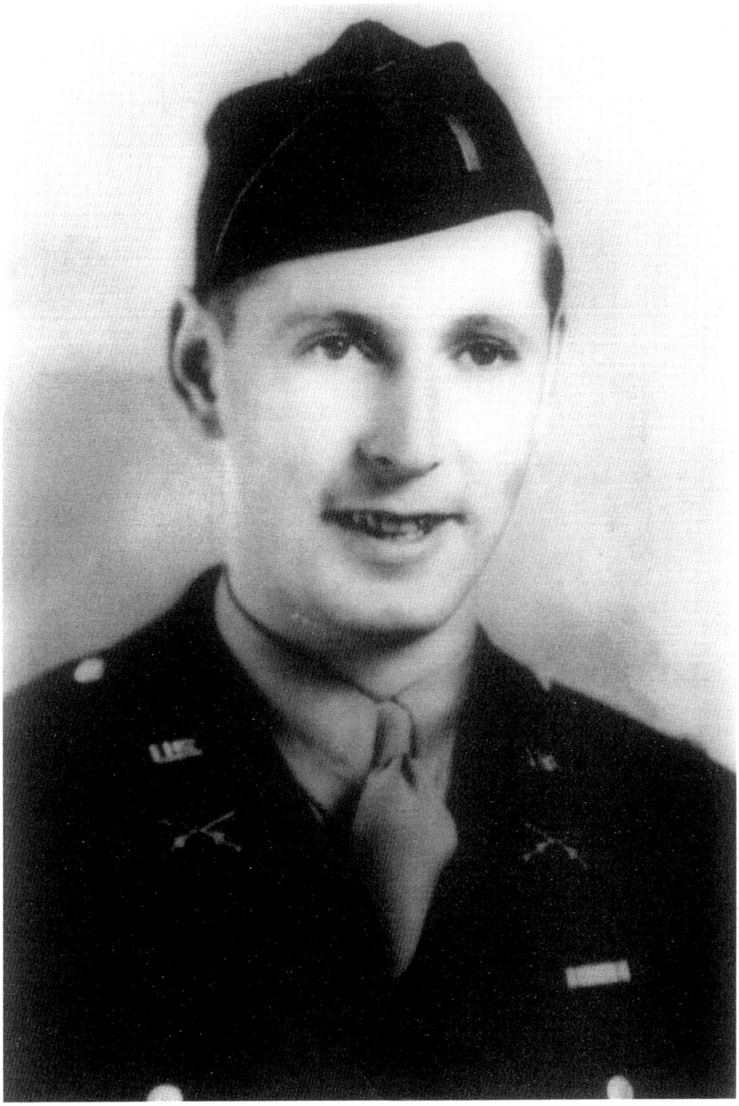

### Robert Craig

Robert Craig graduated from Libbey High School in 1937. He joined the Army in 1941, attending the infantry officer candidate school at Fort Benning, Georgia. He was commissioned as a second lieutenant in December 1942 and sent overseas the following month. He was wounded in action and received a Purple Heart.

Craig was back in action on July 21, 1943, when his company advanced on a mountain village in Favarotta, Sicily. One of the men in the battle, Corp. James E. Hill, recalled the battle. "Lieutenant Craig yelled at me to cover him. Then jumping to his feet he ran head-on through machine gun fire which was coming at him in a steady stream. He reached the gun position miraculously unhurt, and standing over the crew, killed all three of them with his carbine." Later on that day, he deliberately drew the fire of over 100 Germans who had ambushed his platoon, allowing his fellow soldiers to escape. Before he died, he killed five more Nazis and wounded at least three.

For his acts, Craig was posthumously awarded the Congressional Medal of Honor in June 1944. A new bridge built over the Maumee River was named in his honor in 1957.

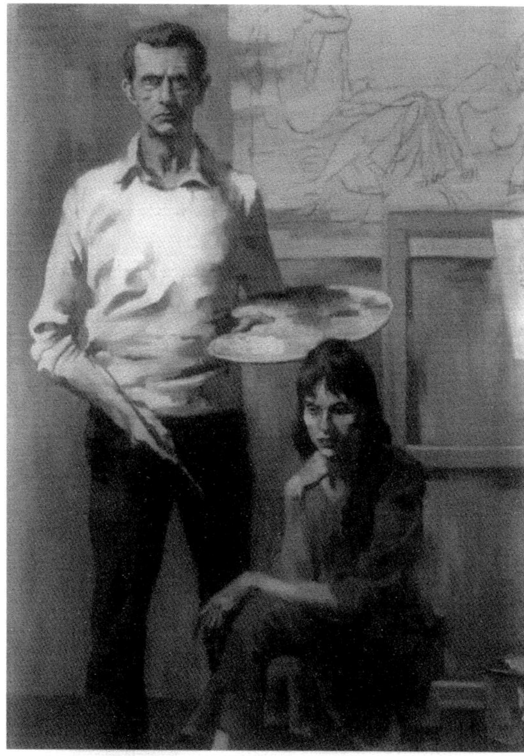

**Adam Grant Self-Portrait**

Adam Grant's artistic talent literally saved his life.

As a young boy in Poland, Grant was arrested by the Nazis and imprisoned in Auschwitz and other concentration camps. He survived by creating artwork for his prison guards. After the war, he came to Detroit, where he got a job designing paint-by-number kits.

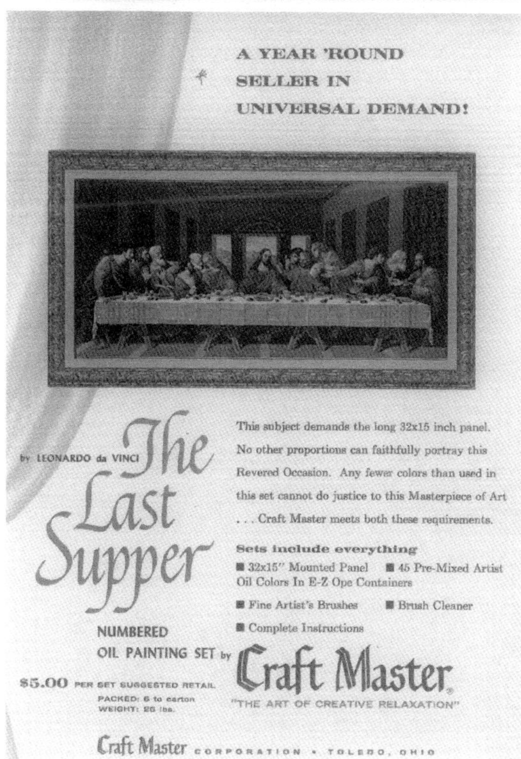


**Advertisement for *The Last Supper* Paint-by-Number, c. 1965**

Adam Grant continued this work with the Craft Master Corporation in Toledo. At a time when paint-by-number kits were one of America's most popular hobbies, Grant designed some of the bestselling kits of all time, including a depiction of *The Last Supper.*

Outside of his professional work, Grant was a successful artist known for his paintings of the female figure, evoking a sculptural quality with lighting effects. Grant's paintings are part of the permanent collection of the Butler Institute of American Art, among other collections, and were featured in exhibits in many places, including Paris, Poland, and Saudi Arabia. Grant died in 1992.

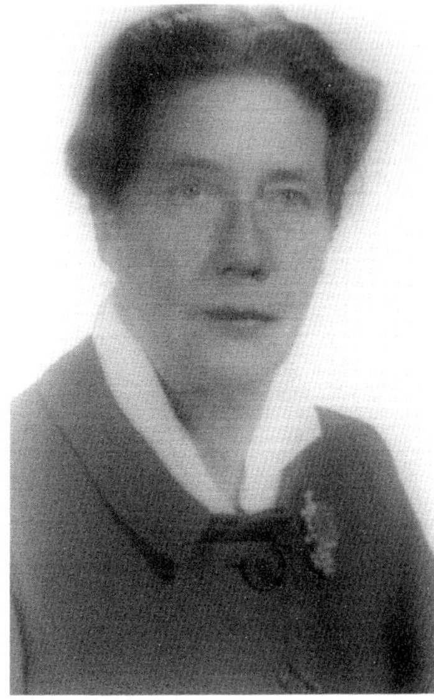

### Virginia Stranahan

Virginia Stranahan lived a life without want. She was born in 1907 to a wealthy family and married into a wealthy family. She and her husband, Duane Stranahan, built a 14,000-square-foot mansion on the Maumee River. (Courtesy of the 577 Foundation.)

### Virginia Stranahan at Her Home

After Virginia and her husband divorced, she wanted to see her home used by the public, and she created the 577 Foundation. It was dedicated to agricultural experimentation and education. She hired artists and gardeners and invited community members to establish their own gardens on the property. On her death at the age of 90 in 1997, Virginia Stranahan gave her home to the 577 Foundation, where today it continues to serve as a community resource. Despite her life of privilege, she left behind a legacy that serves many in its unique educational efforts. (Courtesy of the 577 Foundation.)

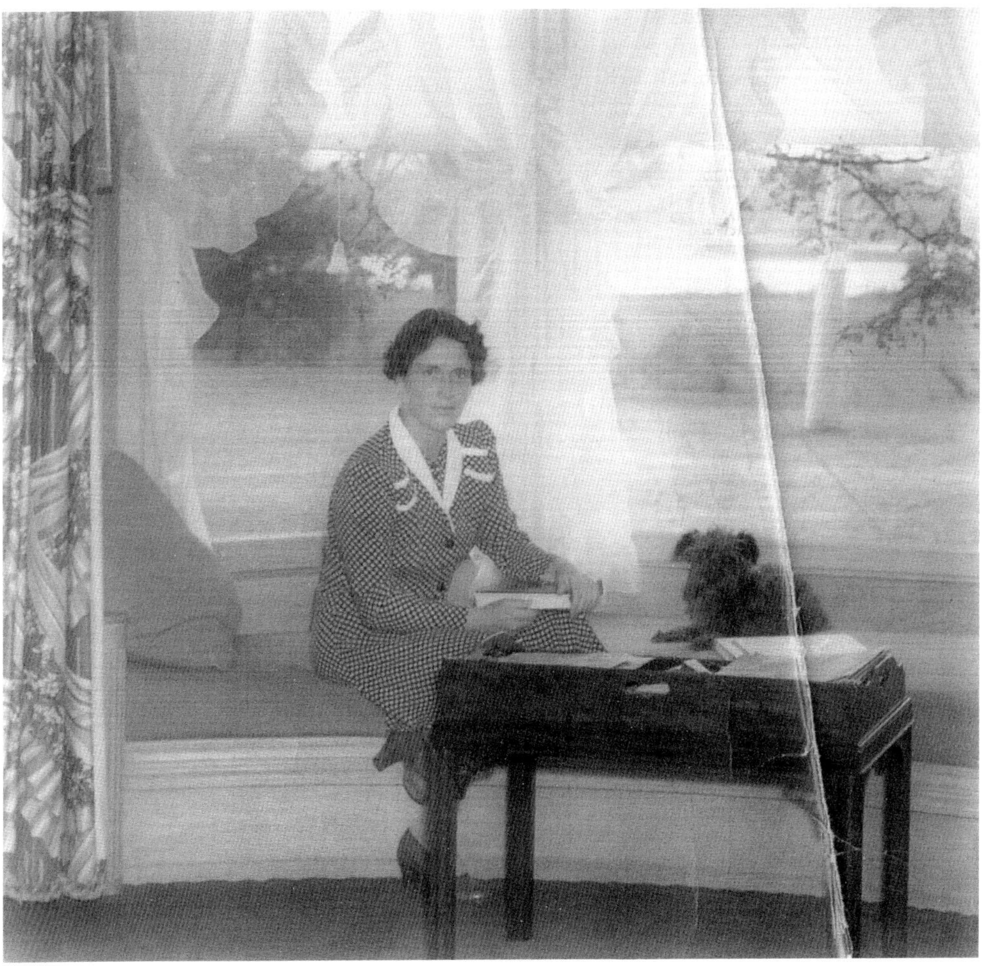

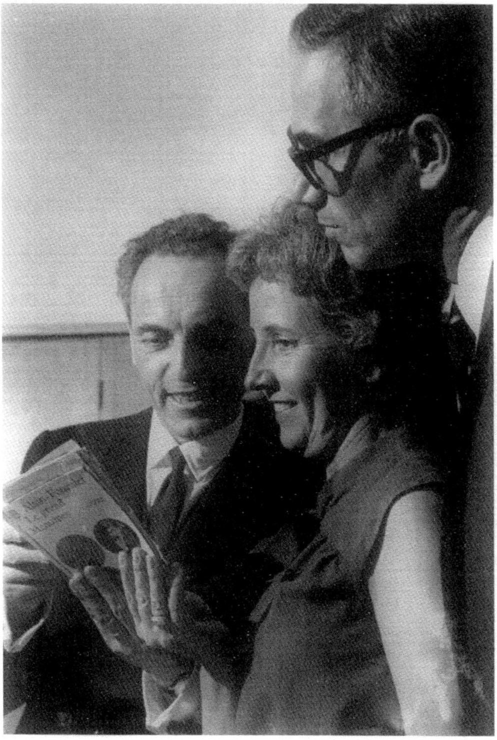

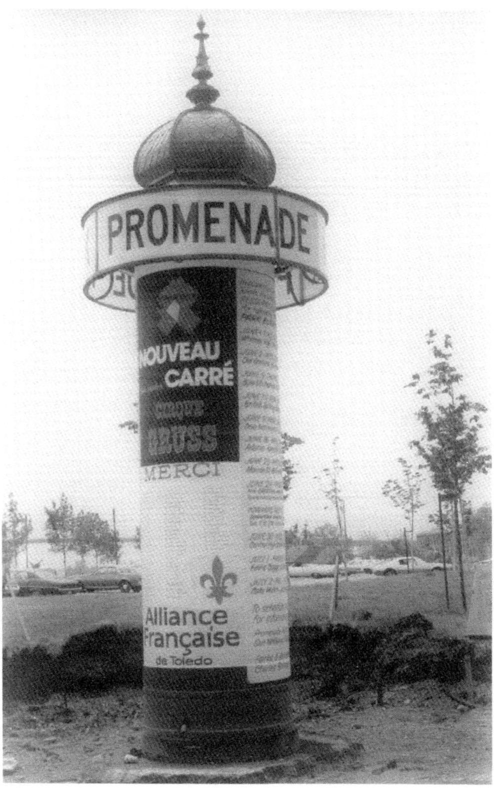


### Betty Mauk

Betty Mauk took her first trip to France when she was 18 years old and returned at least 50 more times during her life. She worked tirelessly to bring a French influence to her hometown of Toledo, especially along the riverfront.

In 1964, she was the guiding force behind the founding of the Toledo chapter of Alliance Française, an organization that still today teaches French language courses and celebrates French culture.

In 1972, Betty Mauk almost singlehandedly changed the landscape of the downtown by working to create Promenade Park, which sought to bring some of the beauty of the Parisian riverfront to Toledo. It included an authentic French kiosk (which Mauk bought at her own expense), and La Creperie, a food stand she operated that sold French pancakes. Mayor Harry Kessler appointed her to the committee in 1973 that was planning downtown redevelopment in recognition of her efforts. She died in 2012 at the age of 93.

# INDEX

# INDEX